Ben Cohen

Some Of My Best Friends

A Journey Through Twenty-First Century Antisemitism

The Berlin International Center for the Study of Antisemitism (BICSA):
Studies in Antisemitism/ Studien zum Antisemitismus, Vol. 4/ Band 4

Ben Cohen

Some Of My Best Friends

A Journey Through Twenty–First Century Antisemitism

Berlin: Edition Critic, 2014

This book is a publication of

EDITION CRITIC

Sophie-Charlotten-Str. 9–10
14059 Berlin
Federal Republic of Germany
www.editioncritic.de
Phone +49 (0)30 42096371
Fax +49 (0)3212 141 5566
E-mail: editioncritic@email.de

Edition Critic thanks all journals and publications for giving us the permission to reprint the following articles by Ben Cohen. Each piece contained in this volume specifies the original publisher.

More information provided at the German National Library,
Deutsche Nationalbibliothek Frankfurt and Leipzig, http://dnb.d-nb.de
Library of Congress Cataloging-In-Publication Data

Ben Cohen
Some Of My Best Friends – A Journey Through Twenty–First Century
Antisemitism

Holocaust*Holocaust remembrance*Judaism*Israel*Zionism*Antisemitism*
anti-Zionism*Islamism*bistro antisemitism*UK and Israel*US and the Middle East

viii + 215 pages – 6'' x 9'' (15.24cm x 22.86cm) *Index*
Softcover
ISBN 978-3-9814548-9-5 (Softcover)
ISBN 978-3-9815919-0-3 (E-Book)
$25/18€/£15

For Aline, Jonah and Samuel, with love and devotion

In memory of my beloved grandfather, Haham Dr. Solomon Gaon

Contents

i

Introduction

Wisdom is the principal thing;
therefore get wisdom:
and with all thy getting
get understanding.
 – Proverbs 4:7

It is not difficult, these days, to find uncomplicated antisemites. By "uncomplicated," I mean those antisemites who are quite happy, proud even, to be described as haters of Jews, and who actively identify with the past tormentors of the Jewish people. Such individuals and groups are distinguished by the fact that they are easily located, as a simple search of the internet's extremist hinterland will relay. Also noteworthy is the accompanying political promiscuity, in that antisemitism nestles comfortably among Islamists, neo-Nazis, conspiracy theorists, ultranationalists and other believers of similar hue.

The articles and essays of mine collected in this volume hardly ignore these uncomplicated antisemites – particularly those in the Middle East, where antisemitic depictions of Jews and Holocaust denial are a staple of the discourse of both Shi'a Iran, the Sunni Islamists and even those Arab regimes that have survived the upheavals of the last few years. Nonetheless, my primary concern over the last decade or so has been with those whose in the west whose antisemitism is decidedly complicated, not least because such people angrily resist the label "antisemite," depicting it as a smear to blunt criticism of the State of Israel, or of the actions of supporters of the State of Israel who live outside its borders.

What is involved here is the difference, as I wrote in the February 2012 essay for *Commentary* magazine that is included in this collection, between what I call "bierkeller" and "bistro" antisemitism. The crude, violent antisemitism incubated in the German bierkellers where the Nazis guzzled beer and shouted themselves hoarse was a hallmark of the twentieth century. Polite, modulated, ostensibly reasonable antisemitism, often calling itself "anti-Zionism," and expressed in the progressive chatter across the tables of fashionable bistros, is a hallmark of the twenty-first.

Making the case for the existence of this functional antisemitism – that is, the kind of antisemitism that refuses to be called by its name, because its authors do not wish to be tarred with history's debris – has not been a simple task. I say this not because of any lack of confidence in my arguments (in fact, I would readily submit that the antisemitism denial that has distinguished the twenty-first century debate on this subject is itself a form of antisemitism, conjuring up images of Jewish tricksters engaged in emotional and moral blackmail.) Rather, it has not been simple because the net effect of antisemitism denial has been to banish any form of consensus on what this term means, and to encourage skepticism when it does appear. As the Israeli journalist Anshel Pfeffer wrote dismissively in *Haaretz* in February 2014, "Something funny happened to anti-Semitism on the way to the 21st century. It stopped being about persecution and open vilification of Jews, which was something the goyim did to us and we had no control over. It became something we define ourselves, something we discover and too often invent where it isn't at all clear it even exists."

And yet, as the articles and essays reproduced here document, a phenomenon perceived by many people, Jews and non-Jews, as "antisemitism" clearly does exist. Are we to believe that those who perceive antisemitism as a living discourse are this century's equivalent of flat-earthers, preferring the superstitions of memory over the exactitudes of science? For those of us engaged in researching and combating antisemitism, the answer must be a defiant no, and our arguments are duty-bound to back up that assertion.

My hope, in introducing this collection, is that I have both untangled the discursive twists of the antisemitism debate and exposed antisemitism's promiscuity. I have long argued that we live in age of Jewish empowerment, distinguished by the existence of a strong, democratic Jewish state, and the reality that Jews enjoy full civil rights in nearly all the countries where they live in substantial numbers. Yet we also live in a globalized age, and in following the trajectory of antisemitism, I've found it cropping up in Venezuela and Hungary, Turkey and Scotland, the United States and South Africa, and many other points in between. Instead of lazily scorning the complexity of contemporary antisemitism as a largely invented phenomenon, I have tried to understand what drives it and whether we are fated to live with it, in one form or another, for the forseeable future. Whether I have been successful in this endeavor is something that those who read my work must judge for themselves.

***

In the decade that I've been writing about the issues addressed in this book, I've been fortunate to work with some extraordinary people. To the following, I owe an enormous debt of gratitude.

In the United Kingdom, my dear friend Henry Peirse indulged my passion for writing while providing me with both a job and a meaningful challenge in my role as a senior editor with *Global Radio News*. Winston Pickett, formerly of the Institute for Jewish Policy Research, was and remains a constant source of encouragement and ideas. Mark Gardner and Dave Rich at the Community Security Trust were similarly supportive from the beginning, and have remained good friends and colleagues. I also want to record my gratitude to David Hirsh and Ronnie Fraser for their sterling work against the academic boycott of Israel, to my old school chum David Toube and his colleagues at the indispensable *Harry's Place* blog, and to Anthony Julius, Eve Garrard and Alan Johnson for their tirelessly brilliant contributions to the ongoing antisemitism debate. Much the same can be said of my former professor at the University of Manchester, Norman Geras, who sadly passed away in October 2013.

In Israel, I've been hugely fortunate to benefit from the friendship of Dr. Manfred Gerstenfeld of the Jerusalem Center for Public Affairs, who published some of my first essays on antisemitism. I also owe profound thanks to Professor Robert Wistrich of the Hebrew University, to Esther Solomon, the opinion editor of *Haaretz* newspaper, to Professor Gerald Steinberg of NGO Monitor, and to the columnist and academic Petra Marquardt-Bigman.

In the United States, my home since 2004, I've been privileged to have the backing and the insights of a vast number of friends and colleagues. It was an early ambition of mine to one day write for *Commentary* magazine, and I want to thank Abe Greenwald, Jonathan Tobin, John Podhoretz, Seth Mandel and the entire editorial team for publishing my essays and articles in the finest political journal in the English language. I've also been lucky enough to work with Bari Weiss in her editorial roles at both *Tablet* magazine and the *Wall Street Journal*; heartfelt thanks to her and to Allison Hoffman and Alana Newhouse at *Tablet*, and to Sohrab Ahmari and David Feith at the *Wall Street Journal*. Thanks, as well, to Margot Lurie at *Jewish Ideas Daily*, Amy Schwartz at *Moment* magazine, and David Hazony, Josh Block and Omri Ceren at *The Tower* magazine. At JNS.org, a Jewish wire service for whom I write a weekly syndicated column, I want to thank my brilliant editor, Jacob Kamaras, as well as the indefatigable founders Russel Pergament and Josh Katzen. Among my many friends in the world of Jewish advocacy, I want to single out Shula Bahat, who welcomed me to the American Jewish

Committee in 2007, and has remained a valued friend and debating partner ever since, as well as Kenneth Bandler, Graham Cannon and Rabbi Gary Bretton-Granatoor.

I want to express my gratitude to Rabbi Mark Gottlieb, Suzanne Garment, Eric Cohen, Aylana Meisel, Neal Kozodoy and Michael Doran for involving me with the compelling work of the Tikvah Fund. Profound thanks, as well, to Clemens Heni and his capable team at Editions Critic in Berlin for conceiving this volume and for organizing the material contained herein. The following individuals have also been bastions of friendship and insight: Chris DeVito, Marco Greenberg, Michael Weiss, Andrew Apostolou, James Kirchick, Steve Baum, Ceil Goldman, Adam Holland, A. Jay Adler, Terry Glavin, Jonathan Narvey, Michael Ledeen, Barbara Ledeen, Diego Arria, Banafsheh Zand-Bonazzi, Hillel Neuer, Gary Emmanuel, Alan Mittleman, Noah Pollak, Gary Rosenblatt, Ben Evansky, Dovid Efune, Karl Pfeifer, Gregg Mashberg, Ed Joseph, Benjamin Weinthal, John-Paul Pagano, Aryn Chapman, Walter Reich, Sammy Eppel, Leopoldo Martinez, and Rabbi Marc Angel of Congregation Shearith Israel in New York.

Three wonderful individuals have been a constant source of support and advice: in Israel, my father, Edward Cohen; in Argentina, my friend, colleague and frequent writing partner, Eamonn McDonagh; and here in New York, my friend and former AJC colleague, Michael Geller. Our long and considered conversations and email exchanges have, it is my hope, made me a better writer and thinker, and for that, and much else besides, I thank the three of you from the bottom of my heart.

My greatest debt is to my darling wife, Aline, and my two sons, Jonah and Samuel, whose love serves as a daily reminder to me of what is good in this world.

New York City, April 2014

Foreword, by Anthony Julius

Anthony Julius is a British lawyer and author, and a leading expert on antisemitism. His books include T.S. Eliot, Anti-Semitism and Literary Form (Thames and Hudson, 2003) and Trials of the Diaspora: A History of Anti-Semitism in England (Oxford University Press 2010).

Ben Cohen is an advocate of Israel's cause and a commentator on the Middle East scene. Are these positions compatible? The correct answer to this question draws on an ancient quarrel. It is quarrel that resonates in our own times. We have not, indeed, moved beyond its terms. As in other ancient quarrels, the adverse parties are no less than Plato and Aristotle.

Plato's position was clear, and has much to commend it. Advocates – in Plato's language, rhetoricians and sophists – cannot be trusted. They are experts in counterfeiting; they make the phoney appear genuine. They are experts in deception; they make the vicious appear virtuous. They are thus immoral – manipulative, untrustworthy, fraudulent, obfuscating. They have no place in any well-ordered society. Aristotle's position was just as clear, but subtler. Every vocation or profession has its own specific ethical obligations. These are additional to the general ethical obligations binding on us all. Advocacy is a profession or vocation, honourable in itself, and has chief among its specific ethical obligations, the following two. First, they must represent their client's interests with zeal. Second, they must advocate those interests truthfully. The way Aristotle reconciles these duties – and, of course, they are in tension with each other – is by proposing the following formula: The advocate must make the best possible case. Critically, "possible" here means consistent with the truth.

Aristotle was right. Plato's position shuts out even the possibility of lawyers, or the possibility of ideologues, in a well-ordered society. And that is absurd: litigants must be represented, different political positions must be advocated. One cannot imagine any decent society (let alone, a well-ordered one) in which political differences could not be ventilated, or defendants in trials championed.

But the test of honesty has to be met. Notwithstanding the heat of the presentation, the urgency and passion of the argument, truth has to be given its due. Ben Cohen meets that test. In a political milieu in which lies are routinely deployed in defence of indefensible positions, Cohen is unusual in his restraint. He is both a stalwart defender of Israel's essential interests and an engaging commentator on the Middle East scene. He can be read with profit by both friends and enemies of the various parties in that region.

Chapter One: The UK, Jews, and Israel

The Persistence of Antisemitism on the British Left

Jewish Political Studies Review, October 2004

Although egalitarian, cosmopolitan, and internationalist principles are common to all variants of socialist doctrine, these have not immunized the Left from antisemitism. What the German socialist leader August Bebel denounced as the "socialism of fools" is as old and as resilient as the Left itself, even if its original thesis, famously expressed in Kautsky's prognosis[1] that the Jews would disappear with capitalism's demise, has turned out to be a fallacy. Like other forms of antisemitism, left-wing antisemitism has survived by mutating; whereas once the Jewish question (or problem) was viewed through the prism of economics, now it belongs to the realm of politics. The orthodox Marxist notion[2] that the Jews – as an economic agent – perform a distinctive function within a system designed for the extraction of surplus value has been replaced by the anticolonialist notion that the Jews – as a national collective – are integral to the maintenance of American hegemony on a global level.[3] Accordingly, there has been a conceptual shift on the Left from the politics of class to the politics of identity; and, again accordingly, a practical alignment with those forces, most notably the Islamist movements, opposed to this hegemony.

As a result of this alignment, three points warrant consideration. First, visceral opposition not to Israel's security policies alone but to its very legitimacy means that, as in Islamist discourse, the terms "Jew," "Israel," and "Zionist" are increasingly interchangeable in contemporary left-wing discourse; second, this discourse has been standardized and globalized;[4] third, this discourse is increasingly finding recognition outside the activist margins, for example, among politicians broadly described as "progressive," among prominent academics, and in liberal media outlets. In the United Kingdom, the phenomenon of left-wing antisemitism has been somewhat overshadowed by the attention paid to similar problems elsewhere in Europe, particularly in France, Belgium, and The Netherlands. Nevertheless, the antisemitism of the British Left deserves closer examination, not least because Britain was the former Mandate power in Palestine and a Labour government was in office when the State of Israel was created in 1948. The aim of this article, therefore, is to take a long view of the development of antisemitism on the British Left. While much of the analysis concentrates on

attitudes toward Zionism, it needs to be stressed that in the United Kingdom, as elsewhere, hostility toward Zionism and Israel often functions as a
Trojan horse for antisemitism.

The primary argument underlying this article is that the classic antisemitism associated with the xenophobic Right and its leftist version are
linked by a profound enmity toward the empowered, autonomous Jew. For
the extreme Right, antisemitism is based on a dark fantasy about the malign
effects of Jewish power, which integrates the financial and the political
spheres. In the leftist imagination, the only good Jew is the invisible Jew, one
who is assimilated totally by his surroundings; by contrast, Jewish national
consciousness is, a priori, reactionary, supremacist, and politically aligned
with imperialism. For many on the Left, the concrete expression of this consciousness, the State of Israel, is the last colonial outpost in the world.

Origins of the "New" Antisemitism

"Why do you come to me with your special Jewish sorrows?" wrote the
Polish Jewish revolutionary Rosa Luxemburg[5] to a comrade. "I feel just as
sorry for the wretched Indian victims in Putumayo, the Negroes in Africa....I
cannot find a special corner in my heart for the ghetto." Those who would
position themselves as Luxemburg's heirs have, perhaps, taken her sentiments a step further. Jewish suffering is relativized or denied outright, while
the supposed crimes of Jewish nationalism are seized upon with gusto.
Moreover, in the collective heart of the modern Left there is a "special corner" for the Palestinians, whose particular narrative of exile has elevated
their trials far above those of other unfortunate nations.

It is at the farthest reaches of the Left, where there is a fixation with
the Palestinians, that we find the brashest expressions of antisemitism.
Among the mosaic of groups that compose the "antiglobalization" movement, as well as among the remnants of the New Left, antisemitic rhetoric
and symbolism is rife. The UN World Conference against Racism in Durban
in September 2001, the conferences organized by the World Social Forum in
India and Brazil, and the marches in several European cities against the U.S.-
led intervention in Iraq are all examples of public events where Jews have
been actively denigrated. Such displays have commonly been presented as
manifestations of the "new antisemitism," generally dated back to September 2000, when the second Palestinian intifada began. Decidedly, this "new"
antisemitism, which would deny selfdetermination to the Jews even as it
celebrates this principle for other nationalities, is driven by the Left, and not
the Right. Even so, it is far from new.[6]

In the British case, it should be borne in mind that contemporary manifestations of leftist antisemitism are loosely related, if at all, to the hostility – rooted in a conflict between indigenous and immigrant workers rather than opposition to Zionism – that Jews encountered from sections of the British labor movement at the turn of the 20th century. In addition, among some British social democrats there is a parallel tradition of solidarity with the Jews and Israel. As in other countries, the adversarial position toward Zionism was the effect of an encroaching New Left agenda during the 1960s and 1970s, so that by 1982 W.D. Rubinstein could state: "Fringe neo-Nazi groups notwithstanding, significant antisemitism is now almost exclusively a left-wing rather than a right-wing phenomenon."[7] Rubinstein also identified the factors that distinguish current leftist discourse as anti-Semitic, in particular the questioning of Israel's legitimacy as a state. This strategy of delegitimization was accompanied by a steady buildup of pro-Palestinian opinion. In a case study of the United Kingdom, Rubinstein noted that as early as 1969, pro-Palestinian groups were being formed within the Labour Party; by 1978, one-sixth of Labour's parliamentary contingent was identifiably pro-Arab. These developments reflected the growing influence of the far Left within and outside the party's ranks.[8]

Much of the ire directed toward Zionism on the British Left drew strongly on motifs found in Soviet propaganda, specifically the equation of Zionism with Nazism and the accusation that the Zionist movement collaborated with the Nazis or even engaged in the killing of Jews to further its own ends. Rubinstein cites the example of the British Anti-Zionist Organization (BAZO),[9] a left-wing group active on university campuses during the late 1970s and early 1980s. In an especially insidious example of the collaboration charge, BAZO claimed that the *Struma*, a ship carrying Romanian Jewish refugees to Palestine that was sunk by the Soviets in 1942, was in fact destroyed by Zionists because the sole survivor, David Stoliar, went on to fight for the Haganah.

Aside from the facile logic involved here, claims like this one, and those contained in the play *Perdition* discussed below, demonstrate the difference between the anti-Zionism of the *ancien* Left and that espoused by its new incarnation. As Robert Wistrich has argued, in becoming a "code word for the forces of reaction in general," Zionism has assumed a global importance for the contemporary Left that not even Marx and Lenin could have foreseen. Consequently, "[t]he extreme left in western societies not only denigrates Israel and Zionism in a systematic manner, but its irrational hostility frequently spills over into contempt or antipathy towards Jews and Judaism as such."[10]

The Lebanon War of 1982 afforded many instances of leftist publications in Britain engaging in ferocious attacks on Israel that drew on classic antisemitic images and themes. These attacks bore striking similarities to the antisemitic crudities evident during the formative years of English socialism. In 1884, for example, *Justice*, the newspaper of the Social Democratic Federation, railed against the "Jew moneylenders who now control every Foreign Office in Europe."[11] Almost a century later, the newspaper of the Workers Revolutionary Party – an organization distinguished by the presence of the actress Vanessa Redgrave among its members and for the generous funding it received from Libya – employed similar terms when it opined that it was "Britain who sold the Palestinian people out to Zionist money power."[12] Aside from the typical association of Jewish influence with financial muscle, what is arresting about this statement is the exaggeration of the power of Zionism to the extent that it, and not the British Mandate, is the starting point for what passes as an analysis of the origins of the Arab-Israeli conflict.

A related tendency is the ascribing of collective guilt for Israel's actions. As this is an important feature of the "new" antisemitism, it should be remembered that this was also pronounced during the Lebanon War. A British anarchist paper captured the two prongs of this argument – that all Jews are responsible for what Israel does and that Jews are therefore responsible for their own misfortune – extremely well.[13] The massacres at the Sabra and Shatila camps, blamed automatically on Israel, could not fail to spark "acts of revenge" across the world; it was not fanciful to assume that the targets of revenge would be Jewish communities. The consequent claim, namely, that Zionism is the "monster" that fuels antisemitism, holds the Jews themselves accountable for prejudice against them. This recasting of Zionism as a causal factor of antisemitism, rather than an authentic Jewish response to it, is a uniquely leftist contribution to antisemitic doctrine. It is, moreover, intimately linked to the accusation of Zionist collaboration with the Nazis. As Rubinstein points out, whereas for the neo-Nazis the Shoah is a hoax, for the far Left "[t]he Holocaust now emerges as the Jews (or Jewish nationalism's) greatest crime – the autogenocide of the Twentieth Century."[14]

Perdition: A Dress Rehearsal

In 1986 the play *Perdition*,[15] by the Marxist playwright Jim Allen, brought the accusation of Zionist-Nazi collaboration to the British public's attention for the first time. Until that point the Left's discussion of Jews and Israel, like most of its discussions, had been conducted internally, with leaders defining the doctrine and foot soldiers repeating it to each other. Now, a thesis that had been dismissed by scholars of the Shoah was suddenly granted a wider audience. *Perdition* was based on a well-known trial brought to the Jerusalem district court in 1954.[16] The defendant in the trial was an elderly Hungarian Jew, Malkhiel Grunwald, who was charged with defaming the Hungarian Zionist leader Rudolf Kastner when he accused him of collaborating with the Nazis as they prepared to exterminate Hungary's Jews in 1944. Kastner's intent had been to negotiate a deal whereby the German army would be supplied with ten thousands trucks in exchange for a stay of execution. But according to Grunwald, Kastner had facilitated, through his negotiations with Adolf Eichmann, the destruction of Hungary's Jews while enriching himself personally. The court found in favor of Grunwald. Kastner himself was assassinated just before Israel's Supreme Court overturned the Jerusalem court's decision.

In the hands of a talented dramatist, this story could have probed the nature and limits of the moral choice confronting the leader of a beleaguered community, as well as the complex motives of the survivor who made these allegations. In Allen's hands, any nuances and subtleties were purged. In his own words, *Perdition* was a tale of "privileged Jewish leaders" collaborating "in the extermination of their own kind in order to help bring about a Zionist state, Israel, a state which itself is racist."[17] The announcement by London's Royal Court Theatre that it intended to stage the play sparked a furious public debate. Many Jewish scholars and leaders pointed to gross distortions and inaccuracies in the text, asserting that *Perdition* was little more than standard antisemitic conspiracy theory with a leftist tinge. European Zionists, the play charged, betrayed Europe's Jews while "all-powerful American Jewry" (a line from the play) discreetly approved the strategy. Indeed, the text was replete with lines that equated the power of Zionism with that of Nazism ("the Zionist knife in the Nazi fist") and highlighted the selfishness of Jewish leaders ("To save your hides, you practically led them to the gas chambers of Auschwitz").

In January 1987 the artistic director of the Royal Court, Max Stafford-Clark, declared that his doubts about *Perdition* were grave enough for him to cancel its performance. Although Stafford-Clark made the decision on his own, left-wing activists were quick to point to a Zionist "conspiracy."[18] The film director Ken Loach, a close colleague of Allen, claimed that the theater had caved in to pressure from prominent British Jews such as Dr. Stephen Roth, Lord Weidenfeld, and Lord Goodman; men, Loach said, "who can pay their way." For anyone exploring the recent history of antisemitism on the British Left, the *Perdition* affair is seminal for at least two reasons. First, the immense press coverage the affair generated meant that extreme anti-

Zionist claims won wider attention, particularly among Britain's liberally inclined intelligentsia; as the past was interpreted through the prejudices of the present – the perception of Israel as a racist, militarist state – it is not surprising that these claims were given serious and sometimes sympathetic attention. Second, the affair rehabilitated the old canard of the nefarious, transcendental power of Jewish individuals and organizations, whether manifested in wartime Hungary (the subject matter of the play) or modern-day London (the reason for the play's cancellation). Since 2000, a similar discourse of uncompromising anti-Zionism, which carries both implicit and explicit warnings about the dangerous extent of Jewish power, has resurfaced in Britain. As has been demonstrated thus far, its authors belong to the far Left, but those who echo it are spread, politically and demographically, more widely.

Antisemitism and the Liberal-Left Elite

In January 2002 the *New Statesman*, an august journal of the British Center-Left, published a cover story about the "Zionist lobby" in Britain.[19] The magazine's cover displayed a golden Star of David stabbing a pliant Union flag and carried the legend: "A Kosher Conspiracy?" In the days and weeks that followed, Jewish and non-Jewish critics excoriated the *New Statesman* for its revival of antisemitic iconography. The magazine eventually ran a qualified apology from the editor, Peter Wilby, who conceded that the cover "used images and words in such a way as to create *unwittingly* the impression that the *New Statesman* was following an antisemitic tradition that sees the Jews as a conspiracy piercing the heart of the nation" (emphasis added).[20]

Wilby's assertion that the *New Statesman* did not realize the historical import of the imagery it used must be regarded as disingenuous. Is it really credible that no one among the culturally sensitive editorial staff of a political weekly would have been struck, in examining the cover before it went to press, by the echoes of the *Protocols* or the agitational rhetoric of Maurras or Streicher? That no one at the *New Statesman* was aware of the Left's own antisemitic idiom, from Fourier's "parasites" to Stalin's "rootless cosmopolitans"? These points were never addressed by the magazine.

The article on the Zionist lobby itself, by Denis Sewell,[21] amassed evidence for one conclusion and then ended with another. After writing about the web of clients assembled by an Israeli arms dealer, including the Shah of Iran and Indira Gandhi; after claiming that this same arms dealer was financially supporting a pro-Israeli lobbying group in London; and after pointing to instances of journalists at *The Times* and the *Daily Telegraph* allegedly being censored by media barons with Zionist sympathies, Sewell ended his piece with the argument that the Zionist lobby was ineffective and "clueless" because it opened itself up to criticism by accepting funds from a man involved in the sale of weaponry. No such sophistry was evident in the accompanying article by John Pilger, the extreme left-wing journalist.[22] Pilger has been a stalwart critic of Tony Blair's project to remake "old" Labour as "new" Labour, whereby many long-established socialist principles were abandoned and a greater distance was placed between the party and the trade unions. For Pilger, as for many on the Left, Blair's personal sympathy with Israel reflects the party's sharp turn to the right, as well as being emblematic of British subservience to American foreign policy. Indulging in the conspiracy theorizing beloved of the far Left, Pilger identified Blair's friendship with "wealthy Jewish businessman" Lord Levy, who also serves as his envoy to the Middle East, as the principle reason for his support of the Sharon "regime." Hence, the *New Statesman* gave us two contrasting views of Jewish power. For Sewell, it is incompetent, whereas for Pilger, it is ruthless and proficient; for both writers, though, Jewish power undoubtedly exists in the shadows of political life, manipulating and shaping policy as it tries to escape scrutiny.

This stress on the intersection of Jewish power with Jewish wealth was evident during the furore over *Perdition*, demonstrating that it is one of the more favored antisemitic themes of the Left and is easily revived. Indeed, in 2003 the veteran Labour MP Tam Dalyell told a *Vanity Fair* journalist that Blair's views on the Middle East had been subverted by a "Jewish cabal" that included, along with Lord Levy, Peter Mandelson, a key ally of the prime minister, and Jack Straw, the foreign secretary (both Mandelson and Straw have Jewish ancestry, but neither is Jewish).[23] Moreover, this highlighting of Jewish influence is not restricted to the British Left's appraisal of their own country's Middle East policy. Numerous denunciations of American foreign policy under the Bush administration have dwelt upon the Jewish origins of the neoconservatives in Washington. In 2004, a former BBC Middle East correspondent was even more brazen. At a speech in Glasgow, Tim Llewellyn accused President Clinton's former Middle East envoy Denis Ross of hiding behind "a lovely Anglo-Saxon name." He went on to say that Ross is "not just a Jew, he is a Zionist...a Zionist propagandist."[24]

The passage of the anti-Zionism of the extreme Left to the Center-Left, along with its attendant disdain for Jewish concerns, is visible in other media outlets. A good deal of attention has been paid to the BBC, which, despite a public broadcasting remit and "Producer Guidelines" that are meant to enforce impartiality, has been consistently biased in its reporting on the Middle East. One analyst has suggested that to understand why this is the case, the BBC's own culture needs to be examined: "It is full of reporters holding left-wing, so-called 'liberal' viewpoints, including very negative ones about Israel. They then recruit people under them who have a similar outlook. In this way, the liberal left-wing system propagates itself."[25]

Similar criticism has been directed at the United Kingdom's two main liberal dailies, *The Guardian* and *The Independent*, both of which regularly publish comment questioning Israel's legitimacy and portraying it as a pariah state.[26] Although both papers have, on occasion, acknowledged the Jewish community's anxieties about their reporting, they have also, on occasion, been dismissive.[27] For example, Paul Foot, Britain's leading leftist commentator until his death in 2004, wrote in his *Guardian* column: "Especially pathetic on the part of our apologists for Israeli oppression is their bleating about antisemitism. For the sort of oppression they favour is the seed from which all racialism, including antisemitism, grows."[28]

This brief survey of attitudes toward Jews on the British liberal-Left would not be complete without some mention of the campaign for an academic boycott of Israel, begun in April 2002 by the biology professor Steven Rose. As in the media, liberal and leftist viewpoints are disproportionately represented in Britain's universities. Despite the profusion of human rights crises around the world, from Sudan to North Korea, it is the Palestinian cause that has seized the imagination of Britain's leftist academics and has fueled calls for a boycott; one practical result has been the reporting of a number of cases of discrimination against Israeli scholars and researchers in British academic institutions. The boycott campaign is perhaps the most transparent illustration of the Left's determination to depict Israel as the ultimate rogue state.

The Red-Green Alliance

The spillage of anti-Zionism into antisemitism noted by Wistrich is an increasingly perilous feature of British political life, as it is elsewhere in Europe. This tendency has manifested itself everywhere from the literary pages of liberal newspapers to resolutions on the Middle East passed by trade unions, as well as in the escalating calls for an academic boycott of, and economic sanctions against, Israel. It has been argued here that any examination of antisemitism on the British Left without a strong sense of historical context is compromised, but it is equally true that the conditions that enable the expression of anti-Jewish sentiment on the Left have never been as permissive as they are now. To understand why this is the case, it is necessary to explore in greater detail an issue raised at the beginning of this article: the growing intimacy between the Left and the Islamists.[29] The very existence of this alliance represents a critical shift for the Left. Radical socialism and radical Islam are far from obvious bedfellows, and a strict focus on the key texts of both does not yield any synergies. Even so, text and doctrine cannot be regarded as the sole substance of politics. Otherwise, one cannot explain why the left-wing mayor of London, Ken Livingstone, known for his previous support of feminist causes, would enthusiastically host an obscurantist Muslim cleric, or why a party claiming allegiance to Trotskyism would join forces with a group identified with the Muslim Brotherhood.[30]

Demography partially explains this shift. There are approximately 1.5 million Muslims in the United Kingdom, and the population is growing. Many British Muslims originate from Pakistan and Bangladesh, and their ranks have been swelled by arrivals from other Muslim countries, notably in the Arab world. In tandem, there has been a corresponding political radicalization. Some British Muslims identify with groups like al-Muhajiroun, which openly declares its support for Osama bin Laden (indeed, the first foreign homicide bombers to carry out an operation in Israel were two British Muslims). Many more identify with the ostensibly moderate Muslim Association of Britain (MAB), which, despite forswearing terrorism, proudly declares its support for Hamas.

Since the end of the Cold War, the Left has been groping for a mass response to the "New World Order"; by allying with the Islamists it may have found one. Of all the marches held in Europe in 2003 opposing the Iraq War, the largest took place in London, involving over one million protestors. An outgrowth of this march was a new political party, Respect, sponsored by the Socialist Workers Party, MAB, and George Galloway, a Scottish MP expelled from the Labour Party in part because of his links with Saddam Hussein's regime. Although Respect failed to win any seats in the 2004 local and European parliamentary elections, it enjoyed a strong showing in those areas of the country, such as East London and the Midlands, with large Muslim populations. Galloway, in particular, is known for his detestation of Israel; of only a handful of principles expressed in Respect's founding document, solidarity with the Palestinians is one. At the same time, Galloway has rejected accusations of antisemitism.[31] Such denials, however, ring ever more hollow for the following reason: despite all the demonization of Israel and Zionism that the British Left has engaged in for the last four decades, leftist groups stopped short of organizational alignment with anti-Semites. With the advent of Respect, this is no longer the case. MAB's admiration for Islamist ideologues such as Sayid Qutb and Sheikh Ahmed Yassin, who expressed their loathing for Jews as Jews and not as Zionists, has begged some sort of clarification from its left-wing partners; but none has been forthcom-

Ben Cohen

ing, save for the standard response that the participation of several Jews in the Palestinian solidarity movement renders accusations of antisemitism inadmissible. What is not recognized is that these Jews, whether acting as individuals or through organizations such as Jews for Justice for Palestinians,[32] have no real base inside the British Jewish community and only identify as Jews for the purpose of disavowing Israel.

Fear of alienating Muslim activists and voters is certainly one reason for the reluctance to acknowledge and condemn Muslim anti- Semitism. Mindful of the importance of the Muslim vote in London, Ken Livingstone, the mayor of London, offered his hospitality to the Egyptian Muslim cleric Yusuf al-Qaradawi, who visited the British capital in July 2004. Despite being confronted with al-Qaradawi's antisemitic pronouncements – he has declared, for example, that there can be no dialogue with Jews "except by the sword and the rifle"[33] – Livingstone continually dismissed objections to his presence in the United Kingdom as "Islamophobia." Gay rights activists, once an important base of support for Livingstone, were similarly dismissed when they expressed displeasure at Qaradawi's visit. Thus did the new Islamist-leftist constellation in Britain reveal those political constituencies that are excluded as well as included: Muslim distaste for those issues that were at the heart of the Left's agenda, such as women's emancipation and homosexual rights, has finally won out. As well as the electoral imperatives of local politics, geopolitics is another explanatory factor for the Left's startling shift. Opposition to the United States is axiomatic to the Left's credo, even if that means joining with other currents with which there is little ideological commonality. This necessarily affects the Left's attitude toward the Jews. In this regard, the "socialism of fools" derided by Bebel might be said to have given way to the "useful idiots" phenomenon derided by Lenin.[34]

Much has changed, but much has stayed the same. The denial of victimhood to the Jews, the plundering of the Shoah to condemn Israel,[35] the conspiratorial portrayal of Jewish power and the inherent illegitimacy of Jewish self-determination, are all constants. However, the antisemitism distinctive to the British Left has integrated, ideologically and organizationally, with its Islamist counterpart. Consequently, British political discourse in the mosque, the street, and the salon has been infected. This last assertion is not intended to subsume peculiarities and differences into a single framework; rather, the aim has been to discern a general pattern of leftist antisemitism in Britain that, ominously, continues to develop.

Notes (all online sources were accessible at the day of the first publication of this article)

1. Kautsky argues that the disappearance of the Jews is also a desirable outcome: "We cannot say we have completely emerged from the Middle Ages as long as Judaism still exists among us. The sooner it disappears, the better it will be, not only for society, but also for the Jews themselves." Karl Kautsky, *Are the Jews a Race?* (Jonathan Cape, London, 1926), also available at: http://www.marxists.org/archive/kautsky/1914/jewsrace/index.htm.
2. For a classic exegesis of this view, see Karl Marx, "On the Jewish Question," in *Early Writings* (London: Penguin, 1992).
3. The view that Zionist imperatives control U.S. policy in the Middle East is increasingly finding favor on the Left, as several scholars have noted. See, for example, Shlomo Lappin, "Israel and the New Antisemitism," *Dissent*, Spring 2003.
4. See Daniel Goldhagen, "The Globalization of Antisemitism," *Forward*, 2 May 2003.
5. Quoted in Walter Laqueur, *A History of Zionism* (New York: M.J.F Books, 1997), p. 435.
6. For an incisive perspective on the novelty of the "new" antisemitism, see Anthony Julius, "Is There Anything 'New' in the New Antisemitism?" in Paul Iganski and Barry Kosmin, eds., *A New Antisemitism? Debating Judeophobia in 21st-Century Britain* (London: Profile Books, 2003).
7. W.D. Rubinstein, *The Left, the Right and the Jews* (London: Croom Helm, 1982), p. 9.
8. *Ibid.*, p. 56.
9. *Ibid.*, p. 110.
10. Robert Wistrich, "Left-Wing Anti-Zionism in Western Societies," in Robert Wistrich, ed., *Anti-Zionism and Antisemitism in the Contemporary World* (London: Macmillan, 1990), p. 48.
11. See Steve Cohen, *That's Funny, You Don't Look Antisemitic: An Anti-Racist Analysis of Left Antisemitism* (Manchester: Beyond the Pale Publishing, 1984), p. 20.
12. *Ibid.*, p. 42.
13. *Ibid.*, p. 53. The newspaper in question was the now defunct *Big Flame*.
14. Rubinstein, The Left, p. 115.
15. *Perdition* was published in 1987 by the anti-Zionist publishing house Ithaca Press (London).
16. See Leora Bilsky, "Judging Evil in the Trial of Kastner," *Law and History Review*, Vol. 19, No. 1 (2001).

17. Quoted in David Cesarani, "The Perdition Affair," in Wistrich, *Anti-Zionism and Antisemitism*, p. 54.

18. *Ibid.*, p. 57.

19. See Winston Pickett, "Nasty or Nazi? The Use of Antisemitic Topoi in the Liberal-Left Media," in Iganski and Kosmin, *A New Antisemitism?* pp. 148–166.

20. *The New Statesman*, 11 February 2002.

21. *Ibid.*, 14 January 2002.

22. *Ibid.*

23. Dalyell later said: "I am fully aware that one is treading on cut glass on this issue and no-one wants to be accused of antisemitism, but, if it is a question of launching an assault on Syria or Iran … then one has to be candid." See http://news.bbc.co.uk/1/hi/uk-politics/2999219.stm.

24. *Jewish Chronicle*, 25 June 2004.

25. Trevor Asserson, "What Went Wrong at the BBC," *Jerusalem Viewpoints*, No. 511, 15 January 2004. Asserson's detailed research is available at www.bbcwatch.con.

26. See, e.g., Gerald Kaufman, "The Case for Sanctions against Israel," *The Guardian*, 12 July 2004. Kaufman is a Jewish Labour MP who has become a virulent opponent of Israel.

27. Upholding its liberal principles, *The Guardian* ran a fairly critical review of a book by the Israeli journalist Daphna Baram, *Disenchantment: The Guardian and Israel*, which the newspaper itself published. The reviewer, Bryan Cheyette, observed that Baram had "something of a tin ear when it comes to the experiences of Jews as a minority in the diaspora." Brian Cheyette, "What Became of Zion?" *The Guardian*, 24 July 2004.

28. Paul Foot, "In Defence of Oppression," *The Guardian*, 5 March 2002.

29. See especially Dave Hyde, "Europe's Other Red-Green Alliance," *Zeek*, April 2003, available at http://www.zeek.net/politics-0304.shtml.

30. Anthony Browne, "This Sinister Brotherhood," *The Times*, 11 August 2004.

31. In a 2002 speech at Cambridge University, Galloway declared: "We shouldn't allow a group of gangsters called Zionists to hold us to ransom on the issue of antisemitism." See http://www.cambridgeclarion.org/Galloway.quest.12jul2002.html.

32. Many British Jews were scandalized when, in December 2003, Jews for Justice for Palestinians held a Christmas-carol service in central London. Among the carols they sang was "Little Town of Bethlehem," rewritten to condemn IDF operations in that town.

33. See http://www.memri.org/bin/latestnews.cgi?ID>SD75304.

34. Lenin (supposedly) referred to those western leftists who unconditionally defended the USSR as "useful idiots."
35. A notorious example of the abuse of Holocaust imagery involved the poet and critic Tom Paulin, who, after telling *Al-Ahram* in 2002 that "Brooklyn-born" Jewish settlers should be shot, wrote a poem that described Israeli soldiers as the "Zionist SS." See David Cesarani, *The Left and the Jews, the Jews and the Left* (London: Profile, 2003), p. 75.

Evaluating Muslim-Jewish Relations in Britain

Jerusalem Viewpoints, February 1, 2005

British Muslim organizations are becoming far more vocal on foreign policy matters. Two positions would appear to be axiomatic: opposition to the Iraq war and Britain's continued involvement in Iraq, and a resolute anti-Zionism which both delegitimizes the State of Israel and scorns Jewish anxieties when it comes to antisemitism.

Prior to the furor over Salman Rushdie's novel *The Satanic Verses,* national origin was the principal component of Muslim immigrant identity in Britain. The Rushdie Affair introduced an overarching Muslim identity over these distinct communities. By the end of 1988, a UK Action Committee on Islamic Affairs (UKACIA) had been formed to coordinate protests against Rushdie. By January 1989, Muslims in the northern English city of Bradford were burning copies of the book in public. It can be argued that alleviating the social plight of British Muslims does not necessarily require legislation which characterizes the policy focus as a problem of discrimination against a *religious* minority. Moreover, a number of studies have questioned the assumption of an organic link between deprivation and Islamist politics. More sensitive social policies and better employment prospects will not, by themselves, dilute the appeal of the radical Islamist agenda. A November 2004 poll conducted by *The Guardian* demonstrates that it is political and religious issues, rather than economic and social ones, which energize Muslim activism in the UK. According to the poll, 88 percent of Muslims want to see schools and workplaces incorporate Muslim prayer times as part of their working day – a demand all but unknown among other religious groups.

The key issue which divides the British Jewish and Muslim communities is the conflict between Israel and the Palestinians. Jews are confronted with a rigid Islamist standpoint which concedes no legitimacy to the State of Israel and which justifies terrorist violence against Jews in the name of Palestine, regardless of whether the victims carry Israeli passports. The separation of the secular and religious domains is a prerequisite for both successful Muslim participation in the institutions of Europe and for reform of the Muslim world itself. At the present time, Britain and other EU states are trying to reach a modus vivendi with an Islamic communal infrastructure that does not accept this separation.

Perceptions of British Muslims

Anyone studying the dynamics of the Muslim community in the United Kingdom is confronted with three distinct images. There is the image of the Muslim as fanatic: Islamist clerics indulging in toxic anti-Western and anti-semitic rhetoric and endorsing the path of violent *jihad* in front of cheering crowds of youthful supporters. There is the image of the Muslim as victim: highly vulnerable, particularly in the aftermath of the 9/11 atrocities, to physical abuse, verbal insults, and the vandalism of mosques and community centers, and disproportionately exposed to poverty and discrimination. Finally, there is the image of Muslim as citizen: advancing communal interests and concerns through the established channels of British political life and forging an identity which harmonizes a devotion to Islamic beliefs with a commitment to the country in which 45 percent of the community was born.

Given these distinct perceptions, it is helpful to be cognizant of the different trends which are at play within the Muslim community. That there are, among non-Muslims, radically different readings of what Muslims in Britain represent testifies to the difficulty of forging a cogent British Muslim identity. In tandem, there is a prevailing view among many politicians and commentators that, in relation to other minorities, attempts to foster a greater sense of belonging to Britain among Muslims have been comparatively less successful.[1] There are a number of reasons for this. British Muslims are, in ethnic terms, far more heterogeneous than other religious minorities. In addition to native-born Muslims, there are large communities originating from South Asia, the Middle East, and Southeastern Europe. This alone complicates the nature of British Muslim identity. Moreover, the combination of social disadvantage along with the penetration of anti-Western beliefs and values into many Muslim communities has served as a brake on greater integration.

Nevertheless, Britain remains confident of its image as a tolerant nation able to integrate different groups. Politicians of all stripes are keen to demonstrate that minorities can advance themselves in what Home Office Minister Fiona McTaggart has described as a "fantastically diverse society." Indeed, Michael Howard, the first Jewish leader of the Conservative Party since Benjamin Disraeli, eulogized Britain's openness during a keynote speech to the party's 2004 conference.[2] Born in Wales to Romanian Jewish immigrant parents, Howard related that his grandmother had perished in a Nazi concentration camp. If not for Winston Churchill and for Britain, he mused, he too would have shared his grandmother's fate. Howard concluded that he – literally – owed Britain his life; his goal now was to give the country "just a tiny bit back of what Britain has given me."

While some Muslim leaders have made clear their desire to contribute positively to Britain, they are also adamant that a greater sense of belonging cannot be achieved unless certain Muslim demands are met. A notable current demand, which has the support of the government, seeks to outlaw "religious discrimination." This expands existing race relations legislation by making it an offense to target someone because of their religious beliefs. Consequently, there are concerns, which the government has denied have any basis, that the measures will impact negatively on freedom of speech. Previous legislation covered only Jews and Sikhs, as they are defined as racial as well as religious groups; the new laws seek to close a perceived loophole by offering protection to religious groups, foremost among them Muslims, who are multi-racial in composition. A number of critics, such as the Labour Peer Lord Desai, have repeatedly said that new legislation is unnecessary, since existing laws already provide a robust defense for an individual discriminated against on racial or religious grounds.[3]

More broadly, Muslim organizations are seeking greater backing for Islamic education in the state sector. They are calling for the introduction of courts, based on sharia law, to deal with divorce, inheritance, child custody and similar status issues.[4] In addition – and this is of particular relevance to relations with the Jewish community – Muslim organizations are becoming far more vocal on foreign policy matters. Much of the focus is on the Middle East and two positions would appear to be axiomatic: firstly, opposition to the Iraq War and Britain's continued involvement in Iraq; and secondly, a resolute anti-Zionism which both delegitimizes the State of Israel and scorns Jewish anxieties when it comes to antisemitism. Underscoring all of this is a determination by Muslim communal organizations to group legitimate political criticism with illegitimate racial and religious slurs: all amount to expressions of Islamophobia.

A serious examination of the state of Muslim-Jewish relations in Britain needs to recognize that the emergence of a Muslim political consciousness is a critical element of the narrative; for those Muslims under the age of 25 especially (a massive 70 percent of the total population), an Islamic political and cultural identity exercises a powerful attraction. Therefore, we will first examine the development of Muslim consciousness in Britain and its current manifestations before considering the implications for relations with British Jews.

The Emergence of Muslim Political Consciousness in Britain

While there has been a discernible Muslim presence in the United Kingdom since the beginning of the nineteenth century, the mass immigration of Muslims to the UK coincided with the dismantling of the British Empire. Muslims, as well as Hindus and Sikhs, arrived in large numbers from India and Pakistan from the late 1940s onwards. Like immigrants from the West Indies, they mainly found work in the public sector, in factories, in transport and similar fields. A large number also started small businesses, such as shops and restaurants. Racism and discrimination were an ugly fact of life from the beginning. The 1970s was a particularly unpleasant period, due to an upsurge in agitation by the neo-Nazi National Front following an influx of Asian refugees expelled by Idi Amin's regime in Uganda.

Among those immigrants to the UK of the Muslim faith, there was a gradual process of institution-building. During the 1960s and 1970s, student societies, educational trusts, and welfare bodies were formed, and a Muslim journal, *Impact,* began publication. But it was not until the late 1980s that a definably Muslim political consciousness emerged in Britain. The catalyst for this was what became known as the "Rushdie Affair." Prior to the furor over Salman Rushdie's novel *The Satanic Verses,* national origin was the principal component of Muslim immigrant identity. Of course, to uninformed or prejudiced outsiders, there was not much difference between a Pakistani and a Bangladeshi with British citizenship. However, a host of factors – linguistic, cultural, historical, and religious – demarcated the identity of a British Muslim whose roots were traceable to Karachi in Pakistan from the identity of a British Muslim who originated from Sylhet in Bangladesh. That Bangladesh had fought a bitter struggle for independence from Pakistan in 1971, during which up to one million Bengali civilians were murdered by rampaging Pakistani troops, only shored up this particular divide. It should also be noted that these divisions are still intact. Commenting on the internal splits among British Muslims, Humayun Ansari observes that "tensions persist between belief in the unity of the Muslim *umma*" – the global Muslim community – "and the conflicting ties that distinguish these communities."[5]

The Rushdie Affair effectively introduced – some might say imposed – an overarching Muslim identity over these distinct communities. Rushdie's novel challenged the very foundations of Islam by questioning the divine origins of the Qu'ran and the authority of the Prophet Mohammed. What was regarded by many Muslims as a work of blasphemy galvanized the Muslim communal bodies, which had been developing over the previous three decades, into action. By the end of 1988, a UK Action Committee on Islamic Affairs (UKACIA) had been formed to coordinate protests against Rushdie. Three main demands were directed at Rushdie's publishers, Penguin Books: first, that all copies of the book be pulped; second, that an unqualified public apology be offered to the "world Muslim community"; and third, that damages be paid equal to the returns on copies of the book which had already been sold. By January 1989, Muslims in the northern English city of Bradford were burning copies of the book in public. The following month, Iran's Ayatollah Khomeini issued a *fatwa* from Tehran exhorting Muslims to kill Rushdie. With the fatwa now in play, the British government observed developments in the Muslim community with growing alarm. In a letter to UKACIA's Iqbal Sacranie, now the Secretary-General of the Muslim Council of Britain (MCB), the then Home Affairs Minister, John Patten, pointed out that the same liberty which permitted Muslims to protest guaranteed Rushdie's right to freedom of expression. UKACIA's reply anticipated the current religious discrimination legislation by asserting that there was no "right to commit sacrilege and insult and abuse the deeply held sanctities of other people."[6]

Still, UKACIA committed itself to working within the law, through lobbying and forging political alliances, though this approach was not universally adopted. Some prominent Muslim radicals, such as the late Kalim Siddiqui of the Muslim Institute in London, openly endorsed Khomeini's *fatwa*, with the result that Rushdie was forced to live with a 24-hour guard. Buoyed by the campaign against Rushdie, Siddiqui then launched the so-called "Muslim Parliament of Great Britain." The basic concept behind the Parliament was what Siddiqui called a "non-territorial Islamic state"; effectively, the provision of Islamic education and community services to enable Muslims to survive within what Siddiqui and his supporters regarded as an inherently hostile environment which would eventually give way to an Islamic state.[7] UKACIA and the Muslim Parliament represented two different schools of thought with regard to Muslim political activity in Britain. UKACIA argued that Muslim interests were best served by working within, rather than against, the system – an approach continued by the umbrella group which it spawned, the MCB. The Muslim Parliament, on the other hand, was far more oriented towards the Islamist political currents in the Middle East and Pakistan. Even though the Parliament dissolved shortly after Siddiqui's death in 1996, its political legacy survives through the radical Muslim organizations which are present on the current British scene. Importantly, these two approaches do not face off as adversaries; while there are differences and disagreements, the Muslim mainstream in Britain cooperates with the radical tendencies on both an institutional and political level, as will be demonstrated.

British Muslims: Ethnic Composition, Social Position, and Political Orientation

The most recent UK national census, conducted in 2001, determined that there are 1.6 million Muslims in Britain.[8] According to the census, 43 percent are of Pakistani origin, 17 percent are Bangladeshi, and another 9 percent originate from India. Additionally, 4 percent are British converts, while 6 percent are from African or Caribbean backgrounds. The remaining 21 percent include Arabs, Iranians, Turks, and Kurds from the Middle East and North Africa; East Africans; Balkan Muslims from Bosnia-Herzegovina, Albania, and Kosovo; and Muslims from other Asian countries. As well as exhibiting a strong degree of ethnic diversity, British Muslims are also comparatively young. Indeed, out of all the country's religious groups, British Muslims have the youngest age profile: one-third are under sixteen, compared to one-fifth for the population as a whole.

A recent report by the Open Society Institute examines "the deprivation, disadvantage and discrimination that many UK Muslims experience in their daily lives."[9] While the report does not conceive of British Muslims as anything other than social victims, and while it uncritically endorses many of the proposals of British Muslim leaders (for example, the religious discrimination legislation), the raw data gathered by the OSI in itself suggests why the British government is now anxious to seize the policy initiative, particularly as it observes worsening relations with Muslims in other EU countries like France and The Netherlands. For example, unemployment is proportionately much higher among British Muslims, standing at 38 percent. Substandard housing is another problem, with 42 percent living in overcrowded accommodations, compared with 12 percent for the population as a whole. The report also cites a survey conducted by Muslim community groups in which 80 percent of respondents said they had been subjected to "Islamophobia," which encompasses the full range of verbal and practical discrimination.[10]

Yet it can be argued that alleviating the social plight of British Muslims does not necessarily require legislation which characterizes the policy focus as a problem of discrimination against a *religious* minority. Moreover, a number of studies have questioned the assumption of an organic link between deprivation and Islamist politics.[11] More sensitive social policies and better employment prospects will not, by themselves, dilute the appeal of the radical Islamist agenda. In that sense, it is worth examining how British Muslims perceive their own position and their attitudes towards the wider British society. A November 2004 poll conducted by *The Guardian* newspaper demonstrates that it is political and religious issues, rather than economic and social ones, which energize Muslim activism in the UK.[12] According to the poll, 88 percent of Muslims want to see schools and workplaces incorporate Muslim prayer times as part of their working day – a demand all but unknown among other religious groups. In a related area, 61 percent of Muslims want the introduction of sharia courts to decide civil issues within their own communities. Notwithstanding the caveat that such courts should not contradict British law, such a measure would certainly strengthen the conservative, theocratic elements among British Muslims.

While 40 percent of British Muslims feel they need to do more to "integrate" into British society, how this is to be achieved is not specified. In terms of political affiliations, the poll reinforces the impression that judgments of Muslim voters are principally made on the basis of perceived anti-Muslim bias in British government policy; considerations unrelated to direct Muslim concerns do not seem to register. This has impacted strongly on the ruling Labour Party. In 2001, 75 percent of Muslims voted for Labour as it won a second term in office. By the reckoning of *The Guardian* poll, this support has collapsed to 32 percent as a result of the conflict in Iraq and Prime Minister Tony Blair's continued backing for the war on terror. Support for the Conservatives has also slipped among Muslims, from 25 percent to 16 percent. This has occurred despite Michael Howard's attempts to distance himself from the Iraq War – on the grounds that Blair allegedly manipulated intelligence regarding the threat posed by Saddam Hussein – as well as his support for conservative moral values and his denunciation of Islamophobia. A full 41 percent of Muslim voters now identify with the Liberal Democrats, who are now situated as the left-wing opposition in Britain. In September 2003, the party's candidate won the election for the Brent East parliamentary constituency in North-West London, overturning a Labour majority of 13,000, due largely to Muslim voters who make up 12 percent of the electorate. In a triumphant post-election declaration, the Muslim Public Affairs Committee (MPAC) – a body which Jewish community officials view with great concern because of its incendiary attacks upon "Zionists"[13] – urged Muslim activists to leave the Labour Party and join with the Liberal Democrats, which had "actively been encouraging Muslims as parliamentary candidates." Smaller parties also make a showing. The Respect Party, so far the foremost political expression of the burgeoning alliance between the British far left and the Muslim Association of Britain (the British branch of the Muslim Brotherhood), commands the support of 4 percent of Muslims. Formed by Scottish MP George Galloway after he was expelled from the Labour Party because of his association with Saddam Hussein's regime in Iraq, Respect has made every effort to conform to the Islamist agenda – even denying that it is a secular organization after a delegate to its 2004 conference claimed that such a designation would be "Islamophobic."[14] The notoriously anti-Zionist Galloway – boosted by his victory in a libel case against the *Daily Telegraph*, which had accused him of receiving funds from Saddam Hussein – will contest Bethnal Green and Bow in East London in the 2005 general election, a constituency with more Muslim voters than any other in the country. Galloway is building his campaign by pointing out that the sitting Labour MP, Oona King, supported the war in Iraq. For her part, King has attempted to mollify Muslim anger by comparing the situation of Palestinians in the Gaza Strip to Jews facing the Nazi onslaught in the Warsaw Ghetto.[15]

Humayun Ansari writes that there is a growing awareness among British Muslims of their electoral clout, "especially in constituencies where they have the potential to alter the balance of power."[16] In both the 1997 and 2001 elections, communal leaders exhorted Muslims to vote and disseminated information on candidates in the forty or so constituencies with a significant Muslim vote. The 2005 election is certain to see this trend repeated. Thus, despite their concerns about Islamophobia, Muslim leaders are well aware that their community now enjoys unprecedented political influence.

Muslim Organizations in Britain: A Profile

During the 1980s and 1990s, a number of domestic and international issues – including the Rushdie Affair, the Gulf War of 1991, the Bosnian War of 1992–95, the ongoing calls for state support for Muslim education, and growing concern about Islamophobia – underscored the need, as far as Muslim leaders were concerned, for a Muslim representative body in Britain. Accordingly, the Muslim Council of Britain (MCB) was created in 1996. A cursory examination of the MCB's structure reveals that it is quite similar to the main Jewish representative organization in Britain, the Board of Deputies of British Jews. A member of the Board has confirmed that the Jewish body provided some guidance to the MCB, mainly on constitutional matters, during the initial stages of its formation.

The MCB's Aims and Objectives stress that the body seeks to promote Muslim unity in Britain and a "more enlightened" appreciation of Islam. In the wake of major reports on Islamophobia in 1997, 2001, and 2004, all of which endorsed calls for legal sanctions against religious discrimination, the campaign against Islamophobia remains central.[17] Currently, the MCB has around 380 affiliates, comprising mosques, community and professional organizations, and cultural associations. However, the emphasis placed on cordial relations with the British government has meant that the MCB is viewed with suspicion by some Islamist groups. Other groups, such as the Saudi-backed World Association of Muslim Youth (WAMY), do not place overt political involvement at the center of their activities, focusing instead upon the religious dimension. Still, many of MCB's affiliates, such as the Federation of Student Islamic Societies (FOSIS), echo the core belief that Muslim interests are best served through political participation.

One organization affiliated with MCB which has achieved a major public profile is the Muslim Association of Britain (MAB). Although it is an Islamist organization linked to the Muslim Brotherhood, MAB has played a major role in both the movement against the Iraq War and the Respect party. This participation reflects a tendency in Islamic political thought which regards Europe as part of the *Dar al Sulh* (the domain of truce) rather than, as the *jihadists* would have it, the *Dar al Harb* (the domain of war).[18] Hence, MAB, like the MCB, believes that British Muslims have a duty to engage politically; however, MAB does not regard existing British political institutions as having any inherent legitimacy. Political participation is simply one means of carrying out the fundamental duty of *dawa*, or proselytizing the Muslim faith. Yet it would be a mistake to regard dawa as mere outreach; underlying it as a concept, as Alyssa Lappen points out, is the view that other faiths are inferior to Islam.[19] For its part, MAB has said that those who abandon the Islamic faith are deserving of the death penalty.[20] One of MAB's leading figures is Azzam Tamimi, a Palestinian who heads the Institute of Islamic Political Thought in London. A Hamas sympathizer, Tamimi served as an advisor to Sheikh Ahmed Yassin, the Hamas leader successfully targeted in Gaza in 2004 by Israeli forces in an anti-terrorist operation. In an interview with the BBC, Tamimi declared that, given the opportunity, he would become a homicide bomber.[21] Such sentiments are fervently endorsed by MAB, which actively praises Islamists like Yassin and the late Sayid Qutb of the Muslim Brotherhood, who expressed his sympathy for Hitler's efforts to exterminate the Jews of Europe. The MCB, which is always quick to dissociate itself from terrorism, and which unambiguously condemned the 9/11 atrocities, has neither remarked on MAB's enthusiasm for radical Islamists nor condemned Tamimi's announcement on the BBC, despite the fact that MAB is an affiliate. Therefore, it is no exaggeration to conclude that Islamist politics have pierced the heart of the Muslim communal infrastructure in Britain. In many ways, this is hardly suprising. As Gilles Kepel points out, London – or "Londonistan," as some Islamists have called it – has been "a sanctuary for global Islamist extremism beginning in the 1980s."[22]

Muslim-Jewish Relations in Britain

Since the onset of the second intifada in September 2000, relations between the Jewish and Muslim communities in Britain have been disfigured by tension and mistrust, much to the chagrin of Jewish leaders.[23] As a member of the Board of Deputies explained, "our position was that the problems of the Middle East should remain in the Middle East." This perspective was not shared by the Muslim communal organizations. By allowing the Israeli-Palestinian conflict to cloud their relations with British Jews, Muslim leaders were kowtowing to the Islamist notion that the Palestinian cause is the principal rallying point for the *umma*. Thus, while British Jewish leaders recognize that there are different theological and political viewpoints running through the Muslim community, on the key issue which divides them – the conflict between Israel and the Palestinians – Jews are confronted with a rigid Islamist standpoint which concedes no legitimacy to the State of Israel and which justifies terrorist violence against Jews in the name of Palestine, regardless of whether the victims carry Israeli passports.

Indeed, the issue of Palestine is at the core of the confusion regarding British Muslim organizations and terrorism. The mainstream organizations, notably the MCB, have all been vocal in their condemnation of terrorist outrages, whether perpetrated in Iraq or elsewhere. When British engineer Kenneth Bigley was kidnapped by terrorists in Iraq in September 2004, an MCB delegation went to Baghdad to try and secure his release. Although Bigley was eventually decapitated, the MCB was able to portray its initiative as an exercise in responsible citizenship. Moreover, they were boosted by frequent media interviews with Paul Bigley, Kenneth's brother, who insisted that President Bush, Prime Minister Blair, and the Israeli occupation of the West Bank and Gaza Strip were the real culprits behind Kenneth's grim fate. Such condemnation does not, however, extend to those acts of terrorism committed against Jews and Israelis. For example, no British Muslim organization condemned the November 2003 attacks on Jewish targets in Istanbul; by contrast, two bombings against British targets in the city a few days later, one of which claimed the life of the British consul-general, were denounced.

Attacks against Jewish civilians in Israel, meanwhile, generally tend to be justified as acts of resistance. The logic is transparent: since Palestine has been usurped by Zionists, civilian Israelis can never be victims of terrorism in the manner of citizens of other states. Moreover, Israel alone is responsible for the bloodshed in the region. As an MCB press release stated: "Israel's unlawful occupation of Palestine has for decades spread seeds of hatred in the Middle East, hatred which has extended into the world far beyond."[24] This last phrase – "world far beyond" – is particularly ominous, implying that the hatred which would lead to an attack on a Jew outside Israel is the responsibility not of the perpetrator but of the Jewish state. Such attacks have already manifested in Britain. Data gathered by the Community Security Trust (CST), the Jewish community's security organization, shows a definitive correlation between the number of anti-Jewish incidents in the UK and the renewed conflict in the Middle East. In 2003, 609 incidents were reported, including physical assault, abusive behavior, and desecration of holy places.[25] According to the CST, there is a recognition among police specialists at Scotland Yard who are researching antisemitic crimes that, while not all incidents are confined to Muslim or Arab perpetrators, tension in the Middle East directly influences the troughs and peaks of violence against Jewish targets.

In terms of antisemitic or Judeophobic statements and outbursts, the incitement against Jews which prevails in the Arab and Muslim world, especially in the media, has impacted upon Muslim-Jewish relations in Britain. The MCB, as well as groups like MPAC and the Islamic Human Rights Commission (IHRC), have accused Israel of committing genocide and have spoken darkly about the "Zionist lobby." Criticism of "neoconservatives" – meaning those Jews working in foreign policy for the Bush Administration – is routine. Jewish complaints that such language and imagery are redolent of antisemitic conspiracy theories fall upon deaf ears, both among British Muslims and, to a great extent, in the liberal media. A favored tactic among Muslim activists is to call for a boycott of Israeli goods and institutions. The boycott has a long pedigree in the Muslim world, having first been introduced by the Arab League in 1945 against "Jewish products and manufactured goods." Thus, despite frequent protests from contemporary advocates of the boycott that their target is the State of Israel, and not the Jewish people, the historical origins of the boycott reveal it to be an unambiguously anti-Jewish measure introduced three years before Israel's creation.

Of special note is the ongoing campaign for an academic boycott of Israel. As in other countries, the drive to boycott Israeli universities and academics has been enthusiastically seized upon by leftist academics in

Britain, among them biologists Steven and Hilary Rose, philosopher Ted Honderich, and others. The MCB was an early and enthusiastic supporter of the boycott. In July 2002, Iqbal Sacranie was quoted by the Iranian news agency, IRNA, as saying that the academic boycott "is a clear message to Israel that it is committing moral outrage."[26] Israel is singled out by British Muslim leaders as a target for a boycott because they subscribe to the Islamist dogma that, since Jews have no right to a state of their own, the State of Israel lacks legitimacy.

Two episodes in 2004 reveal the extent to which Jewish-Muslim relations have deteriorated as the result of the adoption of Islamist positions on Palestine by the British Muslim leadership. In June, an Interfaith Prize awarded to Iqbal Sacranie by Sir Sigmund Sternberg, a noted Jewish advocate of interreligious dialogue, was abruptly withdrawn following Sacranie's accusation that Israel was engaged in "ethnic cleansing" and "creeping genocide" against the Palestinians. Statements issued by both the MCB and MAB supporting Sacranie's decision not to retract his original remarks maintained that it was unreasonable for Jewish concerns over anti-Zionism to influence interfaith dialogue – a clear example of how Muslim organizations delegitimize not just Israel, but Jewish identification with Israel. The July visit to the UK by the Qatar-based Islamist Sheikh Yusuf al Qaradawi further poisoned Muslim relations with Jews and other groups, including Hindus, Sikhs, and lesbian and gay activists. Protests from all these communities regarding Qaradawi's xenophobic and antisemitic views – he has declared, for example, that there can be no dialogue with Jews "except by the sword and the rifle" – were greeted with uniform anger by Muslim organizations. The MCB declared that "the smear campaign against Dr. al Qaradawi is being orchestrated by the Zionist lobby who are evidently angered by Dr. al Qaradawi's staunch opposition to Israeli state brutality against the Palestinian people."

This position was backed by Ken Livingstone, the left-wing Mayor of London, who publicly embraced Qaradawi and denounced a coalition of groups opposing the visit as "Islamophobic."[27] As Reuven Paz has demonstrated, Qaradawi has emerged as a leading Islamic authority for Muslim Brotherhood groups.[28] In 2003, he founded the World Council of Muslim Clerics, headquartered in Dublin. At a meeting in November 2004 in Beirut, the Council adopted a 14-point declaration which backed the insurgency in Iraq and underlined the centrality of Palestine by claiming that it is "the duty of all Muslims to support the Palestinians by all means of Jihad, by finance, propaganda and self-sacrifice." Such radicalism, Paz observes, should be taken as a "warning sign by the West." A first step towards such recognition

might be to question the "moderation" of those Muslim communal organizations which endorse Qaradawi's views and denounce his critics in the most
fearsome terms. In such an environment, are there any reasonable prospects
for a meaningful dialogue between Muslims and Jews in Britain? Jewish
leaders note that there is continued dialogue about issues of mutual religious concern, such as circumcision and *kashrut/halal,* the latter issue having been targeted by Britain's vocal animal rights lobby. For example, in
2003, Muslims and Jews jointly worked against demands for the pre-stunn-
ing of animals, which would violate the requirements of both *kashrut* and
halal slaughter. There are also exercises in mutual understanding undertaken by such bodies as the Maimonides Foundation, Three Faiths Forum, and
Alif/Aleph. According to one of the leaders of Alif/Aleph, there is plenty of
informal contact and discussion, particularly on university campuses, places
better known as key centers of anti-Zionist activism led by Muslim and leftist students.

Conclusion: Separation or Integration?

Among both Jewish leaders and analysts of Muslim politics, there is an understanding that the British Muslim community cannot be reduced to its
jihadist elements, in the form of clerics such as Omar Bakri Mohammed and
Abu Hamza al-Masri, or groups such as Hizb ut Tahrir and the (currently
dormant) al-Muhajiroun. There is also a recognition that British Muslim
identity is complex and malleable. Yet the political orientation of the British
Muslim mainstream remains a source of strong concern.

In Britain and much of Western Europe, it is increasingly acknowledged that the multiculturalist model has failed. What is needed – as the
Commission for Racial Equality, for one, has pointed out – is a model which
encourages integration rather than communal separation under the rubric
of shared values, such as democracy and "the common currency of the English language."[29] Yet Britain appears to be heading in the other direction;
one of the potential problems of the religious discrimination legislation is
that, while providing extra protection from crude Islamophobic actions, it
may end up as a gateway for further demands which actually encourage
greater separation and the strengthening of Islamist positions. The call for
shari'a courts, for example, is a key demand of Qaradawi and his acolytes.
For any British government to concede on this and other points would be a
grave mistake, leading to further social fragmentation.

Initial indications are that the British government, mindful of the collapse in its status among Muslims, is doing its utmost to accommodate the
political agenda of the Muslim leadership. In an article for the *Muslim Week-*

ly,[30] Mike O'Brien, the Energy Minister, launched an attack on Michael Howard and Dr. Evan Harris MP, a Jewish Liberal Democrat who has opposed the
religious discrimination legislation, for not standing up for the rights of
Muslims. "Ask yourself," O'Brien wrote, "what will Michael Howard do for
British Muslims? Will his foreign policy aim to help Palestine?" That O'Brien,
by placing it at the top of the list, acknowledges that Palestine is the main
priority for Muslim political activists, is telling indeed. What is also telling is
that the two politicians criticized by O'Brien are both Jews. Harris himself
wondered aloud whether O'Brien had named him specifically because he is
the only Jewish Liberal Democrat MP, resulting in an indignant denial of
antisemitism from O'Brien.[31] In the same article, O'Brien handed the credit
for the religious discrimination legislation to the successful lobbying of the
MCB. "The Muslim Council of Britain has been at the forefront of lobbying
the Government on issues to help Muslims," he said. "Recently Iqbal Sacranie, the General Secretary of the Council, asked Tony Blair to declare that the
Government would introduce a new law banning religious discrimination.
Two weeks later, in the middle of his speech to the Labour Party Conference,
Tony Blair promised that the next Labour Government would ban religious
discrimination. It was a major victory for the Muslim community in Britain."
It would not be fanciful to assume that similar "victories" lie on the horizon.
Responding to O'Brien's article, MPAC stated that the minister would con-
tinue to be regarded "as a friend of the Muslims so long as he refuses to
break under the zionist (sic) pressure for an apology."[32]

As Gilles Kepel has argued, the separation of the secular and religious
domains is a prerequisite for both successful Muslim participation in the
institutions of Europe and for reform of the Muslim world itself.[33] At the
present time, Britain and other EU states are trying to reach a modus vivendi with an Islamic communal infrastructure that does not accept this separation. As long as that remains the case, rigid Islamist thinking will continue to
be a powerful current within the Muslim community, with the result that
Jews will be regarded as *dhimmis,*[34] and not as fellow citizens.

*Notes (all online sources were accessible at the day of the first publication
of this article)*

1. See, for example, David Pryce-Jones, "The Islamization of Europe," Commentary, December 2004.
2. Philippe Naughton, "Howard goes right with crime, EU and immigration
pledges," *The Times,* 5 October 2004.
3. In an interview with *The Times,* Lord Desai said: "Religion is not a defined
thing. How can you decide what counts as a religion? Should we extend

protection to scientology? If one Muslim insults another from a different sect, we would have a lot of problems. And how do you protect freedom of speech? How do you decide when criticism is reasonable and when it becomes incitement to hatred?" See Jack Shamash, "Start of Ramadan signals move for tolerance," *The Times,* 16 October 2004.

4. See "UK Muslims Want Civil Cases Resolved by Sharia: Poll," *FAIR Daily News Digest,* 1 December 2004; http://www.fairuk.org/dnd/2004/12/DND 20041201Wed.htm#1.

5. Humayun Ansari, *The Infidel Within: Muslims in Britain since 1800* (London: Hurst and Co., 2004), p. 4.

6. The exchange is available at http://www.salaam.co.uk/the meofthemonth/september03_index.php?l=1.

7. See http://www.islamicthought.org/mp-is1.html. See also Ansari, *op. cit.,* p. 205.

8. Detailed breakdowns are available at http://www.statistics.gov.uk/ census2001/.

9. See "Muslims in the UK: Policies for Engaged Citizens," Open Society Institute, Budapest and New York, 2004.

10. A report issued in January 2005 by the Crown Prosecution Service determined that, out of 44 religiously-motivated hate crimes prosecuted in the year to April 2004, 22 involved Muslims and 5 Jews. Given the relative proportion of these communities to the overall population, one can conclude that Jews are just as vulnerable to such crimes as Muslims. Yet the entire focus of the report has been on Muslim fears. See http://news.bbc.co.uk/1/ hi/uk/4184931.stm.

11. See, for example, Daniel Pipes, "God and Mammon: Does Poverty Cause Militant Islam?" *National Interest,* Winter 2002.

12. Alan Travis and Madeleine Bunting, "British Muslims want Islamic law and prayers at work," *The Guardian,* 30 November 2004.

13. MPAC publishes a list of prominent Jews in the media at http://www. mpacuk.org/content/view/176/34/

14. See "Anti-war Catholic MP to court Muslim voters," *FAIR Daily News Digest,* 6 December 2004; http://www.fairuk.org/dnd/2004/12/ DND20041206Mon.htm#4

15. King made the comparison in her article, "Israel can halt this now," *The Guardian,* 12 June 2003, which ended with a call to boycott Israeli products.

16. Ansari, *op. cit.,* p. 244.

17. See "Islamophobia: A Challenge for us all," published by The Runnymede Trust in1997 and launched by then Home Secretary Jack Straw, and the two

reports on Islamophobia issued by the Commission on British Muslims and Islamophobia in 2001 and 2004.

18. Gilles Kepel, *The War for Muslim Minds: Islam and The West* (Cambridge, Mass.: Harvard University Press, 2004), p. 255.

19. Alyssa A. Lappen, "The Dawning of Dawa," FrontPageMagazine.com, 15 July 2003.

20. See Nick Cohen, "Muslim is not a dirty word: Why do we define so many minorities by one faith?" *New Statesman,* 4 October 2004.

21. A partial transcript of the interview is available on Professor Martin Kramer's weblog, "Sandstorm." See http://www.geocities.com/martin kramerorg/2004_11_04.htm.

22. Kepel, *op. cit.,* p. 242.

23. See Ben Cohen, "British Jews Keep Wary Eye on Future," *Jewish Week,* 7 January 2005.

24. The press release is available at http://www.mcb.org.uk/ mcbdirect/searchresult.php?ann_id=324.

25. See "Annual Review: Antisemitism and Jewish Communal Security in Britain in 2003," The Community Security Trust.

26. "UK Muslims Call For Widening of Academic Boycott Against Israel," *Tehran Times,* 13 July 2002.

27. Twelve prominent individuals, including representatives of the Hindu and Jewish communities, signed the initial letter of protest to Livingstone. See http://www.londoncommunity coalition.org/.

28. Reuven Paz, "Qaradawi and the World Association of Muslim Clerics: The New Platform of the Muslim Brotherhood," Project for the Research of Islamist Movements (PRISM), Occasional Papers, Vol. 2, No. 4, November 2004.

29. Kepel, *op. cit.,* p. 245.

30. Mike O'Brien, "Labour and British Muslims: can we dream the same dream?" *Muslim Weekly,* No. 61, 7–13 January 2005.

31. See Melissa Kite and Tony Freinberg, "Minister denies antisemitism after attack on Howard," *Daily Telegraph,* 9 January 2005.

32. See http://www.mpacuk.org/content/view/256/26/.

33. Kepel, *op. cit.,* p. 295.

34. The term *"dhimmi"* derives from Islamic law and enshrines the subordinate but tolerated status of Jews and Christians living under Muslim rule. See Bat Ye'or, *The Dhimmi: Jews and Christians under Islam* (London: Fairleigh Dickinson University Press, 1985). I use the term here more loosely, to

describe the haughty, dismissive, and scornful attitude towards Jewish aspirations and concerns which is prevalent among many Muslim leaders.

Vidal Sassoon, Streetfighter

Tablet Magazine, May 10, 2012

Rabbi Israel Elia, head of the venerable Spanish and Portuguese Synagogue in London's Maida Vale district, remembers the day when he met Vidal Sassoon, one of the congregation's most celebrated sons. Elia had been quietly working in his office on a spring morning two years ago when an anxious colleague relayed the news that a film crew had gathered outside the building. The rabbi went to investigate.

"At the head of the crew, there was a smartly dressed man with delicate, graceful features," Rabbi Elia recalled yesterday. "He walked over to me and introduced himself as Vidal Sassoon. He was making a film about his life and career." Pointing to an annex at the side of the synagogue, Sassoon explained that the building had housed the orphanage where he spent his childhood. "So, I took him inside," Elia said. "He told me, 'I want to show you where my dormitory was.' We entered a room and he looked around. He was excited: 'Yes, this was it, this was the dormitory.' I looked at him and said, 'Vidal, your dormitory is now my office.' He threw his arms around me and hugged me, telling me about the kindness of our community, how his accomplishments would not have been possible without that generosity."

Such were the inauspicious beginnings of a man who, through an international chain of hair salons and a bewildering array of grooming products, revolutionized women's style in the decades that followed World War II. The son of a Turkish Jewish father and a Ukrainian Jewish mother, Sassoon was born in Shepherd's Bush, West London, in 1928. Known to its residents as "The Bush," it was a neighborhood with a tough reputation, home to large immigrant communities from Ireland, Poland, and other points east and west.

Sassoon was still in diapers when his father walked out on his mother, Betty. Destitute and unable to cope, Sassoon's mother learned that there was an orphanage at the Spanish and Portuguese synagogue, approximately two miles away. One day in 1933, she turned up with the young Vidal in tow and placed him in the care of the oldest Jewish community in England. Having been implanted in the orphanage, Sassoon joined the synagogue choir. During his visit with Rabbi Elia, Vidal went up to the elevated box where the choir still sits. "He started to recall one of his favorite tunes," said Elia. "I figured out that it was *Yimloch Adonai*, one of the songs we sing on Shabbat. We sang it together." (As a child growing up in the same synagogue, I remember being drafted into the same choir and grumbling about it. One of the adults admonished me, "Vidal Sassoon used to sing in this choir, so if it's good enough for him, it's good enough for you!"). By his own account, Sassoon's years at the orphanage were happy ones. (Sassoon, unlike his younger brother Ivor, was never bitter toward Betty, with whom he remained close.) But when the Luftwaffe began its nightly bombing raids on London, he was evacuated, along with thousands of other children from the city, to the countryside. Returning to London at the age of 14, he entered the hairdressing trade that was to make his reputation, starting out as an apprentice at a barber's shop in the Whitechapel district of East London.

As he threw himself into his new vocation, Sassoon further cemented his attachment to the Jewish community. "He wasn't religious, but he was extremely proud to be a Jew, and he was a dedicated Zionist," Rabbi Elia said. In the immediate postwar years, London's Jews faced a new threat from the remnants of British Union of Fascists, a Hitlerite party led by Sir Oswald Mosley, whose black-shirted followers had regularly clashed with Jewish immigrants in the East End during the 1930s. Sassoon recalled England's hostile political atmosphere earlier this year: "Antisemitism was absolutely rife," he said in a podcast for the Holocaust Memorial Museum. "I mean, it was nothing for another kid to say to you, 'Dirty Jew.' And although England was a good place to be, especially with Churchill and the fight against the Nazis, there was always that sense of the Jews being second-class citizens."

In 1947, the fascists again began menacing London, this time under the tutelage of Jeffrey Hamm, head of an organization of thugs calling themselves the "Association of British Ex-Servicemen." For Sassoon, this was not a fate to be accepted lying down. As a response to Hamm's provocations, a gathering of young Jews known as the 43 Group – named for the number of people in the room at their founding – announced that the fight back had begun. Among them was the slender, if wiry, Sassoon. As Hamm's followers gathered on street corners bellowing that "not enough Jews were burned at Belsen," Sassoon and his comrades, armed with knives, coshes, and knuckledusters, set about breaking up fascist meetings. In another interview, Sassoon remembered turning up for work one morning with a black eye. "I just tripped on a hairpin," he explained to the worried customer who had just settled into a barber's chair for a haircut.

Encouraged by his ardently Zionist mother, Sassoon's exploits with the 43 Group led him to a higher calling. In 1948, as the British Mandate was drawing to a close, Sassoon arrived in Palestine where he joined the Palmach in the fight for Israel's independence. In the manner of the young men and women who had flocked to Spain in the previous decade to fight on the Republican side during the Civil War, Sassoon's decision to participate in the Zionist struggle for independence, like that of the other volunteers who came from Europe and America, was rooted in a commitment to Jewish pride and honor. "That was the best year of my life," Sassoon later told a British newspaper. "When you think of 2,000 years of being put down and suddenly you are a nation rising, it was a wonderful feeling. There were only 600,000 people defending the country against five armies, so everyone had something to do." Sassoon served in combat. "I wasn't going over there to sit in an office," he told the *Jewish Chronicle*. "I thought if we don't fight for a piece of land and make it work, then the whole Holocaust thing was a terrible waste. But this way at least we got a country out of it."

Shortly after Israel won its independence, Sassoon was back in England. Slowly but confidently, the former streetfighter and soldier turned himself into an international celebrity. His trademark hairstyle, the boyish, geometric bob-cut named for the actress Nancy Kwan, who first wore it, was especially popular with the skinny, waif-like stars of the day. But his most famous cut of all was a pixie crop for the actress Mia Farrow for her 1968 film *Rosemary's Baby*. Mingling with the A-list, Sassoon relocated to Los Angeles, embracing a lifestyle that doubtless would have furrowed the eyebrows of the elders at the Spanish and Portuguese synagogue. "In those days," he matter-of-factly told an interviewer last year, "having sex was the same as having dinner." At the same time, Sassoon remained anchored in his Jewish identity, and wary of any threat to Jewish security. In 1982, he created the Vidal Sassoon International Center for the Study of Antisemitism at the Hebrew University in Jerusalem. "We had several heart to heart talks in recent years," Professor Robert Wistrich, the center's long-time head, told me. "He was shaken by the Shoah and by his experiences in postwar England. He was absolutely driven by the sense that one had to do something because antisemitism was always there beneath the surface. The way he saw it, antisemitism, the Shoah, was presented as a righteous act. It wasn't an academic point of view, it was a moral one based on his own experience." Rabbi Elia concurred: "After we finished our tour of the synagogue and the orphanage, we sat in the kitchen for a meal prepared by my wife. He was passionate, asserting that Jewish people should always be on guard, ready to defend themselves."

Elia interprets Sassoon's dedication through the Judaic concept of *hakarat hatov* – acknowledging of the goodness of others. "It was something he carried with him from the orphanage onwards. It's a very Jewish attribute."

The Courage of Ronnie Fraser

"Contentions" @ Commentary Magazine, November 1, 2012

I first met Ronnie Fraser, an unassuming lecturer in mathematics at one of London's further education colleges, in 2002. Sitting at a table in a small central London cafe, Ronnie barely sipped the cappuccino in front of him as he laid out for me, in urgent tones, the growing support among British academics for a boycott of their Israeli colleagues, along with the vicious strain of antisemitism underlying their campaign.

I can admit, now, that a large part of me wanted to believe that Ronnie was exaggerating. The boycott was certainly wrong and definitely misguided, but could one really argue that British academics, six decades after the Holocaust, were trafficking in the kinds of antisemitic conspiracy theories that would not have been out of place in the pages of *Der Stürmer*? The answer, in short, was yes. As it turned out, Ronnie's prognosis was entirely correct; not only did the academic boycott of Israelis become the most pressing concern inside the leftist-dominated University and College Union (UCU), it did so in ways that led many of its Jewish members to conclude that they themselves were its principal target. And so, from 2005 onwards, a motion to implement, extend and refine a boycott of Israel's academic sector became a fixture at the annual conferences of the UCU, which were transformed into festivals of antisemitic bombast. To give one example, as pro-Israel academics mused over the prospect of a legal challenge to the boycott, one boycott advocate, a faculty member at London University's prestigious University College, declared that any legal action would be financed by those with "bank balances from Lehman Brothers that can't be tracked down." A neo-Nazi couldn't have put it more venomously.

Nonetheless, Ronnie Fraser never shied away from confronting this toxicity head-on. This week, he brought his case to an employment tribunal, charging that the boycott amounted to a breach of Britain's anti-discrimination legislation. The *Jewish Chronicle* today reports: "A Jewish academic repeatedly broke down in tears as he told an employment tribunal that he had suffered a decade of harassment while opposing a boycott of Israel." Maths lecturer Ronnie Fraser, whose parents escaped Nazi Germany, said he felt a special responsibility to challenge the University and College Union after it rejected a widely-accepted definition of antisemitism. The grandfather-of-nine wept as he took the oath at London's Central Employment Tribunal on Wednesday. He said he had felt threatened by the union's anti-Israel policies and a catalogue of events that had left him "hurt, upset and insulted." "This case is not about Israel-Palestine. It's not about me. It's about fellow Jews. We have been forced out. We have been humiliated. It has been horrendous and relentless against us," he said.

Later the tribunal was briefly halted when Mr Fraser again wept while explaining how he believed his grandparents had been killed at Auschwitz. "They died as a result of antisemitism and this is my way of saying 'never again.' I don't want my four children and grandchildren having to suffer what they did," he said. The significance of Ronnie Fraser's action is simply explained. For more than a decade, antisemitic hate speech has cowered behind the imperative, as boycott advocates would have it, of engaging in "solidarity" with the Palestinians. By raising his complaint within a legal forum, Ronnie's aim is to expose the true nature of this sordid rhetoric. Win or lose, Ronnie Fraser is truly deserving of the designation of a hero. With little more than a modest lecturer's salary to support him, he has flung himself into the frontline battle against antisemitism, thereby achieving more than all the established Jewish communal organizations, particularly here in America, combined. As "Engage," another brave organization fighting the boycott, noted in its report of Ronnie's remarkable speech to the UCU last year, his remarks to an audience filled with boycott advocates were met with "stony silence." If any notion of justice still prevails in the United Kingdom, the employment tribunal cannot afford to react similarly.

How British Justice Failed Ronnie Fraser

"Contentions" @ Commentary Magazine, March 28, 2013

On Monday night, as Jews around the world sat down for the first seder of the Passover holiday, anti-Zionists in the United Kingdom and elsewhere held a very different celebration to mark the comprehensive dismissal of a discrimination case brought by Ronnie Fraser, a Jewish math teacher, to an employment tribunal in London.

As I reported back in November, Fraser's courageous battle against antisemitism in the labor union to which he belongs, the University and College Union (UCU), propelled him into a courtroom showdown with the advocates of an academic boycott of Israeli institutions of higher education. Fraser's argument rested on the contention that the union's obsessive pursuit of a boycott negatively impacted its Jewish members. A series of ugly episodes – among them the posting of a claim, on a private listserv run by the UCU, that millions of dollars from the failed Lehman Brothers' bank were transferred to Israel, as well as the address given by a leading South African anti-Semite, Bongani Masuku, to a UCU conference – convinced both Fraser and his lawyer, the prominent scholar of antisemitism Anthony Julius, that the union had become institutionally antisemitic and was therefore in violation of British laws protecting religious and ethnic minorities. The tribunal's judges, however, didn't agree, issuing what London's *Jewish Chronicle* described as a "blistering rejection" of the entire case. As the news spread, anti-Semites on the far left and extreme right crowed that the verdict was a "crushing defeat" for the "Israel lobby" (in the words of the *Electronic Intifada*) and the just deserts of a "whiny Jew" (in the inimitable phrase of the neo-Nazi bulletin board, *Stormfront*). The miniscule Jewish anti-Zionist organization Jews for Justice for Palestinians dutifully lined up behind this chorus, declaring that Fraser's "mission" to prove himself a "victim" had failed.

Why did the Fraser case collapse in such spectacular fashion? In part, the problems were technical and procedural; several passages in the verdict argued that the UCU's officers were not themselves responsible for the specific instances of antisemitism Fraser's complaints highlighted, while another lazily bemoaned the "gargantuan scale" of the case, asserting that it was wrong of Julius and Fraser to abuse the "limited resources" of the "hard-pressed public service" that is a British employment tribunal. The verdict also contained extraordinary personal attacks on the integrity of Fraser's witnesses, among them Jewish communal leader Jeremy Newmark and Labor Party parliamentarian John Mann, and even insinuated that the plain-speaking Fraser was unwittingly being used as a vassal by the articulate and florid Julius!

Ultimately, though, highly partisan political considerations decided the outcome. After dismissing all 10 of Fraser's complaints as an "impermissible attempt to achieve a political end by litigious means," the honorable judges then leveled some acutely politicized accusations of their own. Fraser and his supporters were accused of showing a "worrying disregard for pluralism, tolerance and freedom of expression." Their broader conclusion, that it "would be very unfortunate if an exercise of this sort were ever repeated," is clearly designed to discourage other potential plaintiffs from pursuing complaints against the UCU. Most disturbing of all is paragraph 150 of the verdict, which will doubtless become shorthand for one of the most insidious attempts to redefine antisemitism ever devised. After accepting that British law does protect "Jewishness" as a characteristic of individuals, the judges went on to say that "a belief in the Zionist project or an attachment to Israel ... cannot amount to a protected characteristic."

This excerpt of the verdict should not be understood as protecting the rights of anti-Zionists to free speech. It is, rather, about protecting anti-Zionists from accusations of antisemitism by arguing that anti-Zionism is, by definition, not antisemitic. Of course, elsewhere in the verdict, opposition to Zionism is conflated with "criticism of Israel," which has the neat effect of making Fraser and those who think like him – as Julius pointed out, a clear majority of Jews – appear radically intolerant. But when the core themes of anti-Zionism are unmasked–the denial, uniquely to the Jews, of the right of self-determination, the portrayal of Israel as a racist, and therefore illegitimate, state, the presentation of the Palestinians as victims of a second Holocaust, and the use of the term "Zionist" as a codeword for "Jew" – we move far beyond the domain of permissible policy criticism into open defamation.

More fundamentally, the verdict denies Jews the right to determine those elements that comprise their identity and leaves the definition of what constitutes antisemitism to (often hostile) non-Jews. (As I argued in a February 2012 Commentary essay, that has been the case ever since the term was first coined in the 1870s.) As Fraser himself noted in a statement emailed after the verdict was delivered, "[F]or the court to say that, as Jews, we do not have an attachment to Israel is disappointing, considering we have been yearning for Israel for 2000 years and it has been in our prayers all that time." Fraser added that the verdict "highlighted the need for Anglo-Jewry to urgently adopt and publicize its own definition of antisemitism."

The lesson of the Fraser debacle is simply this: a single employment tribunal in the United Kingdom has created a precedent which will be invoked by every Jew-baiter around the globe; namely, that when Jews raise the question of antisemitism in the context of visceral hostility toward Israel, they do so in bad faith. That such a bigoted principle can be established in a democracy famed for its enlightened judicial methods is, perhaps, the most shocking realization of all. So, yes, Ronnie Fraser was defeated. But so too was British justice and fair play.

Ed Miliband Defends His Father's Legacy

Tablet, October 2, 2013

Ed Miliband, the leader of Britain's Labour Party, is among the most senior Jewish politicians since Benjamin Disraeli – and some corners of the British press continue to wonder, as they did in Disraeli's time, whether the son of an immigrant is fully trustworthy.

Last weekend, the right-wing *Daily Mail* newspaper published a story about Miliband's father, Ralph, headlined "The Man Who Hated Britain." In it, the paper revisited the Shakespearean 2010 standoff between Miliband and his elder brother, David, for the Labour leadership, offering its own, distinctive interpretation of the conflict between the two brothers couched in an attack on a diary entry a teenage Ralph Miliband, a refugee from the Nazis, wrote criticizing British society.

For the *Mail's* correspondent, Geoffrey Levy, all roads lead back to Ralph. Levy's piece began with an anecdote about the young Ralph, "a Jewish immigrant who, with his father, had fled to London from Belgium just weeks earlier to escape the Nazi Holocaust," standing at the tombstone of Karl Marx in London's Highgate Cemetery, swearing an oath that that he "would be faithful to the workers' cause." In essence, the paper detects the whiff of a Marxist plot, sourced to the grave of a man who died in 1994. Ralph Miliband went on to become one of Britain's leading Marxist academics, teaching at the London School of Economics, Leeds University and Brandeis University. Both David and Ed grew up within the framework of their father's politics, which neither ever explicitly abandoned. The brothers worked as interns at *The Nation* magazine in New York, before embarking on political careers in the Labor Party that saw them serve in ministerial posts in the governments of Tony Blair and Gordon Brown.

According to Levy, any doubts about their father's trajectory belonged to David, not Ed. "In his explosive memoirs, serialised last week in the *Mail*, Gordon Brown's spin doctor Damian McBride argued that Ed Miliband was obsessed with maintaining his father's legacy," Levy wrote. "Winning the leadership was Ed's 'ultimate tribute' to his father." The article carried uncomfortable overtones of the middle of the twentieth century, when much of the British press portrayed Jewish immigrants as subversive ingrates. In that regard, it's worth noting that British leftists, many of whom have a decidedly tin ear when it comes to understanding the contemporary twists of antisemitism, never tire of reminding us that in the bad old days of fascism, the *Daily Mail* supported Oswald Mosley's blackshirts as they terrorized the Jewish community in London's East End. Today, Ed Miliband submitted a wounded reply to the attack on his father, which was in turn answered by a *Mail* editorial defending the original piece. It's clear that Miliband too detects the unpleasant insinuation of immigrant disloyalty. "He arrived here as a 16 year-old boy – a Jew – having walked 100 kilometres with his Dad from Brussels to Ostend to catch one of the last boats out before the German soldiers arrived," Miliband wrote. "Then he joined the Royal Navy. He did so because he was determined to be part of the fight against the Nazis and to help his family hidden in Belgium. He was fighting for Britain." Not surprisingly, the *Mail's* clumsy attempt to depict Ed Miliband's turn to the left as a loving gesture directed at his deceased father raised the hackles of Britain's more influential commentators. The Mail's "continuing campaign against the late Ralph Miliband violates every cherished British notion of fair play," declared Jonathan Freedland in *The Guardian*. Norman Geras, a distinguished academic who has consistently challenged the British left's import of classic antisemitic tropes into its hostility toward Israel, asserted that "Ralph's stature in the public domain was also something of which [David and Ed] could be justly proud. No smear campaign against him will be able to erode that."

Lost in this controversy is the notion that it is possible to be alarmed by Ed Miliband's political direction without invoking his father. In many ways, the Obama Administration's debacle over Syria can be traced back to Ed's eleventh hour campaign, back in August, to defeat Prime Minister David Cameron's bid to secure parliamentary backing for military action against the Assad regime. Ed's success led to the gruesome sight of Labour parliamentarians cheering the vote just days after Assad's chemical weapons murdered hundreds of civilians in the town of Ghouta. If Ed Miliband does become Britain's Prime Minister, and if he leads Britain back into the social-democratic statist system undone three decades ago by Margaret Thatcher, only a hardened conspiracy theorist would reduce that outcome solely to Ralph's malign influence. But that, for those who don't read it, is the *Daily Mail* for you.

Soccer's 'Y' Word Controversy

Tablet, October 4, 2013

Tottenham – pronounced Tot-num – is a rather bleak neighborhood on the northeastern edge of London. The area was never historically Jewish, though it abuts the heavily ultra-Orthodox neighborhoods of Stamford Hill and Lower Clapton. Yet, somehow, the local soccer team, Tottenham Hotspur – or, more familiarly, Spurs – became known as England's Jewish club.

For decades, Tottenham fans – both Jewish and not – have embraced the signs and signifiers of Judaism, wearing Star of David T-shirts, waving Israeli flags and chanting the word "Yiddo!" at their own players while calling themselves the "Yid Army." The chants and songs range from devastatingly witty to abysmally offensive: When the German superstar striker Jurgen Klinsmann, who now coaches the U.S. national team, signed for Tottenham in 1994, the Spurs crew turned to *Mary Poppins* for inspiration. "Chim Chiminee/Chim Chiminee/Chim Chim Cheroo," they chorused, "Jurgen was a German/But now he's a Jew."

For fans of Tottenham's rival clubs, all this is the proverbial red rag to a bull. One of the nastiest Jew-baiting songs involves a rewrite of "Spurs are on their way to Wembley," a chart topper released in 1981 to celebrate the club's participation in the final of the Football Association Cup competition at the famous stadium on London's outskirts. "Spurs are on their way to Wembley/ Tottenham's gonna do it again," went the original. "Spurs are on their way to Auschwitz/ Hitler's gonna gas 'em again" goes the revised version. There are other perversities, too. "Aga Doo Doo Doo," a torturous novelty song that was popular in the 1980s, is rendered, "Gas a Jew Jew Jew." And, more recently, the routine spectacle of non-Jewish fans of Tottenham's opponents making hissing noises – an imitation of the gas chambers at Auschwitz – at non-Jewish Spurs fans brandishing the Star of David in reply. Yet earlier this month, Britain's Football Association decreed that it was Spurs fans who were at risk of prosecution for using the term "Yid." "Those fans claim that use of the term is a 'badge of honour' and is not intended to be offensive," the association said in a statement. "By using the term in this manner, fans may be clouding the issue by making it harder to differentiate its use by these fans and by those who use the term in an intentionally offensive manner."

The ensuing public debate went all the way up to Prime Minister David Cameron, who told the *Jewish Chronicle*, "There's a difference between Spurs fans self-describing themselves as Yids and someone calling someone a Yid as an insult. You have to be motivated by hate. Hate speech should be prosecuted but only when it's motivated by hate." But the FA has plenty of reason to take a firm stand against even the slightest whiff of antisemitism. Over the last 20 years, the English game has been largely cleansed of its fouler aspects as commercial imperatives have taken over. Today, the FA's Premier League – which has given the world David Beckham, originally of Manchester United – is an international phenomenon, and two decades after the United States declared itself a football-friendly country by hosting the quadrennial World Cup, it is looking to establish itself alongside sporting juggernauts like the NFL, the NBA, and MLB. Sports fans who might once have derided the game as a paleolithic form of basketball, and as symbolically un-American as communism, are now being told, aggressively so, that that they simply don't understand what they've been missing. And it is the English Premier League, whose broadcast rights were purchased by NBC for $250 million, that serves as soccer's flagship in America. In the commercials that showcase forthcoming matches, there are two common techniques to entice curious Americans. You'll see flashes of spectacular action on the pitch: screaming shots toward goal, bicycle kicks, mid-air battles between thrusting heads seeking the ball, all accompanied by strangled howls of awe from the commentator's box.

You'll also see the supporters. A television montage typically includes a sea of fans with clenched fists held high, close-ups of faces contorted with anticipation or excitement or downright misery, flags, banners, and scarves billowing from the top of the stadium to the edge of the playing field. Because, you see, it's all about "passion" – a word that's bandied around a great deal – without peer. "Forget *Downton Abbey*," one NBC tagline exhorted, "the real English drama starts here." In the absence of country piles and feckless gentry, it's in the FA's interest to smooth out the historically rough edges of its signature product. Scratch the surface of England's soccer culture, and the images of lovable ebullience and booming humor are paralleled by a darker history of grotty stadiums, racist hooligans taunting black players with monkey noises, and regular displays of appalling violence involving rival fan organizations known as "firms." "You want to get rid of things that will antagonize your audience, and obviously antisemitism is one," said Simon Kuper, the author of *Soccernomics* and other best-sellers on soccer. "That would be more relevant in the U.S. than, say, in the Asian countries."

***

For Ivor Baddiel, one of Britain's leading comedy writers and a Jewish fan of Chelsea, the FA's new zero-tolerance approach to racism was an unprecedented opportunity to deal with the use of what is now referred to as "the 'Y' word." Three years ago, Baddiel explained, he and his brother David, also a comedian, were at a Chelsea game when the scoreboard flashed the news that Tottenham were losing in their match. Predictably, the derogatory "Yid" chants followed. "From behind us, we heard this lone voice chanting, 'Fuck the Yids, fuck the Yids,' said Baddiel." Someone tapped him on the shoulder and said, 'Actually, there's quite a few Jewish people here.' At the top of his voice, he starts shouting, 'Fuck the Jews, fuck the Jews.' I'm not in any way hard, but for the first time in my life I cracked, and I confronted him."

The Baddiel brothers then teamed up with the anti-racist organization *Kick It Out*, producing a video in which leading footballers past and present urged fans to stop engaging in behavior that would, under Britain's stringent laws against hate speech, subject them to criminal charges if they called someone in the street or in the supermarket a "Yid." If abusing some-one with the 'N' word is no longer acceptable, the video argued, shouldn't the same principle apply to the 'Y' word as well? According to Kuper, that depends upon who's saying it and why. Tottenham fans, as the FA recog-nized, use the word as a badge of pride, unlike their opponents, who use it as hate speech. "I think common sense shows which chant is more malicious. We're talking about hate speech, and it doesn't seem to me that calling your-self 'Yid Army' is hate speech," said Kuper. He also cited the example of Ajax (pronounced Ai-yax), the Amsterdam club whose Jewish pedigree is just as tenuous as Tottenham's but whose fans behave in much the same way as Spurs faithful. "Ajax fans calls themselves Super Jews and wave Israeli flags, and fans of other Dutch clubs shout antisemitic abuse at the Ajax fans," Ku-per said. "If you wave an Israeli flag and say, 'This is who we are,' it might be absurd, and it might make no sense, but it's not hate speech. If you chant songs about Auschwitz, that is hate speech."

Baddiel argues that the word, popular with the black-shirted fascists who harassed Jews in London's East End during the 1930s, is intrinsically a form of hate speech, no matter who wields it. That is why he hopes that Spurs fans can be educated out of their "Yid" fixation. "I'd rather have that than banning orders and censorship and that sort of thing," Baddiel said. "Tottenham fans are not identifying because they are proud to be Jewish, they are doing it because they are proud to be Tottenham fans." What that means, he argued, is that it's up to Jews who aren't part of the Tottenham side to make clear to the team's fans that "Yid" is a slur that's unacceptable in any context. "It's not their word to reclaim," Baddiel said. "It's our word to reclaim if we want to. You can't have a group of non-Jews reclaiming it just because they're Tottenham fans." The tide of history appears to be on Bad-diel's side, insofar as the days when attending a soccer game caused you to fear for your life are rapidly drawing to a close. All-seater stadiums, a family atmosphere, and lucrative sponsorship deals have made English soccer more safe and more tolerant, though nostalgists will bemoan that, as a spec-tacle, the game has become somewhat anodyne as a consequence.

That's why those who want to catch the last gasp of the 'Y' word, as well as the occasional sight of an Israeli flag fluttering on the terraces, would do well to tune in to a Tottenham game sooner rather than later. By this time next year, both the Yid Army and its enemies may well have been van-quished.

Norman Geras: 1943–2013

Tablet, October 18, 2013

There is one memory of Norman Geras – the distinguished academic, prolific author and blogger, and doughty fighter against antisemitism and racism, who passed away in England earlier today – that has stayed with me for the last twenty-five years. It was a dreary afternoon in the northern English city of Manchester, late in 1988. About twenty students, nearly all of us professed Marxists, had gathered for Geras's weekly university seminar on Marxism. As we discussed how class interests manifest in politics, one participant, who clearly wasn't a Marxist, opined that not every owner of the means of production was hellbent on class warfare. Could we not accept, in his inimitable phrase, that there were "cuddly capitalists?"

Immediately, there were dismissive grunts and sycophantic glances in Geras's direction. Surely the great Professor, on whose every word we hung, would rip this insolent pawn of the hated bourgeoisie a new one? But Norman Geras was not that kind of man. He answered with clarity and sympathy, artfully guiding the student through whatever text it was we were examining. In those few moments, the aspiring revolutionaries in his classroom were taught a salutary lesson on the enduring bourgeois values of respect, tolerance and kindness. Geras was, to be sure, a Marxist and a man of the left. His books included a study of the Polish-Jewish revolutionary Rosa Luxemburg and an important treatise entitled "Marx and Human Nature," in which he argued that Marx did, in fact, accept that there was such a thing as human nature, and that socialists consequently needed to grasp the ethical implications of this position. Later in his life, Geras grappled on a daily basis with those ethical implications. A stalwart opponent of Stalinism during the Cold War, in its aftermath he emerged as perhaps the most tenacious critic of the western left's embrace of dictators and tyrants from Slobodan Milosevic to Hugo Chavez, by way of Saddam Hussein. The platform he used to express these views was, at least at the time he launched it, a novel one: a blog simply entitled "Normblog." During the decade or so of the blog's life, its austere design never once received a makeover, yet each day, thousands of readers would flock to read the latest posts by "Norm," the name by which Geras became universally known. Norm's interests–reviews of books and films and music, interviews with other bloggers about why they blog, ruminations on political philosophy, reminiscences of his favorite cities, observations about cricket, a sport he truly loved – more than anything else brought to mind the phrase flung by Stalin's prosecutors against the Jews they loathed. For Norm, who was born in what was then Southern Rhodesia, and who spent the bulk of his life domiciled in the United Kingdom, was truly a "rootless cosmopolitan."

In challenging the orthodoxies of the left, Norm adopted stances that were denounced as heretical by his comrades in the Marxist academy, most especially the editorial board of the *New Left Review*, a journal he was long involved with before they parted ways over the issue of supporting authoritarian regimes in the name of "anti-imperialism." In a 2004 post, "The last word on the Iraq war," Norm restated the case for the toppling of Saddam's regime in unabashedly moral terms. "The most powerful reason in its favour was a simple one," he wrote. "The regime had been responsible for, it was daily adding to, and for all that anyone could reasonably expect, it would go on for the forseeable future adding to, an immensity of pain and grief, killing, torture and mutilation." This sensibility was carried over into his writings on antisemitism, a subject he addressed with increasing frequency and urgency, given the vogue among some of his fellow academics for boycotting their Israeli colleagues, and more generally depicting Israel as the source of all evil. And in doing so, his Jewish identity was placed front and center.

In arguably his finest book on moral philosophy, "The Contract of Mutual Indifference," Norm gently chided Rosa Luxemburg for her declaration that she had "...no special corner of my heart reserved for the ghetto." "A Jewish socialist ought to be able to find some special corner of his or her heart for the tragedy of the Jewish people. A universalist ethic shorn of any special concern for the sufferings of one's own would be the less persuasive for such carelessness." What of Marx's own antisemitism? Again, Norm's instinct was to confront its existence, rather than ignore it. "The only reason for not facing up to these things," he wrote, referring to Marx's characterization of a rival thinker as a "Jew ni**er," "is to protect Marx's reputation as a thinker. But this is not a good reason, because it's no protection; what's there is there."

"What's there is there." That may well be Norman Geras's epitaph. Through his unfailing insight and disarming honesty, Norm was unique. And now that he is gone, it is safe to say that we will not see his like again.

Chapter Two: The Middle East and Israel in Context

The Hezbo(ti)lla

The Huffington Post, June 18, 2010

Behind the rush to send further flotillas to the Gaza Strip, a power game between Islamists of various stripes is emerging. While Turkish, Palestinian, Iranian and Hezbollah flags have all been spotted at rallies and port side gatherings in support of the flotillistas, these scenes of apparent unity belie a more conflicted reality beneath.

Turkey's government, having cast itself as a kind of neo-Ottoman guardian of the Palestinians, is the object of much goodwill among Gazans. That has irked the Iranians, the principal sponsor of the Hamas regime, into a display of one-upmanship: Last week, Tehran announced that it was sending its own flotilla under the protection of the Iranian Navy – a pledge it subsequently backed away from. Not to be outdone, the Syrian dictator, Bashar al-Assad, seized on the recent flotilla clash to start beating the drums of war. In an interview with the *BBC*, Assad said that the Israeli raid on the Mavi Marmara had ruled out any prospects for peace in the near future. Such bellicosity suggests that Assad wants to claim the mantle of his late father, Hafez, as the "lion" of the region. As Syria both hosts the exiled Hamas leadership and has been the object of recent American overtures, Assad has at least two reasons to believe he can do so. Amidst all this jockeying, there is another player, under-analyzed since the initial flotilla furor, but nonetheless critical to its outcome: the Lebanese terrorist movement, Hezbollah.

Like Hamas, Hezbollah is wedded to the idea of an unyielding war against the Jews ("if the Jews all gather in Israel, it will save us the trouble of going after them worldwide," Hezbollah leader Sheikh Hassan Nasrallah famously declared.) And like Hamas, it is also locked in struggle with a rival Arab leadership. For Hamas, it's the Palestinian Authority; for Hezbollah, the Lebanese state. In legal and political terms, Hezbollah is an outlaw. The group is shunned by western states as an interlocutor, is militarily stronger now than in 2006, when the United Nations Security Council passed Resolution 1701 demanding that it disarm, and remains the most immediate threat to Lebanon's integrity. Just this week, a top Hezbollah financier was arrested in a region of Paraguay well-known for smuggling and organized crime. Craving both its weapons and international legitimacy, Hezbollah recognizes that there are times when a slice of political respectability can come in very useful. The flotilla campaign has provided Hezbollah with an opportunity to show its "humanitarian" side and to align itself with Turkey. The wily Nasrallah understands that, for all the current tensions between Turkey and the west, Ankara is in a much better position to strengthen his hand within Lebanon than are either of Hezbollah's traditional backers, Iran and Syria. Hence Nasrallah's fulsome praise of the Turkish leadership, which has apparently resulted in an invitation from Prime Minister Erdogan for him to visit Turkey. Even with his supporters chanting "O Allah, O Merciful One, watch over Erdogan," Nasrallah shows no sign of moderating. Nor has he lost any of his customary hubris (the opposition website Syria Truth quoted Nasrallah saying – translation here – that Turkey's "red flag" was "making decisions" based on Hezbollah's "yellow flag"). Hence his decision to back the new flotilla which is reportedly heading to Gaza from Lebanon.

This flotilla is being organized by Yasser Kashlak, a Palestinian businessman based in Lebanon. Kashlak is known for his ties to terror groups, having shared the platform at a January "pro-resistance" conference in Beirut with representatives of Hezbollah, the Popular Front for the Liberation of Palestine, the Syrian Ba'ath Party and the Iranian Vice-President, Reza Mir Tajeddini. Kashlak insists that his flotilla is an independent initiative, but al-Manar, Hezbollah's broadcasting arm, disagrees, noting that the voyage was announced less than a day after Nasrallah appealed for more flotillas to head for Gaza. The assertion of no connection with Hezbollah is further undermined by the presence of Samar Hajj, the wife of a former Lebanese General jailed for his part in the assassination of Lebanese Prime Minister Rafiq Hariri. If the Mavi Marmara saga didn't prove it already, Hezbollah's planned foray into Mediterranean waters demonstrates that the flotilla movement is about many things, but humanitarian aid isn't one of them. Israel's decision to further ease the blockade of Gaza will therefore make little difference. The goal here is to assault Israel with more tenacity than one's rivals. Should that mean dispatching a few martyrs along the way, then so be it.

Bahrain: The Missing 'A' Word

The Huffington Post, February 17, 2011

In all the coverage of the freedom protests in Bahrain, a certain word beginning with the letter 'A' has been strikingly absent. I don't mean 'autocratic.' Nor 'authoritarian.' Both of those have been invoked, and rightly so.

I refer to the word 'apartheid.' The Afrikaner term for 'separateness,' apartheid prevailed in South Africa from 1948 until 1993, when that country was under white minority rule. While apartheid as a system was snuffed out in South Africa, it has survived as a descriptor that is deployed, in the main, by the bitterest detractors of Israel, but is arguably more relevant in the case of another Middle Eastern country: Bahrain.

It's always worth recalling what the original model of apartheid involved. In South Africa, 90 percent of the population was composed of nonwhites (blacks in the main, but also mixed race and Indian communities) who were disenfranchised and deprived of fundamental human and civil rights. Through such measures as the Group Areas Act (1950), the Bantu Education Act (1953), the Reservation of Separate Amenities Act (1953), the Suppression of Communism Act (1950), and the Prohibition of Mixed Marriages Act (1949), the apartheid regime micromanaged the lives of its subjects on the basis of their skin color. Under apartheid, it was the law that determined where blacks could live, what they could study, which seats they could occupy on public transport, what they could say or write publicly, with whom they could share a bed or marry. It was this reliance on law that made apartheid South Africa peculiar. Discrimination is a feature of most countries, but very few enshrine it within a legal framework. In Bahrain, where 70 per cent of the population is Shi'a, and power and wealth are concentrated in the hands of the Sunni minority, the constitution speaks of equality – formally, then, it's very different to apartheid South Africa. Yet when it comes to actual practice, the similarities are striking, as this report from the Bahrain Center for Human Rights (BCHR) makes painfully clear.

Residency rights, for example, are at least partly determined by ethnic origin. The report discusses "one of Bahrain's largest district, Riffa," which occupies "more than 40 percent of Bahrain land, in which a majority of the members of ruling family reside." Shi'a and some Persian origin Sunnis, the report continues, are prohibited from living there. A Reuters report last October highlighted a related problem: the 53,000 Shi'a who have been denied government housing because of their origin, some for as long as 20 years. It's a similar story in the labor market. "Employment in government bureaus does not follow a clear and specific standard, but is governed by family and sectarian connections," the BCHR report says, pointing out that the Shi'a majority occupies, at most, 18 percent of the top jobs in government. When it comes to unemployment, 95 percent of those without jobs are Shi'a. Do these facts about discrimination in Bahrain add up to apartheid? A sober analysis based on the understanding of apartheid as a system, rather than a pejorative term to be thrown at those you don't like, would conclude that the overlap is hardly precise. At the same time, there is no arguing against the claim that Bahrain is a society where inequality is ethnically rooted, and then buttressed by the denial of civic and political freedoms.

Bahrain is not the only Arab country where minorities rule over majorities: Syria is another, as was Iraq under Saddam Hussein. In none of these cases has the word "apartheid" ever been uttered. Those South Africans, such as Bishop Desmond Tutu, who have eagerly franchised the word in the case of Israel have been absolutely silent when it comes to Arab parallels. And believe me, it's not because they are worried about social scientific rigor. This lack of a consistent, trained spotlight on countries like Bahrain, and the absence of a chorus of luminaries ready to denounce each of its repressive actions in colorful, emotive language, is one reason why the rest of the world has only now discovered that there has long been a thirst for freedom in the Middle East. If that heralds a final break with the platitudes and double standards that characterize the voguish, "anti-imperialist" discourse about the region, so much the better.

Another Flotilla Looms, This Time on Land

JointMedia News Service, March 12, 2012

For the global network of anti-Israel activists – those charmers who bring us the annual delight of "Israel Apartheid Week," solidarity flotillas to Hamas-ruled Gaza, and Ivy League conferences dedicated to the destruction of Jewish sovereignty – there is only one cause in the world that counts.

Bashar al-Assad's butchery in Syria? Forget it. The long nightmare of Zimbabwe under the demented rule of Robert Mugabe? They don't want to know. The persecution of Christians, particularly in the Middle East? Not their problem. All they care about is, in the words of the organizers of the forthcoming Global March on Jerusalem, "the policies and practices of the racist Zionist state of Israel." Almost two years after the attack by Islamic extremists upon Israeli commandos who boarded a Turkish vessel that was attempting to break the blockade of Gaza, the same cast of villains is lining up for a march upon Jerusalem. The city that was liberated and unified following Israel's victory in the 1967 Middle East war is now the site, say the march organizers, of "ethnic cleansing" against Palestinians and "Judaization (sic) policies." And so, on March 30, they plan to have 1 million marchers gathering on Israel's land borders, with the aim of converging upon Jerusalem.

And what a motley crew they are. Among the endorsers of the march is the pro-Taliban Islamic Movement of Afghanistan, and alongside the Afghan Islamists you will find the Berlin branch of the Boycott, Divestment and Sanctions (BDS) campaign against Israel – a perfect opportunity to dust down those "Kauft Nicht Bei Juden" ("Don't Buy From Jews") signs brandished by their grandparents and great-grandparents on the streets of Nazi Germany. From Britain comes the "Viva Palestina" organization led by George Galloway, an insidious former parliamentarian with a long-held penchant for tyrants and dictators, among them Saddam Hussein, Syria's Assad family and the Iranian regime. Then there are those described by the organizers of the march, with no hint of irony, as "VIPs." Their number includes the former Malaysian Prime Minister, Mahathir Mohamed, who, in a January 2010 address to a conference of Islamists, bemoaned the fact that "the Holocaust failed as a final solution...Jews survived to continue to be a source of even greater problems for the world." Alongside Mahathir is his fellow Malaysian, Anthony Fernandes, the CEO of Air Asia (an airline readers are duly urged to boycott).

Most disgraceful is the presence of those Christian clergy who round upon Israel while ignoring the appalling plight of Christians in Egypt, Iran and other Muslim countries. There is the South African Archbishop Desmond Tutu, who has energetically pushed the slander that Israel is actually worse than the old apartheid regime in South Africa. Next to Tutu is the Greek Orthodox Archbishop, Hilarion Cappucci, who was imprisoned by the Israeli authorities in 1974 for smuggling weapons to Palestinian terrorists.

Still, as ugly as all this is, one may well ask whether the Global March on Jerusalem is that significant. After all, Israel faces a much graver range of threats, from Iran's nuclear ambitions through to the Hamas and Hezbollah terrorists aiming missiles at Haifa, Ashkelon, Tel Aviv and other cities. With that in mind, I asked Adam Levick, a blogger and pro-Israel activist who has launched a website to expose the agenda of the march – www.gm2j.co – why we should care in the first place. "The organizers and leadership of the Global March to Jerusalem are comprised almost exclusively of terror supporters and extremists who oppose a Jewish state within any borders," Levick told me. "They are intent on organizing a potentially violent provocation." In looking back at the 2010 Gaza flotilla, Levick argues that we ignore such initiatives at our peril. "The true nature of the terrorist-provoked violence on board the Turkish ship was disseminated too late," he said. "We have to do what we can to prevent the Global March on Jerusalem from portraying itself to the media as a non-violent, humanitarian action."

Here we arrive at the heart of the matter. The aim of the marchers is not to promote non-violence, but to instigate violence. More than anything else, they want to put Israel's defenders in the position of having to open fire, so that images of "Zionist brutality" can then be broadcast around the world. If that happens, we can expect all sorts of loathsome comparisons between Israel and Syria, as though there were no difference between a massacre of innocents in the city of Homs and a clash sparked by terrorist sympathizers. Speaking of Syria, it should be pointed out that the Assad regime – at the same time as it continues its assault on Homs – will be enabling marchers to assemble along its border with Israel, exactly as it did last June, when a raging mob attacked Israeli border guards on the Golan Heights. Assad is desperately looking for ways to divert attention from his crimes. That so-called human rights activists like Archbishop Tutu would assist him in doing so is the most terrible indictment of all.

The future looks bleak for Middle East Christians

Ha'aretz, March 22, 2012

Wearing a frown that creased his unreasonably handsome features, George Clooney was handcuffed by police outside the gates of the Sudanese Embassy in Washington, DC last Friday, during a protest against a renewed military offensive by the Khartoum regime in the border areas of newly independent South Sudan. The Hollywood actor was shepherded to a waiting patrol car along with a troupe of civil rights leaders, including several Jewish representatives, who were also detained. The spectacle was a timely reminder that the coalition which crystallized around the genocide in Sudan's Darfur region – in which Jewish communal organizations were heavily involved, together with assorted celebrities and civil rights groups – has endured. South Sudan is the site of a bloody and seemingly endless conflict that has already claimed upwards of two million lives. The country now faces a new round of murder and mass displacement at the hands of its northern neighbor.

How should these latest horrors be contextualized? In a recent interview, Clooney discussed his visit to the Nuba Mountains, the inhospitable terrain that lies at the heart of the current conflict. "Religion is not an issue," he said, when asked about the causes of the war. "In the camps you will find Christians and Muslims hiding together. It is ethnic in nature." Given the increasingly sharp debate about Islam here in America, it shouldn't come as a surprise that the liberal Clooney is keen to avoid talk of a religious war.

Nonetheless, the Islamist character of the regime in Khartoum can hardly be deemed incidental to the conflict. In common with other Arab countries, Arab chauvinism in Sudan is combined with a domineering, supremacist version of Islam. The religious aspect was dramatically underlined at the beginning of March, when Sudan announced that it had stripped around 700,000 of its citizens of their nationality, the vast majority Christian. They have just over two weeks from today to leave Sudan. Those who depart for the south will walk straight into an unfolding humanitarian catastrophe. Those who remain in the north face the prospect of imprisonment or forced deportation.

To this depressing tale of ethno-religious cleansing, we can add the problem of slavery. The government of South Sudan says that there are 30,000 slaves being held in the north, the clear majority of whom, again, are Christians. As far as the north is concerned, there is no slavery in Sudan, a line about as credible as the Tehran regime's insistence that there are no homosexuals in Iran. Instances of Christian persecution can be found in nearly every Muslim country. The death sentence imposed on Youcef Nadarkhani, an Iranian pastor who committed the mortal sin of converting to Christianity from Islam, has highlighted the tenuous situation faced by Iranian adherents of the faith. In Nigeria, Christian churches are bombed with mounting frequency by the Islamist terrorists of Boko Haram, whose name translates as "western education is a sin." In Egypt, the Coptic minority faces violence and discrimination that will likely get worse, given the strong showing by the Muslim Brotherhood and the Salafist parties in the recent elections. In Iraq, Pakistan, Somalia – you name it – reports of Christians being falsely charged with blasphemy or apostasy, along with gruesome tales of beheadings and beatings, are multiplying by the day. Though not every Christian community in the Middle East lives with the scale of terror currently spreading through Sudan, it is legitimate to ask whether Sudan provides a terrifying glimpse of the future for Christians in the wider region. In that sense, it's worth paying to heed to the statement delivered on March 12 by Sheikh Abdul Aziz bin Abdullah, the Grand Mufti of Saudi Arabia, who declared that it is "necessary to destroy all the churches of the region." In the event that their churches are destroyed, the Christians who worship in them will surely follow. It must also be acknowledged that Christians are repressed both by the allies of the west, like Saudi Arabia, and by its adversaries, like Iran and Sudan.

Jews and Christians in America already have an encouraging record of joint campaigning, especially when it comes to Israel advocacy. Both communities now have a duty to raise the banner of Christian persecution, an issue with similar mobilizing potential to the campaign against apartheid in South Africa, or freedom for Soviet Jews. They need to do so with urgency and clarity. We may not have reached a final, genocidal phase yet, but we are headed in that direction.

South Sudan is a Jewish Cause

JNS/The Algemeiner, April 25, 2012

The great Jewish historian, Salo W. Baron, famously criticized the "lachrymose" conception of Jewish history, by which he meant the reduction of the Jewish experience to a series of gory persecutions. This view of the Jewish past often colors our sense of the Jewish present, with the result that we see ourselves as having few friends, or even none at all, in a hostile world which resents the re-establishment of Jewish sovereignty after centuries when Jews were at the mercy of others.

Thinking this way can be dangerous. I say this not because I make light of the threat posed to Israel by Iran, say, or because I don't regard antisemitism in Europe and in the Islamic world as a major problem. I say this because we shouldn't allow the fixations of enemies to divert us from the reality that we do have friends – and that we owe these friends our support when they fall upon dark times. This week, the Islamist regime that has ruled Sudan since coming to power through a military coup in 1989 declared a new war against the neighboring state of South Sudan. The newest member of the United Nations, South Sudan declared its independence in July 2011, following a referendum in which almost 100 per cent of participants opted to separate from the predominantly Arab and Muslim north. For nearly 30 years, Sudan waged a brutal war against the largely Christian, African south, in which around 2 million people lost their lives. Jewish communities around the world, and especially here in North America, need to flex their muscles in support of South Sudan. The ethical imperative is clear, as anyone following the brutal campaign waged by the Sudanese regime in the Nuba mountains in recent weeks would be aware. But there is also a political imperative. Israel was one of the first states to recognize South Sudan. At the end of 2011, Salva Kiir, South Sudan's combative President, visited Israel and spoke of his wish to move his country's embassy to Jerusalem. Israeli aid and development agencies, often assisted by Jewish organizations like the American Jewish Committee's Africa Institute, have, over the years, played a major role in building up the South's economy and infrastructure.

Hence, the bottom line is this: in a region filled to the brim with hateful enemies and fair-weather allies, South Sudan is the only state that can truly be called a friend of Israel. The origins of this friendship stretch back to the early years of the State of Israel, when David Ben Gurion, Israel's first Prime Minister, articulated a strategy known as the "Alliance of the Periphery," whereby the non-Arab and non-Muslim populations in the Middle East – Kurds, Iranians, Lebanese Christians and so forth – were regarded as natural partners in countering the Arab campaign against the Jewish state.

Yet showing support for South Sudan in its hour of need is not Israel's task alone. Jewish communities in the diaspora should also be advocating for a renewed "Alliance of the Periphery." After all, when we hear the blood-curdling declamations of Sudan's dictator, the indicted war criminal Omar al Bashir, against the "insects" running South Sudan, how can we not be stirred by the parallels with the Iranian regime's anti-Israel rhetoric, or the fulminations against the "sons of pigs and monkeys" across the Islamic world, or even the dehumanizing verbal assaults by the Nazis upon the Jews? Throughout much of the conflict over the last decade in the Darfur region of western Sudan, American Jews were a vital base of support and awareness. Synagogues and community centers across the country were draped in "Save Darfur" banners. When 100,000 people turned out for an April 2006 rally on the National Mall in Washington, DC, a huge number of the participants were drawn from Jewish communities. There is no reason why this impressive solidarity should not be reignited for the people of South Sudan. Only this time, we should be explicit that we support South Sudan because we are Jews. Their foes are also ours; for example, many of the organizations that traipse around American university campuses preaching hatred of Israel have also portrayed the Darfur campaign as a nefarious tool of Zionist influence, much to the glee of Sudan's rulers, who quickly jumped on the bandwagon by claiming that talk of a genocide was a Zionist myth.

Sadly, Jews have a tendency to become nervous in such situations. Rather than celebrating our political influence, we seek to bury it behind inter-group and inter-faith coalitions. It is not that such coalitions are unwelcome; the problem is that many Jews apparently believe that the more universal a campaign is, the more acceptable it will be in the court of public opinion, and the less selfish we will look. If we want to boost the pride of our friends, we need to boost the pride in ourselves. For the best coalition of all is still to be formed: one in which Jews, Kurds, Southern Sudanese, Lebanese Christians, Iranian democrats and others seeking to combat the malign in-

fluences of Islamism and Arab chauvinism gather under one roof, supporting each other as equals. As Herzl said, "If you will it, it is no dream."

Fallout from Shalit Deal Continues to Divide Israelis

JNS/Canadian Jewish News, June 19, 2012

Having experienced hijackings, cross-border incursions, gun attacks and
suicide bombings across several decades, Israelis also know too well that
the damage wreaked by terrorist atrocities can reverberate for years after
these insidious acts are committed. Internal divisions often accompany that
lasting damage. In the immediate aftermath of a terrorist attack, the country
invariably unites in grief, but splits emerge when the feelings of those families scarred by terror attacks conflict with decisions that the government
deems to be in the national interest. A prime case in point involves Arnold
and Frimet Roth, whose 15-year-old daughter, Malki, was murdered along
with 14 others when a suicide bomber struck the Sbarro pizza restaurant in
downtown Jerusalem on Aug. 9, 2001. Ahlam Tamimi, a Palestinian woman
who transported both the bomb and the bomber to the restaurant, was subsequently captured and sentenced to 16 life terms in prison.

In October 2011, as part of the deal in which 1,027 Palestinian prisoners were exchanged for Gilad Shalit, the Israeli soldier who spent more
than five years in Hamas captivity, Tamimi walked free. Now living in Jordan, Tamimi has become a celebrity in the Arab world, hosting her own
weekly show on the Hamas satellite TV station, al-Quds. In between extol-
ling the virtues of "martyrdom attacks" against Jews, she celebrates her own
monstrous achievement; on one famous occasion, when she learned that she
had enabled the killing of eight children at the Sbarro restaurant, and not
three as she had previously thought, she turned to the camera wearing a
broad grin of pride. Six months before the Shalit deal, the Roths and their
many supporters implored Israeli Prime Minister Benjamin Netanyahu not
to consider Tamimi's release as part of any exchange. Netanyahu, they say,
did not respond then. Nor did he respond when the Roths challenged Netanyahu's claim that the families impacted by the Shalit deal had been sent a
letter explaining the government's position; they could find no evidence,
they insisted, that such a letter had been sent. Now the Roths are accusing
Netanyahu of ignoring them for a third time. The occasion was the news that
another convicted terrorist, Nizar al Tamimi, had crossed the Allenby Bridge
from the West Bank into Jordan to join his cousin and ertswhile fiancée –
none other than the murderer-turned-TV star Ahlam Tamimi. Nizar, who

was serving a life sentence for the murder of a Jewish resident of the West Bank in 1993, was also released under the terms of the Shalit deal. While Ahlam and Nizar's victims will never recover from the grief inflicted by their grotesque crimes, the Arabic press is reporting that the couple is currently planning their wedding.

This month, the Roths wrote an open letter to Netanyahu pointing out that Nizar al Tamimi's release "was conditioned on the requirement that he remain at all times within the areas controlled by the Palestinian Authority." His reunion with their daughter's murderer came, therefore, as a massive blow to the Roths, who were already aware that Tamimi had previously tried to enter Jordan and been turned back. "I called someone who has a very senior position in the Ministry of Justice," Arnold Roth told me. "He said, 'it's never going to happen,' but advised me to check nonetheless. I chased the Shabak (Israel's security service) for two and a half weeks. When I finally got a reply, I was told that there was a decision to allow Nizar to leave, provided that he doesn't come back within five years." Roth hired a lawyer to challenge the decision, but it was too late – Nizar al Tamimi arrived in Jordan on June 7. "I felt like I'd been hit over the head with a cricket bat," Roth, an Australian who made aliyah, recalled in his conversation with me.

I contacted Israeli government officials to find out their reasoning. After encountering some initial reluctance, I received a call from Mark Regev, Prime Minister Netanyahu's spokesman. "I understand Arnold's pain and the pain of those whose family members have been killed by terrorists, when they see those guilty of these horrendous crimes being released," Regev said. However, he stressed, the current situation is a direct outcome of the Shalit deal. "Everything flows from that," Regev said. "Arnold's position is a legitimate one that we respect. Ultimately, the government chose the path of getting Gilad Shalit out of captivity." Though he was unwilling to discuss the specific details of Nizar al Tamimi's case, Regev did explain the strategic principle behind the government's thinking. "Israel does not have a problem with terrorists leaving," he said. "It's easier for us when hardcore terrorists actually leave. Their ability to hurt us in the future is much more limited." Arnold Roth is not persuaded by this argument. In an email to me subsequent to our conversation, he pointed out that another terrorist released through the Shalit deal, Ibrahim Abu Hijleh, had been rearrested. "If they want terrorists out of the country, why did they explicitly restrict more than 100 of them, including Nizar al-Tamimi, to the area controlled by the PA?" Roth wrote. "That's a decision they took in October 2011. Since they made that decision then, why did they change it now? And without any announcement? And without consulting any of the victims?" Lack of consultation with the victims is a recurring theme among critics of the Israeli government's actions in this sensitive area. "Israeli government decision-making related to the release of terrorists and related issues continues to be highly secretive, often inexplicable, and entirely insensitive to the families of the victims," Professor Gerald Steinberg, the President of NGO Monitor, a leading Israel advocacy organization, told me in an email. "The mass release in the Shalit exchange, and now facilitating al Tamimi's 'family reunification,' has continued the cruel pattern of shutting out the families of the terror victims, while eroding Israeli deterrence against the perpetrators of mass terror." It is against this charged background that the Roths are demanding answers. The Israeli government can, of course, say that it is providing answers; but the problem with those answers is that they raise even more painful questions. Clarity is needed, and that's why Prime Minister Netanyahu should finally sit down in person with Arnold and Frimet Roth. True, such an encounter may well turn out to be a fractious one. That is better than a continuing silence that comes across as cold indifference.

The Real Challenge in the Middle East is Ideology

JNS/The Jewish Week, July 2, 2012

Roger Garaudy, the French self-styled philosopher who died on June 13 aged 98, was an exceptional individual. And I don't mean that as a compliment. Garaudy began his political life as a communist and then converted to Islam, changing his first name from "Roger" to "Ragaa." Along the way, he authored a noxious screed entitled, "The Founding Myths of Israeli Politics," in which he denied the Nazi Holocaust. For his pains, he was fined a hefty sum by a French court for violating that country's laws against Holocaust denial and handed a suspended prison sentence. Following the atrocities of September 11, 2001, Garaudy actively promoted the conspiracy theory that the attacks on New York and Washington, DC, were the work of the U.S. government. Garaudy's great contribution was thus to embrace, in a single lifetime, the principle expressions of totalitarianism in the 20th century: communist, fascist and Islamist. No sensible person, one would imagine, could mourn the death of such a man, nor find any intellectual sustenance in the writings of a conspiracy theorist. Actually, Garaudy had plenty of admirers. The late, unlamented Libyan dictator, Muammar al-Gaddafi, described him as "Europe's greatest philosopher since Plato and Aristotle." Not be outdone, Abdul Halim-Khaddam, the former Syrian vice president and a loyal servant of the Assad dynasty until he fell out with Bashar al Assad in 2005, praised him as the "greatest contemporary western philosopher." Arab conservatives, too, found much to appreciate: In 1986, Garaudy was awarded Saudi Arabia's King Faisal Prize for Services to Islam.

Shortly after Garaudy died, the Federation of Islamic Organizations in Europe (FIOE) lauded his "...humane example; we ask Allah, the Almighty, to receive him with His Bountiful Mercy, and to accept him among the righteous." Their attraction to this peddler of lies is not hard to understand, given that FIOE once claimed that Israel was selling vodka on the Russian market in bottles labeled with a picture of the al-Aqsa mosque in Jerusalem. FIOE is also a European affiliate of the Muslim Brotherhood, the party that embraced antisemitism at its inception and is now, through the person of Mohamed Morsi, in control of the Egyptian Presidency. In Iran, the mullahs awarded Garaudy celebrity status. During the 1990s, he visited Tehran, where he was received with full honors by then President Mohammed Khatami. This event took place, it should be noted, several years before Mahmoud Ahmadinejad became Iran's President; Khatami was widely feted in the West as a moderate alternative to the hardliners around the Supreme Leader, Ali Khamenei. And once Ahmadinejad became President, he quickly organized an international parley of Holocaust deniers in Tehran in 2006. Unable to attend because of illness, Garaudy sent the conference a videotaped message.

Garaudy's legacy was on full display in Tehran again last week, when Iranian Vice President Mohammad Reza Rahimi delivered a speech to an audience of high-ranking diplomats at a UN-sponsored conference on drug trafficking. Did Rahimi address concerns about Iran's role in the transportation of heroin from Afghanistan to the West? No. Instead, he warned shocked delegates that the narcotics trade was run by Jews, acting on the instructions supposedly contained in the Talmud. Rahimi's line – "the book teaches them how to destroy non-Jews, so as to protect an embryo in the womb of a Jewish mother" – could have been written by Garaudy. Of course, this was not the first time that a senior Iranian official uttered such contemptible remarks before an apparently civilized, sophisticated audience. In 2007, Ali Larijani, at the time Iran's chief nuclear negotiator, addressed the Munich Security Conference, a major annual event that brings together leading politicians, military personnel and policy analysts. Asked whether he endorsed Ahmadinejad's denial of the Holocaust, Larijani answered that it was an "open question" as to whether the Nazi slaughter of the Jews had taken place. For all the huffing and puffing that enraged Westerners engage in after being subjected to speeches like these, one might think that they would learn from their mistakes. If you ask Iran to host an international gathering, or if you invite a representative of the Iranian regime to a prestigious event, then speeches promoting Holocaust denial and other conspiracy theories will follow as surely as night does day.

But Western policymakers don't learn from their mistakes for one good reason. They are in denial about the true nature of a political culture in which denial of the Holocaust has become a sacred dogma. In the eyes of too many Western diplomats, the competing forces on the world stage are all rational actors; if some of these actors make outrageous statements, it is because they themselves have been insulted. By focusing on tangible results – creating a Palestinian state, for example, or offering assurances that Iran's nuclear program will not be targeted by a military strike – their hope is that these flights of ideological lunacy will be reined in. What this demonstrates is the enormous gulf between the West and the prevailing systems of belief in the Islamic world. In our culture, someone like Garaudy is a figure to be avoided, or mocked, or both. However, for Arab and Muslim leaders, a European intellectual who tells them the things they are predisposed to believe is manna from heaven. Why should they take German or French diplomats at face value when there are people like Garaudy claiming that everything they say is a pack of lies dictated by a Jewish conspiracy? Until Western leaders grasp that the true challenge posed by the Middle East lies not in tangible elements, like Israeli settlements or water policies, but rather intangible ones in the form of beliefs like those outlined above, there will be no chance of progress. We in the West learned a long time ago that ideas matter. It is high time to apply that insight to the Middle East. Should we arrive at a juncture when conspiracy-mongers like Roger Garaudy are treated with the same contempt as they are in the West, the much-heralded Arab Spring will truly have sprung.

Saints or Sinners? Meet Rachel Corrie's Allies

JNS/Canadian Jewish News, September 4, 2012

I am writing this column with great reluctance. In a rational world, the accidental death of Rachel Corrie, the pro-Hamas activist who was crushed by a bulldozer in Gaza almost 10 years ago, would no longer have a place in the news cycle. Sadly, we do not live in a rational world, and therefore Corrie's fate – along with her insidious group of allies that mushroomed following her death – ontinues to plague us.

Here's what we know: After much careful deliberation, an Israeli court in Haifa finally dismissed a civil suit brought by Corrie's parents, ruling that her death was not a homicide, but a consequence of Corrie's decision to stand in front of an armored bulldozer whose driver could not see her. Further, we know that Israel is a country where the clear separation of powers that is essential to democracy exists. Israel's courts are not beholden to the government or the IDF. Rather, they are robustly independent, unafraid of reaching decisions that might be unpopular with the imperatives of whomever happens to be in government. Case-in-point: In 2003, Israel's Central Elections Committee (CEC) banned Balad, an anti-Zionist party based among Israeli Arabs, from running in the elections of the same year. The CEC argued that Balad's rejection of Israel's character as a Jewish state disqualified the party's participation. But Israel's Supreme Court overruled that decision, thereby allowing Balad to run in the elections. One of Balad's leaders, Ahmad Tibi, praised the court for "blocking the anti-democratic avalanche of the right-wing." Yet, when an Israeli court arrives at a decision that the "Zionism is racism" chorus disagrees with, all of a sudden the entire judicial system is corrupt. In responding to the Corrie verdict, Amnesty International talked, ludicrously, of a "pattern of impunity" when it comes to alleged violations by the IDF. (Clearly, Amnesty does not remember the case of Lt. Col. Ya'akov Gigi, who was imprisoned and demoted in 2008 after being convicted in the wrongful killing of a Palestinian civilian.) Former President Jimmy Carter, who depicts Israel as an apartheid state, dutifully chimed in with similar wording: "The court's decision confirms a climate of impunity, which facilitates Israeli human rights violations against Palestinian civilians in the Occupied Territory." Frankly, we shouldn't expect anything else from individuals and groups like these. They are predisposed to believe the slander that Israeli institutions are built on the principle that Jews are more equal than non-Jews. Still, the cumulative effect of these statements leads unwitting readers to believe that the only issue worth considering is Israel's behavior. Their authors do not – indeed, will not – ask what Corrie was doing in Gaza in the first place, nor do they question the ugly, genocidal politics that this deeply misguided young woman subscribed to. Corrie was a member of the International Solidarity Movement (ISM) – a misnomer if ever there was one, since Palestinians are the sole subject of the dubious "solidarity" which they offer. You will not find ISM volunteers in Syria, documenting the unspeakable atrocities committed by Bashar al Assad's regime. You will not find them in Russia, monitoring the kangaroo court that recently convicted the feminist punk band Pussy Riot to two years imprisonment on the charge of "hooliganism." Nor will you find them in Venezuela, the homicide capital of the world, standing alongside the innocent civilians murdered by gangsters aligned with the tyrant Hugo Chavez.

And you will not find them in these places for two reasons. Firstly, the ISMers have a soft spot for authoritarian regimes, so long as these are sufficiently anti-American. Secondly, they are cowards: Israel and the Palestinian territories are ideal spots for war tourists of this ilk, since, statistically-speaking, there is very little chance of death or injury at the hands of the IDF, and you can get a shower and a decent meal at the end of a day's "solidarity" work. At the same time, the ISM is not stupid. It is an integral part of the current of opinion that has essentially beatified Rachel Corrie. Since she died, her supporters have portrayed her as an unimpeachably noble soul, on a par with – unbelievably – Anne Frank. Writing this week in Counterpunch, an online antisemitic rag that is a favored destination for the ISM, Jennifer Loewenstein had the temerity to conclude, "I believe Anne Frank would have agreed with Rachel's mother, Cindy, who – when asked if she thought Rachel should have moved away from the bulldozer – replied, 'I don't think that Rachel should have moved. I think we should all have been standing there with her.'" Raiding the memories of the Holocaust to score points for the Palestinians is a long-established tactic of the ISM and similar groups. But what really matters here is the moral gulf that separated Anne Frank from Rachel Corrie. Read Anne Frank's diary, and what comes across is a humanism extraordinarily rare for someone so young. Corrie, by contrast, frequently accused Israel of practicing genocide – an absurd claim, given the year on year increase in the Palestinian population – while happily taking up membership in a group that seeks to destroy Israel with what it euphemistically terms the "one-state solution." There are few examples in history of nations giving up their right to self-determination without bloodshed. A single state from the Mediterranean to the River Jordan would have to be imposed on Israelis, and most of them would have to die or be expelled for it to take shape. That bald reality is the true legacy of Rachel Corrie, one that leaves her and her allies not as saints, but as sinners.

Time to Challenge the 'Palestine-Firsters'

JNS/The Algemeiner, November 27, 2012

Between June and October of this year, Palestinian terrorists in the Hamas-controlled Gaza Strip launched almost 260 attacks, the vast majority involving rockets and missiles, into Israeli territory. Come this month, and the barrage multiplied considerably, with more than 100 rockets being fired on

Nov. 11 alone. But it was only when Israel formally began a defensive operation three days later, during which Hamas leaders like Ahmed Jabari, the
terrorists' chief, were successfully eliminated, and airstrikes against key
Hamas targets were undertaken, that the Gaza situation consumed foreign
media coverage to the exclusion of almost everything else.

It's a sobering thought, especially when you consider that more than
200 Syrians were murdered by the Assad regime during the seven days of
Israel's Operation Pillar of Defense, taking the toll of eighteen months of
massacres to well above 40,000. Or that a bloodcurdling 81 prisoners were
executed by the Iranian regime in one 10-day period this month. Twelve
years after the second Palestinian intifada triggered a worldwide movement
to oppose Zionism and Israel on a scale unseen since the Soviet-inspired
campaigns of the 1970s, we've grown accustomed to this kind of dispropor-
tionate – and yes, I use that word deliberately – media response. And we
think, too, that we understand the reasons underlying it. The commentator
Jeffrey Goldberg explained it beautifully in one of his recent columns. Goldberg reported the contents of an email he received from a Syrian friend in
Beirut. "We get very little interest from the international press compared to
the Palestinians," wrote the friend. "What should we do to get more attention?" Responded Goldberg: "My advice is to get killed by Jews. Always
works."

But there is another, historically weightier, factor that needs to be
taken into consideration. I'm referring to the widespread belief that the
"injustice" meted out to the Palestinians in 1948, when the State of Israel
was created, is what lies at the root of the post-World War Two conflicts in
the Middle East. According to this account, everything else that happens in
the region – the extraordinary repression meted out by ruling regimes upon
their own citizens, both before and after the much-vaunted "Arab Spring," or
the vicious civil war within the Islamic world which determines that the
most numerous victims of Islamist factions are fellow Muslims – is just a
side-show to this main event. Many of the proponents of this view in America belong to a school of thought that has turned an antisemitic smear into an
analytical category. I'm speaking, of course, about the term "Israel-Firster,"
so enthusiastically deployed by a cast of characters ranging from the fringe
Jewish blogger, M.J. Rosenberg, through to the contributors to the "Open
Zion" blog edited by the journalist Peter Beinart. These people believe that
the reason the Middle East is in such a mess is because the U.S. administration is under the thumb of a nefarious "Israel Lobby," a cluster of organizations and individuals so influential that they can force the government of the
U.S. to act against its own interests by supporting Israel.

The two most well-known advocates of the "Israel-Firster" stance were both frenetically typing condemnations of Israel into their laptops as the Israeli Air Force struck back against Hamas. I refer to Professors John Mearsheimer and Stephen Walt, authors of the execrable 2008 tome The Israel Lobby, which is probably the clearest exposition of the "Israel-Firster" conspiracy theory that you are likely to read. Writing in the London Review of Books, the same publication that printed the joint Mearsheimer/Walt essay that eventually became The Israel Lobby, Mearsheimer outdid his customarily fatuous assertions. For example, he quoted a now discredited survey that claims a majority of Israelis believe that Palestinians live under a system of "apartheid." He approvingly cited a blog written by another marginal Jewish commentator, Mitchell Plitnick, which described the right-wing Yisrael Beitenu party as "fascist." Most of all, he reproduced the myth, lovingly stoked in Arab capitals for the last 70 years, that the end goal here is a "Greater Israel." Meanwhile, Walt used Mearsheimer's column as a cue to declare his belief that "the one-state outcome" – in other words, the replacement of the State of Israel by a Palestinian state stretching from the Mediterranean Sea to the River Jordan – "looks increasingly unavoidable." Added Walt: "And in that context, even a prolonged, contentious campaign for civil and political rights wouldn't be as pointless as what we are now witnessing." This sort of rhetoric is not only (because of its cavalier support of an outcome that could only be achieved through mass killings of Israelis) morally poisonous. It actually runs counter to the very same American national interests these authors claim to uphold.

What these "Palestine-Firsters," as I call them, seek to deny is the reality that emerged from Israel's latest limited campaign against Hamas. Firstly, that Israel can defend itself quite adequately without a single American soldier on the ground, in marked contrast to the rest of the region. Secondly, that the Obama administration's support for Israel was based on that fundamental tenet of international law that holds that sovereign states have the right of self-defense. Thirdly, that a strong and secure Israel is a critical asset to American interests in the region, as well as the liberal democratic values which both countries represent. For that reason, there is a crying need to supplant the vogueish, Palestine-centered interpretation of the Middle East with one that recognizes that this particular Middle Eastern conflict is not the most important, nor the most dangerous, in the region. As long as we fail to appraise this reality, we will permit regional leaders, like Turkish Prime Minister Recep Tayyip Erdogan, and Egypt's newest pharaoh, President Mohammed Morsi, to divert attention from their own wrongdoings onto the plight of the Palestinians.

An Israel chastised will not end Erdogan's bloody, and largely unreported, onslaught against the Kurdish minority in his country. It will not stop Islamist terrorists from Egypt to Pakistan placing bombs in churches and mosques alike. It will not lead to the defeat of al-Qaeda operatives from Mali to Yemen. What it will do, though, is hurt America. And that is reason enough to turn to the Palestine-Firsters and ask them point blank, where do your loyalties really lie?

More Peace, Less Process: The Key to Israeli-Palestinian Negotiations

JNS/The Algemeiner, May 30, 2013

U.S. Secretary of State John Kerry has already visited the Middle East four times since President Barack Obama named him to the post back in February. Perhaps anticipating the large number of yawns that such a statistic is likely to produce, Kerry directly addressed, during his latest jaunt, the growing number of peace process skeptics on both sides of the Israeli-Palestinian divide. "There have been bitter years of disappointment. It is our hope that by being methodical, careful, patient, but detailed and tenacious, we can lay out a path ahead that can conceivably surprise people, but certainly exhaust the possibilities of peace," Kerry told them. However much Kerry would like us to believe that there are routes to peace that haven't yet been explored, there is a dreary sense of deja vu about his words. Every day, it seems, an American politician declares that time is running out, that windows of opportunity are closing, that the Israeli-Palestinian dimension of the broader Middle East conflict is propelling the region towards apocalypse. Obama himself comes to mind in this regard. In 2010, he told the United Nations General Assembly, "[W]hen we come back here next year, we can have an agreement that will lead to a new member of the United Nations – an independent, sovereign state of Palestine, living in peace with Israel." But it's now 2013, and there is no State of Palestine, only a Palestinian Authority (PA) that shuns direct negotiations in favor of a unilateralist strategy to secure recognition of an independent Palestinian state by everyone except Israel. Moreover, the Palestinians are openly distrustful of U.S. efforts. "I'm hesitant to say we are seeing a miraculous transformation in American policy and its blind strategic alliance with Israel," said the PLO's Hanan Ashrawi upon Kerry's arrival, conveniently regurgitating the widespread myth in the

Arab world that American Middle East policy is determined solely by Israeli imperatives.

Nor has Palestinian rhetoric changed for the better. The eliminationist desires of the Palestinian leadership – and I'm not talking here about Hamas, but about our ostensible peace partner, the PA – remain as ingrained as ever. At the end of April, for example, Rabi Khandaqji, the PA governor of the West Bank City of Qalqilya, reaffirmed that the Palestinians would never abandon the so-called "right of return." Palestinian refugees, Khandaqji declared, would return "to Haifa, Nazareth and Acre" – all cities that lie inside the pre-1967 borders of Israel. This isn't code for the destruction of Israel. It's an explicit call for the destruction of Israel. The traditional approach of American and western negotiators has been to play down this kind of rhetoric as ideological baggage that will disappear once meaningful progress has been made. Time and again, this patronizing, even racist, manner, which treats Arab politicians as tantrum-prone children who say things they don't really mean, has been proved wrong by events. And yet, the template for peace negotiations has barely been modified during the last 20 years. Which is why negotiators at the State Department would be wise to consult an important new paper published by two Israeli academics, Joel Fishman and Kobi Michael, in the academic journal, the Jewish Political Studies Review. Introducing the notion of a "positive peace," Fishman and Michael warn against efforts to create a Palestinian state without worrying about its governance and internal political culture, since this would increase "the chances of bringing into being one more failed and warlike state that would become a destabilizing force in the region."

Positive peace, the authors assert, is not just the about the absence of war, nor about elevating the right of national self-determination above all other considerations. "The real problem," they write, "is that, long ago, the would-be peacemakers, in their haste and fear of failure, did not frame the problem correctly. They failed to ask the right question. In order to avoid disagreement, they concentrated on process and postponed the substantive issues of content. They hoped that the dynamic of congenial negotiations would facilitate a favorable outcome. By taking refuge in process and hoping to keep the negotiations 'on track,' they neglected the real goal: building a stable and sustainable peace, or positive peace."

In the Israeli-Palestinian context, a positive peace entails a complete overhaul of the zero-sum attitude toward Israel that has become institutionalized in Palestinian politics. For decades, the Palestinians have regarded negotiations as simply one of several avenues in pursuing their war on Israel's existence: armed struggle, more accurately defined as terrorism, has been another, while the global Boycott, Divestment and Sanctions campaign is yet another. Fishman and Michael cite the pioneering Israeli scholar Yehoshafat Harkabi's observation that in Arab discourse, the idea of peace with justice is equivalent to the vision of a Middle East without Israel. And in marked contrast to American worries that time is running out, they point out that as far as the Palestinians are concerned, we've got all the time in the world. When the late Yasser Arafat spoke, in 1980, about "a war which will last for generations," he was being sincere. And Arafat's view persists because, in spite of all the economic incentives waved at the PA, the near-metaphysical belief in a struggle to the death has prevailed over the rational, sensible notion of territorial partition. Fishman and Michael should consider writing a second paper about how these realizations might guide policy-makers, so that the peace process is more about peace and less about process. Though they don't say it explicitly, there is a strong sense in the paper that negotiations that are not preceded by meaningful, internal political reform in the Palestinian entity will share the miserable fate of the Oslo Agreement. And if that's correct, then the "path that could conceivably surprise people," as John Kerry put it, begins not with discussions about settlements, water rights or the size of the Palestinian security forces, but with what the Palestinians themselves believe about the world around them – and whether they are capable of change.

Hezbollah: From Terrorism to War Crimes

JNS/The Algemeiner, June 10, 2013

An unexpected obstacle to efforts within the European Union (EU) to designate Hezbollah as a terrorist organization emerged last week when the new Bulgarian foreign minister, Kristian Vigenin, stated in a radio interview that evidence connecting the Lebanese Shi'a organization with last year's murderous assault on a busload of Israeli tourists in the resort town of Burgas was "not conclusive." Vigenin produced no new evidence to counter the conclusion, shared by American, Israeli and British intelligence agencies, that Hezbollah was behind the attack. Yet by casting doubt on Hezbollah's role, Vigenin has opened the possibility that the bitter political divides within this comparatively marginal member of the EU could impact the bloc's Middle East policy as a whole.

For several years, Europe has been out of step with the United States and Israel over Hezbollah. Not applying the terrorist designation to Hezbollah has meant that the organization's supporters in Europe have been able to raise funds for it with impunity. The Burgas attack provided new momentum for British efforts to secure a reversal of this ghastly policy, especially as Bulgaria's previous, pro-western government was in no doubt over who was responsible. Only a fortnight ago, France and Germany, two countries that had long been resistant to the terrorist designation, were signaling a major change of position. Enter the new Bulgarian government, a coalition of technocrats and ex-Communists elected on the basis of public anger with the perceived corruption and incompetence of the prior administration. Those who detect the hand of Russia in this bizarre twist over Burgas are probably not wrong. In eastern Europe these days, governments who distance themselves from America and western Europe are bound to veer towards Moscow. And Moscow doesn't want anyone to touch Hezbollah, given the military support these terrorists and war criminals have given to the Syrian regime of Bashar al-Assad, which President Vladimir Putin and his cohorts energetically support.

This messy political context may, ironically, yield a positive result, in that it's unlikely that the rest of the EU, and particularly the British, will feel obliged to take Bulgaria's clumsy change of heart seriously. Moreover, the Burgas attack is not the only reason to apply the terrorist designation. For one thing, the British government has repeatedly cited the conviction of a Hezbollah operative in Cyprus, Hossam Taleb Yaacoub, for conspiring to launch a Burgas-style attack against Israeli tourists visiting the island – a plan which one terrorism analyst described as "a rare lifting of the veil on how [Hezbollah terrorists] operate." For another – and this is certainly of even greater importance – Hezbollah has become an active element in Assad's murderous war on his own people, which has claimed 80,000 lives. Without the support of Hezbollah units, it is unlikely that Assad's regime could have conquered rebel forces in the western town of Qusair, an outcome that further boosted Assad's morale in a week when his Russian allies announced that they would be providing his regime with S-300 air defense missiles. Indeed, the French have already suggested that policy towards Hezbollah will be determined by events in Syria, rather than the Burgas attack. "Given the decisions taken by Hezbollah and the fact that it has fought very hard against the Syrian population, I confirm that France will propose to inscribe the military wing of Hezbollah on the list of terrorist organizations," the French foreign minister, Laurent Fabius, recently declared. This reference to a Hezbollah "military wing" will without a doubt draw impatient sighs from the Israelis, who correctly point out that since Hezbollah doesn't distinguish between its "political" and "military" wings, neither should anyone else. But if the designation measures are robust enough to override any sly attempts to raise funds for Hezbollah as a political organization, that shouldn't really matter.

Additionally, if the EU doesn't act decisively against Hezbollah, it will face the accusation of complicity not just with terrorism, but with war crimes and crimes against humanity as well. By mobilizing in support of Assad, Hezbollah, as a Lebanese organization, has both crossed an international border for the sole purpose of carrying out military aggression, and participated in some of the ugliest atrocities against civilians witnessed since the Darfur conflict in Sudan. France has said that it has no doubt that the "regime and its accomplices" have used chemical weapons in their offensive. Even the Israel-obsessed UN Human Rights Council has described "murder, torture, rape, and other inhumane acts" as proof that the Syrian conflict has reached "new levels of brutality." It's a far cry from the shameful scenes in European cities in 2006, when left-wing celebrities led demonstrations against Israel's decision to strike against Hezbollah after the terrorists launched missiles at northern Israel, clad in T-shirts bearing the legend, "We Are All Hezbollah." Now, only the most fanatically minded will hold to the conviction that Hezbollah is a legitimate "resistance" organization. Consequently, if the Europeans want to show that they are serious about taking on Hezbollah, they can go one step further than a terrorism designation. They can tell Hezbollah's leader, Hassan Nasrallah, that he, along with his key officers, will be held personally responsible for the abysmal crimes committed by their forces in Syria. Since Assad's atrocities have reached the unspeakable depths visited by other, similar conflicts in recent years – I think in particular of Bosnia, Congo and Rwanda – a war crimes tribunal is an absolute necessity. And the butchers of Hezbollah should be among the first in the dock.

Syria Debate Shows our Moral Decline

JNS/The Algemeiner, September 4, 2013

"Terraced thousands died, shaking scythes at cannon/The hillside blushed, soaked in our broken wave/They buried us without shroud or coffin/And in August the barley grew up out of our grave."

These lines are from the poem "Requiem for the Croppies," by the great Irish poet Seamus Heaney, who died last week. They were pointed out to me by a dear friend of mine, also an Irishman, who instructively observed how Heaney's verse – which commemorated the merciless British crushing of an Irish uprising in 1798 – eerily conjures up the terrible reality of Syria in our own time. Let's recall a few basic facts. Firstly, by the time the Western powers began to seriously consider intervention in Syria, more than 120,000 people had already been killed. Secondly, the use of chemical weapons by Bashar al-Assad's regime at the end of August was decidedly not the first time these had been deployed. Back in June, as I and others reported, the French government declared it had "no doubt" that "the regime and its accomplices" – which include the Islamist terrorist organization Hezbollah – had engaged in chemical attacks against civilian centers. Thirdly – and this is what I want to focus on here – when presented with devastating and credible evidence of chemical weapons use, the response of many Western politicians has been to equivocate and demand further evidence, as though obtaining such proof in Syria's killing fields is a mere walk in the park.

The insistence upon further evidence has been accompanied by other rationalizations for not getting involved, all of them constructed from myth rather than fact. To begin with, there's the view pushed by both left-wing and right-wing isolationists that Syria's warring groups are all as bad as each other, and that the end of the Assad regime will usher in an al-Qaeda one. That view was comprehensively debunked in recent days by the journalist Elizabeth O'Bagy, one of the few foreign correspondents to have spent lengthy periods of time in Syria, who provided an eyewitness account of politically moderate Syrian rebels defending Christian and Alawi villages from both the regime and from Islamist extremists. As little as a month ago, O'Bagy said, she saw "daily protests by thousands of citizens" against Islamists in the north of the country. Her conclusion? "Moderate opposition forces – a collection of groups known as the Free Syrian Army – continue to lead the fight against the Syrian regime." Then there's the slippery slope argument – the idea that we are going to get dragged into a ground war in Syria, just as we did in Afghanistan and Iraq. Given that the operation being discussed is an extremely limited one that will be prosecuted from the air – so limited in fact, that it may not have the desired effect of "degrading," as the Obama Administration puts it, Assad's military capacity – this objection is plainly misleading and a deliberate falsehood. Why are we so determined to remain indifferent in the face of men, women and children convulsing to death from Sarin gas? I have no satisfactory answer, but during this period of the High Holy Days, we are obliged, in my view, to confront this question as we reflect on our moral health. After all, we Jews have spent the last seven decades asking whether more could have been done to avert the Holocaust. Could we not have bombed the railway lines to the concentration camps? Could we not have smuggled more weapons to resistance fighters, both Jewish and non-Jewish? Well, yes, we could have done much more, but we also could have done a lot less. Imagine if the current crop of politicians currently dominating the Syrian debate, from U.S. Sen. Rand Paul (R-KY) to the leader of the British Labor Party, Ed Miliband, had been in office instead of Roosevelt and Churchill. (On second thought, don't.)

Next week, all eyes will be on the U.S. Congress as it considers the White House's request to strike at specific military targets controlled by the Syrian regime. Already, this is shaping up to be a depressing story of weak leadership and moral failure. President Barack Obama didn't have to refer the matter to Congress, just as British Prime Minister David Cameron wasn't obliged to take the matter to parliament, but both have been overwhelmed by the isolationist mood in their respective legislatures. Now, sadly, there are reasons to expect that the vote in Washington will falter along similar lines as the vote in London. As the Washington Post pointed out, both House Speaker John Boehner (R-OH) and Minority Leader Nancy Pelosi (D-CA) are portraying the vote as one based upon "conscience." And when it comes to Syria, there is precious little conscience around these days. I began this article by quoting an Irish writer, and I'd like to end by quoting a Jewish one.

In his searing poem "Shema," Primo Levi, the literary titan who survived Auschwitz, addressed "You who live secure/In your warm houses":

I commend these words to you.
Engrave them on your hearts
When you are in your house, when you walk on your way,
When you go to bed, when you rise.
Repeat them to your children.
Or may your house crumble,
Disease render you powerless,
Your offspring avert their faces from you.

Who Does Iraq's Jewish Archive Belong To?

JNS/The Algemeiner, September 17, 2013

A few years ago, in response to a Palestinian critic who made a disparaging remark about the fact that I don't speak Arabic, I felt compelled to write an article explaining why that is the case. I said that under different circumstances, I could have been born in an Arab country and grown up speaking Arabic. My father's family had been settled in Iraq for generations, but they fled to England in 1941 – the same year that Baghdad's Jews were convulsed by a June pogrom known as the *farhud* – presaging a much larger exodus of Iraqi Jews over the next decade.

Among my father and his relatives, there was little nostalgia for the old country, and therefore no reason, as they saw it, to ensure that their children born outside Iraq learned Arabic. It's not that they didn't appreciate the centrality of Iraq to Jewish history; this was the land where the *Talmud Bavli* (Babylonian Talmud) was completed, where scholarship flowed from the Jewish academies of Sura and Pumbedita (now the city of Fallujah, site of some of the most brutal fighting during the war in Iraq), and where, in modern times, Jewish merchants flourished alongside Jewish writers and musicians. Yet there were also more recent memories of Iraq, uglier and sharper. The *farhud* – a word which Edwin Black, the author of a fine book on the subject, translates as "violent dispossession" – cast a pall over relations between the Jews and their Muslim neighbors, and the mistrust deepened because of the support of many ordinary Arabs for Hitler's Nazi regime. During the 1950s, antisemitic legislation and property confiscation forced the departure of the majority of Iraq's Jews, but the small remnant who stayed were not immune from persecution. In 1969, the Ba'ath Party fascists ruling Iraq executed 11 Jews on trumped-up charges of spying, transporting Iraqis from all over the country to Baghdad to watch the gruesome spectacle of a public hanging. Since these images are seared into the minds of Iraqi Jews, it doesn't take a huge leap of the imagination to understand why the vast majority wouldn't consider returning there even if they could, and therefore why there are vibrant Iraqi Jewish communities in cities like Tel Aviv, New York, and London, but not Baghdad or Basra. Indeed, the break with the mother country is so irreparable that Iraqi Jews are of one mind when it comes to the current controversy over whether the United States should return an archive of Iraqi Jewish treasures to the Iraqi government: it absolutely should not do so.

The archive of books, photographs, scrolls, writings and communal documents, including one item that dates back to 1658, was discovered by American troops in Baghdad in 2003, as they combed through the flooded basement in the headquarters of Saddam Hussein's much-feared *mukhabarat*, or secret police. Lyn Julius, a London-based writer and advocate on behalf of Jewish communities from the Arab world, has noted that the archive was seized by Saddam's henchmen from the Bataween synagogue in Baghdad, in 1984. If the archive was stolen from its Jewish guardians at gunpoint, why on earth would the State Department, which has spent millions of dollars lovingly restoring its contents, return it to the Iraqi government? Simply because that government has suddenly decided that the archive constitutes, as one Iraqi representative put it, "part of our identity and history"? Or because the U.S. feels duty bound to respect an agreement it made at the time to return the archive? Julius and other advocates on behalf of Iraqi Jews make a strong case that returning the archive essentially involves restoring stolen property to those who stole it. Instead, they say, the archive should sit with its rightful owners themselves, the close-knit Iraqi Jewish communities spread around Israel and the countries of the West. On moral and legal grounds, I cannot counter this position. But here's a confession: I wish I could.

I wish I could envisage the sight of the archive on display in a Baghdad museum, much as it will be at the National Archives in Washington next month, with crowds of schoolchildren gathering to learn about the great community that lived among their great-grandparents. I wish I could organize a family trip to Iraq to see that hypothetical exhibition, safe in the knowledge that what is being shown belongs to our community, and that we are sharing it with the other ethnic and religious groups among whom we lived. I wish I could discover where my grandparents resided, in much the same way that American Jews of Polish or German extraction freely go on visits to these and other countries in Europe, walking the same streets trodden by their ancestors. I even wish that I were eligible to reclaim the Iraqi citizenship my grandparents lost, just like those descendants of Jews from Poland and Germany who can now obtain the passports of those countries not as a privilege, but as a right.

Most of all, I wish that after being displayed in Baghdad, the archive could go on a tour whose first stop would be the Israel Museum in Jerusalem, or Beit Hatfutsot in Tel Aviv. What better symbol of reconciliation could there be? All that, sadly, is a pipe dream. Iraq today is not Germany, a country that solemnly commemorates the barbarism of the Nazis and is home to a thriving Jewish community. As far as the Jews are concerned, Iraq now – with the important exception of the Kurdish region, whose people have a noble record of aiding Jews in plight – is the same Iraq of yesteryear, where populist antisemitism runs deep, hatred of Israel is a doctrine, and denial bordering on contempt overwhelms any discussion of the Iraqi Jewish exodus of the 20th century. So, yes, those Jews who say that Iraq has done nothing to deserve the return of stolen Jewish property are correct. Still, I can't help wishing that would not be the case.

Ben Cohen

Why Yair Lapid is Wrong on the Peace Process
and Israeli Recognition

JNS/The Algemeiner, October 17, 2013

I'll confess that when I first read about Israeli Finance Minister Yair Lapid's disagreement with Prime Minister Benjamin Netanyahu's insistence that the Palestinians recognize Israel as a Jewish state, I felt a degree of sympathy. Not for the substance of the argument, but for the manner in which Lapid expressed it.

"My father didn't come to Haifa from the Budapest ghetto in order to get recognition from Abu Mazen (Palestinian Authority President Mahmoud Abbas)," Lapid said Oct. 7 at New York's 92nd Street Y. "Darn right," I grunted at my Mac. The core ethos of Zionism, as Lapid himself explained, is that we Jews are no longer the passive objects of other nations' histories. We make our own history and we define ourselves, for we are, as the Israeli national anthem *Hatikvah* declares in its penultimate line, "a free people in our own land." But however much we might appreciate Lapid's healthy dismissal of the opinions of those who deny the legitimacy of Jewish national aspirations, it is precisely because of those same aspirations that his argument is dangerously flawed. When you study what others call the Israeli-Palestinian conflict, and what I prefer to call the Palestinian war against Israel's legitimacy, it should be painfully apparent that it is the intangible aspects of this long dispute that have confounded a final agreement, and not the tangible ones.

What I mean is this: if this dispute were solely about sharing a territory, equitable distribution of water rights, common security arrangements, and so forth, we might well have arrived at a resolution by now. When you look at other protracted conflicts that have largely been resolved – such as the one in Northern Ireland between mainly Catholic Irish nationalists and mainly Protestant Unionists and the British government – success has stemmed from the basic fact that each party recognizes the other's legitimacy. However revolting the terrorist actions of the Irish Republican Army, its leaders never sought the dissolution of the United Kingdom. Equally, the loyalist fanatics who terrorized innocent Catholics in Belfast and Derry did not seek to destroy the Republic of Ireland.

For that reason, the Northern Ireland peace process was able to focus on tangible goals, like the disarmament of terrorist groups and a formula for power sharing, rather than getting bogged down in a competition about historical rights. That's not to deny the obvious existence of historical wounds, merely to observe that they were overcome. By contrast, what nags in the context of the Israeli-Palestinian conflict is the rejection by the Palestinian side of the entire Zionist enterprise. Regardless of whether they are sitting at the table with Israeli negotiators, or gallivanting around the U.N. demanding unilateral recognition, the essential Palestinian message has, for more than a century, been that the Jews really have no right to be here in the first place. The Palestinian campaign for the so-called "right of return" is the clearest example of what I'm describing. Abbas and the PA, as Yair Lapid really should know, repudiate Israel's Jewish character because they refuse to give up on the idea that Israel's Jewish society will eventually be overwhelmed by the descendants of the Arab refugees of 1948 "returning" to a country that they have never set foot in.

As long as the Palestinians reject Israel's Jewish character, they will insist on the "right of return." That's why we don't have the luxury of saying, "damn what you think." Recognition of Israel as the historic homeland of the Jewish people should not be demoted to the status of an afterthought, something we'd like to achieve if we can, but won't worry about if we can't. It is, rather, the key reason why this conflict has persisted for so long. As the Oslo process of the 1990s demonstrated, you can only go so far by not tackling these fundamental ideological objections on the Palestinian side. Indeed, negotiating with Palestinian leaders as if these objections don't exist simply encourages Abbas and others to raise them at delicate moments. That way, they can portray the Israelis as intransigent occupiers, safe in the knowledge that the rest of the world regards the Palestinians as blameless victims. That is why Netanyahu's unwavering stance on the need for Palestinian recognition of Israel's Jewish character should be welcomed as a gesture of peace, not an excuse to perpetuate the status quo. Peace is only possible if the Palestinians revise the historical narrative that currently leads them to denigrate Israel as the "Zionist entity." "Ah," you say, "that'll never happen." And you may be right. But that's a subject for another time.

Saudi Arabia Woes Play Well for Israel

JNS/The Algemeiner, October 29, 2013

Ah, Saudi Arabia! The country that spawned 15 of the 19 terrorists that executed the atrocities of September 11, 2001. The country we in America are told is an ally, even though, when it comes to values, we have virtually nothing in common with the reactionary oil billionaires running the place. The country whose oil supplies us, for the moment, with about 13 per cent of our annual energy needs. The country with one of the most abysmal human rights records in the world, which bans any religion other than Islam, which imports slave labor from the Indian subcontinent, and which subjects women to what can only be described as gender apartheid. That's why it's hard to feel any sympathy with the Saudis when it comes to their current spat with the Obama Administration. Sadly, however, the continued threat posed by Iran and its Syrian and Hezbollah allies, and the absence of any coherent Middle East strategy on Washington's part, compels us to hold our noses and pay due attention to the Saudi complaints. Earlier this month, the Saudis refused to take up one of the ten seats on the U.N. Security Council reserved for non-permanent members. There was a rare agreement among regional analysts that this was an odd move to make, but most of the attention focused on the explanation the Saudis offered as to why.

Prince Bandar bin Sultan, the Saudi intelligence chief, said that frustration with the U.S., and not the U.N., was the reason for the Saudi decision. Two justifications were given: firstly, the tiresome ritual objection that the Palestinian question remains unresolved, something the Saudis feel duty-bound to cite in order to underline their Arab credentials. Secondly – and now we're getting somewhere – a profound frustration with Obama's Syria policy, which the Saudis correctly feel will simply empower the Iranians at a time when our Administration is being seduced by the overtures of the new President, Hassan Rouhani. Ultimately, there is nothing remotely attractive about either the Saudi or Iranian models of Islamic government. The Saudis impose the fanatical Islamist doctrines of Wahhabism, while the Shi'a Islamist revolution of the Iranians has been a recipe for domestic oppression and regional aggression, carried out by the Assad regime in Damascus and Hezbollah. Yet it is too easy to say, "a plague on both their houses."

In the icy moral universe of geostrategic considerations, there is a clear advantage for Israel built into these Saudi objections. Nearly all the Arab states live in perpetual fear of an Iranian nuclear bomb. Like the Israelis, they don't trust Rouhani or Supreme Leader Ayatollah Ali Khamenei. But if Arab governments are the ones nagging the U.S. about Iran's malicious intentions, it takes the spotlight off Israel and reminds the world that the Iranian threat is a real, ongoing concern for Iran's immediate neighbors. Additionally, the current situation rather forces the Arabs to acknowledge that they have common interests with Israel. That's always been the case – Israel's decision to strike Iraq's nuclear reactor in 1981 resulted in private praise and public condemnation in Arab capitals – but this point is driven home even more explicitly in the Iranian case. Israel's Prime Minister, Benjamin Netanyahu, has already hinted in the Knesset that secret talks have been taking place between the Israelis and the conservative Arab regimes, adding that there is renewed appreciation for Israel's role in maintaining regional security. What's telling is that the assumption that Israel and these Arab regimes would eventually realize their common purpose under American auspices has been exploded. Incredibly, it now looks as if Israel and its Arab neighbors could come together over Iran not just without the U.S., but in spite of it!

All the same, let's not count the Americans out just yet. Obama hasn't reached a deal with the Iranians, and chances are that the current round of making nice with Tehran will go the same way as his previous overtures in in 2010, because any agreement would likely collapse through Iranian reluctance to accept a strict monitoring arrangement of their nuclear facilities. The democratization of the Middle East, and the acceptance of Israel as part of the region, remains a long way off. Absent that outcome, hardheaded calculations based on immediate interests will rule the day. That's why it's helpful that a chorus of Arab voices, led by the Saudis, are telling Obama that Iran under its current regime was, is, and remains the greatest threat to this part of the world.

Chapter Three: BDS – anti-Zionism in action

The Ideological Foundations of the Boycott Campaign Against Israel

Recent discussion regarding the ideological basis for a boycott of Israel, whether in academia or in response to the campaign for the Boycott, Divestment, and Sanctions (BDS) forcefully promoted by a network of Palestinian and international NGOs, has concentrated upon two interrelated issues: first, the thematic overlap between anti-Zionism and antisemitism; and secondly, the emergence of the left as the principal driver of anti-Zionist discourse in Western democracies. This focus should not convey the impression that contemporary antisemitism is reducible only to anti-Zionism, nor that malign notions about the Jewish people are the sole preserve of the left. Antisemitism in its classic form – that is, hatred of Jews largely unrelated to the existence or actions of the Jewish state and rooted in national-religious prejudice – persists in many countries, particularly in Eastern Europe and the republics of the former Soviet Union. Political currents outside the left, most obviously on the extreme right, as well as among the various strains of Islamism, remain ideologically wedded to classic antisemitism and incorporate anti-Zionism on that basis. It is equally true that the extremes of left and right identify increasingly with the portrait of Jewish power as global, transcendental, and unaccountable; that they use the terms "Jew" and "Zionist" interchangeably; and that they admiringly regard Islamism as the primary source of opposition to American and "Zionist" ambitions in the Middle East and, by extension, the world.

However, such mirroring cannot explain and should not obscure the distinctive character of much of the current left discourse on Israel. Indeed, to classify this discourse as simply an instance of extremism is to ignore that its most disturbing aspect – the insistence that Jewish state be quarantined as a necessary step toward its eventual elimination – has penetrated the mainstream of political debate and exchange. What needs to be interrogated, therefore, is the set of ideas that underlie the boycott movement as well as their appeal, both actual and potential. What unifies these ideas is a grand strategy of delegitimization that highlights elements of theory and ideology, history and comparative politics. In opposing the existence of a Jewish state, the boycott movement remains faithful to the long-held opposition of many left-wing ideologues toward Jews asserting themselves as an identifiable, autonomous collective. In advocating the economic, cultural, and political isolation of Israel, the boycott movement borrows from multiple historical legacies, notably the state policy of antisemitism, formally presented as anti-Zionism, practiced in the Soviet Union, as well as the Arab League's three-tier economic boycott of Israel (namely, the boycott of Israeli companies, of companies that engage in business with Israel, and of companies that engage in business with companies engaged in business with Israel). Finally, in demonizing Israel by comparing it with the former apartheid regime in South Africa – a grave deceit that is a core concern of this paper – the boycott movement seeks to force Israel to abandon, internally, its Jewish character and, externally, its sovereignty. The Left's Opposition to Jewish Self-Determination It is this entrenched opposition to Jewish self-determination – in an age, no less, when progressives celebrate the identity politics of marginal, disempowered groups – that has led to the charge of antisemitism being leveled at much of the left. This is commonly and angrily refuted with the counterclaim that opposition to a state is radically different from hatred of an entire people.

But what such a response ignores is the moral flimsiness of a position in which only Israel, out of nearly two hundred states in the international system, is selected for dissolution, and the disregard for the impact such a catastrophe would have upon Jews both inside and outside the Jewish state. As I have argued elsewhere,[1] this position mirrors the disdain with which Jewish concerns have historically been regarded by a large section of the left. This was as true of the period before the emergence of political Zionism as it was after. In its pre-Zionist phase, left-wing antisemitism had a decidedly economic thrust.

For example, Karl Marx's best-known comments about Jews and Judaism were spiced with crude antisemitic language about "huckstering" and "haggling." This characterization of Judaism as a metaphor for capitalism can be found in his 1843 response to Bruno Bauer, "On the Jewish Question." Although Marx actually challenges Bauer's opposition to Jewish emancipation, the overriding thrust of his thesis is that Judaism is identified with an economy based upon monetary exchange and private property. Outside of these parameters, Marx cannot conceive of a space for Jewish existence. Hence his conclusion, "The social emancipation of the Jew is the emancipation of society from Judaism."[2] To the extent that all group identities are constructed around narratives of history or religion or culture, they can be characterized as synthetic or even artificial. Yet for much of the left in the late nineteenth and early twentieth centuries, the objectionable nature of

Jewish identity, in contrast to the identities of other groups, stemmed from its artificiality, which was understood as being economic in origin. Agents of a monetary economy could not constitute a community, much less a nationality: hence the equation of Jewish emancipation with Jewish disappearance, as intimated by Marx. These views partly explain the contempt that marked the exchanges of so many revolutionaries on the perennial "Jewish question." Rosa Luxemburg, herself a Jew, put it baldly in one of her private letters: "Why do you come to me with your special Jewish sorrows? I feel just as sorry for the wretched Indian victims in Putumayo, the Negroes in Africa.... I cannot find a special corner in my heart for the ghetto."[3]

What is supremely ironic is that the contemporary revivers of this negationist approach – those who insist that Zionism represents a surrender to antisemitism, who go on to claim that antisemitism is simply a rhetorical trick to muzzle criticism of the State of Israel, who grudgingly concede that Jewish identity may have, after all, a valid religious component, but stringently reject anything beyond that – present their approach as the key to making Jewish communities secure. From a Jewish perspective, such a position is transparently dishonest. Isaac Deutscher, the Jewish Marxist historian, cogently summarized why in a 1954 interview in which he explained that his original opposition to Zionism "was based on a confidence in the European labor movement, or, more broadly, in European society and civilization, which that society and civilization have not justified."[4] Would such confidence be justified now? It is true that Jews living in postwar Europe have known an unprecedented degree of security, underpinned by a range of tangible factors, from robust laws combating antisemitism to educational programs promoting tolerance and awareness of Jewish history. However, security is not guaranteed by structural measures alone. Since the eruption of the second Palestinian intifada in September 2000, European Jews have undergone a security crisis without parallel in the post-1945 period. In part, this is because of a dramatic increase in anti-Jewish incidents recorded in nearly every European state, intimately related to the troughs and peaks of conflict in the Middle East. But it is also the product of an discursive environment of discourse in which Israel is often portrayed, in general terms, as a rogue state and, in specific terms, as a reincarnation of the one state to have most outraged the liberal conscience in recent memory – apartheid South Africa. Herein lies the paradox. The existence of the State of Israel has been a critical pillar supporting the greater sense of security and confidence that Jews in Europe and elsewhere have enjoyed in the years following the Holocaust.

Despite that, they are told by anti-Zionists that the State of Israel is a critical source of insecurity, for themselves and for the world. In other words, they are told that the principal source of contemporary Jewish misfortune, as well as a primary cause of injustice and disorder in international society, is the Jewish state. In his seminal essay, *Anti-Semite and Jew*,[5] Jean-Paul Sartre provided a description of an abstracted, idealized type closely associated with this convoluted reasoning. Rather provocatively, he named this type the "democrat." In framing the problem, Sartre observed: "The anti-Semite reproaches the Jew with being Jewish; the democrat reproaches him with willfully considering himself a Jew." The "democrat" is a "feeble" protector of Jews, argued Sartre, because while those Jews who discard their Jewish identity acquire a nobility in the eyes of the democrat, those who embrace their identity are by definition a danger, to themselves and to others. The "democrat" in Sartre's essay warns us: "The Jews will come back from exile with such insolence and hunger for vengeance that I am afraid of a new outburst of antisemitism." Such "insolence" may be said to have taken the form of the State of Israel and is what lies behind the ire of today's "democrats." For them, Israel exemplifies the refusal of most Jews to respond to their newly-permissive environments by disappearing, as well as their apparent stubbornness in clinging to the anachronism of the nation-state (especially when their dubious claim to nationality has been indulged at the expense of a genuine nation that has been both colonized and dispossessed). Thus are the historical consistencies of left-wing antisemitism demonstrated; so, too, is the ostensibly precise boundary between anti-Zionism and antisemitism torn down.

Two Stages in the Evolution of Left-Wing Antisemitism

In broad terms, then, one can distinguish two stages in the evolution of left-wing antisemitism. The first predates Zionism, is rooted in the critique of capitalism, and is typified by Marx. The second coincides with the emergence of Zionism and the opposition to Zionism, is rooted in an anti-imperialist paradigm, and is typified by Sartre's "democrat." It is in this second stage, in which Zionism as a movement is regarded as a harmful force on a global scale and the State of Israel is portrayed as a foreign body inserted into the heart of the Arab homeland, that the origins of the apartheid analogy can be discerned. The notion of Zionism as a global threat to colonized nations and as a strategic tool of empire was enthusiastically embraced by the New Left in the 1960s. Given the anti-Stalinist orientation of much of the New Left, it is striking that the representation of Zionism which was so readily adopted was, in fact, a Soviet creation – one, moreover, that was entirely predictable, given the active promotion of antisemitism in the USSR in the wake of the Doctors' Plot of 1948 and the associated campaign against "rootless cosmopolitans." What the Soviet pamphlets demonized as "international Zionism" was a fusion of czarist-era antisemitism with the anti-imperialist bluster of the Soviet regime. In that regard, two distinctly Soviet libels stand out, both of which still claim adherents on the contemporary left. The first concerns the Holocaust. Soviet revisionists engaged, not in the denial of the extermination itself, but in the transfer of responsibility for the extermination. The Zionist movement was accused of collaborating with the Nazis in the implementation of the Final Solution to such a degree that the Holocaust became "the autogenocide of the Twentieth Century."[6] This ugly distortion was echoed in parts of the Western left, most famously in the form of a play entitled Perdition, which almost came to the London stage in the 1980s and remains in active circulation among anti-Zionists today. Based on the 1954 libel trial in Israel involving Rudolf Kastner, who had been accused of collaborating with the Nazis in order to rescue Jews in occupied Hungary, Perdition was, in the words of its late author, Jim Allen, a tale of "privileged Jewish leaders" collaborating "in the extermination of their own kind in order to help bring about a Zionist state, Israel, a state which itself is racist."

The second libel concerns the insidious essence of Judaism and, flowing from that, the global reach of Jewish and Zionist influence. The writings on Zionism churned out by the Soviet state apparatus, camouflaged as social science, portrayed the movement as an organic outgrowth of Judaism's racist doctrines, notably the concept of the "Chosen People." Although the Soviets developed and popularized this inversion of Jewish theology, one does not have to delve into Soviet archives to find examples of it. During the conflict between Israel and Hezbollah in July 2006, the Norwegian newspaper Aftenposten published an article by Jostein Gaarder,[7] a popular Norwegian author, alleging that Israel's military actions in Lebanon were a demonstration of the conceit and hubris that comes with the status of "Chosen People." From the Soviet Union's standpoint, this notion of chosenness elevated Zionism into a transnational foe, along with "racism," "imperialism," and "militarism." Standing in its way, however, were the peoples of Africa, the Arab states, Asia, and Latin America.

The Apartheid Analogy

The delegitimization strategy waged against Israel today, and particularly its apartheid component, owes much to the Soviet Union. As the international campaign against Israel waged by states aligned with the Soviet Union, as well as among the Non-Aligned Movement, escalated during the 1970s, the apartheid analogy came into play. The clearest example of this was Resolution 3379, passed by the UN General Assembly in 1975 with active Soviet encouragement, which categorized Zionism as a form of racism. The resolution also assisted in the creation of a dedicated Palestine bureaucracy within the UN secretariat. Resolution 3379 was significant in that it punctured the Westphalian norms underlying the UN Charter, particularly regarding the sovereign equality of states, through its incorporation of the key tropes of Soviet anti-Zionism. By bracketing Zionism with apartheid and racism, the resolution effectively said that Israel was less of a state and more of a toxic growth within the international system. In its preamble, the resolution approvingly noted "...resolution 77 (XII) adopted by the Assembly of Heads of State and Government of the Organization of African Unity at its twelfth ordinary session, held at Kampala from 28 July to 1 August 1975, which considered 'that the racist regime in occupied Palestine and the racist regime in Zimbabwe and South Africa have a common imperialist origin, forming a whole and having the same racist structure and being organically linked in their policy aimed at repression of the dignity and integrity of the human being.'" The Kampala formulation strongly reflected both the imperatives of Soviet policy (its domestic antisemitism and its embrace of the Arab cause abroad) and the anti-colonialist idiom used to express that policy.

Indeed, 1975 also saw the publication of Valery Skurlatov's notorious tome Zionism and Apartheid, by the state-run Politizadat publishers in Ukraine.[8] Transparently antisemitic in substance and tone, Skurlatov's work expounded on the "organic link" referred to in the Kampala formulation: "Racial biological doctrines, according to which people are divided into 'chosen people' and goyim, have been turned into official ideology and state policy in Israel and South Africa, where the 'inferior' are forcibly separated from the 'superior.' That is what apartheid is." In a shrill conclusion, Skurlatov claimed that in their "death agony," both Zionism and apartheid had adopted Nazi Germany's propensity for "adventurism": "This is why the world's attention now focuses on apartheid and Zionism; their secrets have become known, and the nations have discovered the abominable essence of the 'God-chosen.'" Given that the apartheid analogy was a favorite theme of Soviet incitement against Jews, its persistence in the post-Soviet era is alarming, as is the apparent indifference shown by its current advocates to its totalitarian provenance. What the current advocates have in common with their Soviet precursors is their invocation of the word "apartheid" as part of a strategy to secure Israel's isolation and reverse its international legitimacy; at the same time, their version strives for greater respectability, insofar as it has largely been purged of the nakedly antisemitic foundations upon which the Soviet anti-Zionists based themselves. Instead, the concentration is on the supposed similarities between apartheid and Zionism in terms of state structure and government policy. This shift is one reason why the apartheid analogy has been able to slip from the margins into mainstream discourse in the West. This does not make the analogy any more acceptable. In essence, the apartheid analogy remains a slander, one found all over: in the Iranian press; on Arab satellite television channels; in the academic boycott motions submitted to British academic unions in 2005, 2006, and 2007; in the boycott resolution passed by the representatives of the Sor Trondelag regional parliament in Norway in 2005 (and revoked in 2006); and, most importantly, in the corridors of the United Nations, where many officials still behave as though Resolution 3379, revoked in a curt single-line resolution in 1991, is still on the books. The UN continues to sponsor conferences and meetings, such as the World Conference Against Racism in Durban in 2001, that are little more than excuses to pile opprobrium upon Israel.[9] For many, the definition dictates the solution: Pregnant within the accusation that the State of Israel practices apartheid is the recommendation for Israel's termination.

Distorting the Meaning of Apartheid

One lamentable feature of the present debate is that precious little effort is expended on recalling what apartheid in South Africa actually constituted. Therefore, when applied to Israel, the analogy is, at best, a careless and hasty attempt to graft the structure of one state onto another, simply because tensions and divisions over citizenship, land use, and access to services are a fact of life in Israel (as they are in other multiethnic societies). At worst, it represents the transformation of the word "apartheid" into a sheer pejorative term, removed from its southern African context and stripped of its close historical linkage with Afrikaner nationalism. What, then, did apartheid involve? In the first instance, apartheid involved the enforced domination of the ruling minority belonging to one group over the oppressed majority belonging to another group. In South Africa, 90 percent of the population was composed of nonwhites disenfranchised and deprived of fundamental rights. Such a system of governance has its parallels in the Middle East, but they are not to be found in Israel. The spectacle of minorities ruling over majorities is a common one in the Arab world: in Ba'athist Syria, where the Alawis have long been dominant despite a Sunni majority; in Bahrain, where the Shi'a majority is ruled by a Sunni minority; or, until recently, in Ba'athist Iraq, where Saddam Hussein's dictatorship concentrated Sunni Arabs from the Tikrit region in positions of power. Yet even in these cases, where repressive and authoritarian states have been appropriated by minorities, the analogy with apartheid is inept – unless, of course, the purpose is merely to employ the word "apartheid" as a term of abuse. What made the apartheid system in South Africa peculiar was the manner in which racism was enshrined in law. The only credible parallel would be Nazi Germany following the promulgation of the Nuremburg Laws. Just as the Nazis legally degraded Germany's Jewish citizens, the legislators of apartheid South Africa passed a matrix of laws and regulations that imposed a hellish form of discrimination on the nonwhite majority. Through such measures as the Group Areas Act (1950), the Bantu Education Act (1953), the Reservation of Separate Amenities Act (1953), the Suppression of Communism Act (1950), and the Prohibition of Mixed Marriages Act (1949), the apartheid regime micromanaged the lives of its subjects on the basis of their skin color. Under apartheid, it was the law that determined where blacks could live, what they could (or more precisely, could not) study, which seats they could occupy on public transport, what they could (or could not) speak and write, with whom they could (or could not) share a bed or marry. Therefore, it follows that if apartheid is understood as the rule of racist law, any comparison with Israel – or any other country – needs to begin at the point of the law.

Even a cursory examination of Israeli law reveals an explicit commitment to the principle of the equality of all citizens, regardless of background. On that basis alone, there is no rational foundation for the apartheid analogy. At the same time, the apartheid analogy has evolved in terms of focus and substance. Perhaps mindful that the comparison with the legal culture and practices of the State of Israel undermines rather than supports their case, some advocates of the apartheid analogy – most notably the former U.S. president, Jimmy Carter[10] – base their approach on an analysis of Israel's land policies in the Palestinian territories. From this standpoint, apartheid is interpreted as the state managing land conflicts between competing groups in an inequitable fashion, with resulting human rights violations, as opposed to a discriminatory legal framework regulating citizenship and human rights. This shift in emphasis begs an obvious question that leads, in turn, to other questions. If the fundamental features of South African apartheid are absent, then why use the term? Is the implication that land policies are the crux of the matter, rather than, say, the denial of voting rights to a vast swathe of the population? And if that were the case, why was the key demand of the anti-apartheid movement in South Africa expressed as "one person, one vote"? We will return to these issues shortly, by way of the delegitimization strategy, but first let's examine this revised apartheid analogy on its own terms. In essence, Israel stands accused of reviving the bantustan policy of the apartheid regime in the Palestinian territories. In fact, some detractors, such as UN official John Dugard,[11] assert that Israel's offenses "surpass those" of South Africa, but these claims do not hold up under scrutiny. Devised in the 1940s, the concept of the bantustans, separate "homelands" for blacks, was intrinsic to the racist culture of the apartheid regime and its prescription of separate (and unequal) development for different racial groups. By the 1970s the poverty-stricken bantustans were home to nearly four million blacks, many of whom were forcibly deported and deprived of their South African citizenship. Starved of resources and entirely dependent on the apartheid regime (since the absence of international recognition meant that international aid was not available), the bantustans were nonetheless touted as a permanent solution for South Africa's black population. By transferring the black population in its entirety to the bantustans, the architects of apartheid intended to make sure that pressure for majority rule never reached critical mass.

Applying the charge of "bantustanization" to Israel assumes that Israel's presence in the Palestinian territories is permanent and that it is therefore parceling up the land accordingly – hence the portrayal of the Jewish settler movement as an arm of the state. However, the policies of successive Israeli governments over the last decade have, if anything, indicated the temporary nature of Israel's control over the Palestinian areas. Israel has disengaged fully from Gaza and from outlying regions of the West Bank and has made clear its willingness to consider land swaps in any final status negotiations. On this critical point, the bantustan comparison is found wanting, much as it is in other significant areas. There is, for example, no government policy to forcibly deport Arab citizens of Israel to the Palestinian territories. Nor has the Palestinian Authority been hampered by a lack of international legal personality, as was the case with the bantustans. To the contrary, the PA is near universally regarded, including by Israel, as a state-in-the-making; as a result, it has received billions of dollars in international aid and assistance since its creation. Were the PA really a bantustan, international policy would be to undermine it, so as not to compromise with a creature of apartheid. Instead, policy has oriented toward strengthening and stabilizing the PA.

In sum, the apartheid regime and its bantustans were the product of the application of racist doctrines in law. By any reasonable assessment, neither these doctrines nor such laws can be discerned in the Israeli context. What can be discerned is precisely that which makes Israel unremarkable among multiethnic nations: the fact that complaints of discrimination frequently emerge from the Arab minority, as well as from segments of its Jewish populace. This is not to make light of discrimination nor to claim that Israel's state institutions have always responded to these legitimate concerns with the necessary sensitivity. The overriding point here is that discrimination, however disturbing, is manifestly not the same as apartheid.

The Agenda of Delegitimization

In the same way that the boycott movement frequently abuses the history and meaning of the word "Holocaust," so does it distort the word "apartheid." This comparison is not the result of any rigorous analysis. It is about twisting historically-specific meanings to serve the agenda of delegitimization. This requires that the word "apartheid" be deliberately reserved for Israel, to underline its illegitimacy. There are plenty of other democracies where discrimination is a fact of life; look, for example, at the treatment of the Roma and Sinti ('Gypsy') peoples in the new democracies of Eastern Europe. Yet the Czech Republic is not described as an apartheid state. Hungary is not the target of a boycott. The thesis that Israel resembles apartheid South Africa is a fiction. Moreover, it is a fiction that is politically necessary to preserve the fundamental aim of the boycott movement: not the withdrawal of Israel to the 1967 lines, but its dissolution as a sovereign state. Of course, this is not to suggest that every person who advocates a boycott of Israel necessarily supports this goal, but it is the goal of those who have created the boycott movement and who set its agenda and priorities. It is a goal that is consistent with the broad trajectory described here, which sees in the persistence of Jews and Jewish identity an abnormality and which seeks to eradicate the foundations – territorial, cultural, political – for a conscious, self-defining Jewish existence in Israel and the Diaspora.

Footnotes

1. Ben Cohen, "The Persistence of Antisemitism on the British Left," Jewish Political Studies Review 16:3–4 (Fall 2004).
2. Karl Marx, "On the Jewish Question," in Selected Essays (New York: International Publishers, 1926), p. 97.

3. Quoted in Walter Laqueur, A History of Zionism (New York: Holt, Rinehart and Winston, 1992), p. 435.

4. Isaac Deutscher, "Israel's Spiritual Climate," in The Non-Jewish Jew (London: Merlin Press, 1981), pp. 126–52.

5. Jean-Paul Sartre, Anti-Semite and Jew (New York: Schocken Books, 1948), p. 58.

6. W. D. Rubinstein, The Left, The Right and the Jews (London: Croom Helm, 1982), p. 115.

7. Jostein Gaarder, "God's Chosen People," Aftenposten, 5 August 2006.

8. Theodore Freedman (ed.), Antisemitism in the Soviet Union: Its Roots and Consequences (New York: Anti-Defamation League, 1984), pp. 583–87.

9. For further discussion, see Ben Cohen, "The Right To Exist: Anti-Zionism at the United Nations," Engage Journal, January 2006, available at http://www.engageonline.org.uk/journal/index.php?journal_id=5&article_id=16.

10. Jimmy Carter, Palestine: Peace Not Apartheid (New York: Simon and Schuster, 2006).

11. John Dugard, "Israelis Adopt What South Africa Dropped," Atlanta Journal-Constitution, 29 November 2006.

Progressive? Then Don't Boycott Israel

The Huffington Post, June 25, 2010

It was an expose in the best traditions of investigative journalism: Commerce Department documents obtained under the Freedom of Information Act that detailed how, between 1965 and 1977, more than one thousand American corporations colluded in the economic boycott of a small, embattled country, in a bid to please a group of powerful, oil-producing states. Though the boycott was prohibited under U.S. law, the government consciously looked the other way as these corporations went the extra mile in complying with the boycott. Like when they discriminated against employees deemed to have compromising ethnic ties to the targeted country.

The article in question appeared in 1981. The object of the boycott, organized by the League of Arab States, was Israel. And the magazine that published these revelations was *The Nation*.

How times have changed. Three decades after it named and shamed those American corporations who cozied up to some of the most repressive and reactionary countries on earth, *The Nation* has become the house journal of the American branch of the movement to subject Israel – and only Israel – to a campaign of Boycott, Divestment and Sanctions (BDS for short.) A recent issue of the magazine included a piece by Adam Horowitz and Philip Weiss endorsing BDS with zealot-like enthusiasm. Rich in distortions and half-truths, the article was at its most preposterous in depicting BDS as a grassroots movement assembling Palestinians, anti-Zionist Jews, human rights advocates and labor unionists in a moral crusade against Zionism. Scratch beneath this complacent self-image and you quickly understand that the origins of the BDS movement have more in common with a black shirt than a rainbow flag. Horowitz and Weiss point out that there is an established boycott tradition among the Palestinians, citing their embargo against the Jewish community in Palestine during the upheavals of 1936. What they don't mention is that the 1936 boycott was accompanied by a paroxysm of violence against Jews and their property. Nor do they mention that the Palestinian leadership, under Haj Amin al Husseini, the Mufti of Jerusalem, was unashamedly pro-Nazi. Indeed, the policy of simultaneously boycotting and beating the Jews had been introduced by Hitler when he assumed power three years earlier.

In 1945, al Husseini's Nazi-derived policy was formalized by the Arab League Council, which declared a boycott of "Jewish" and "Zionist" goods. In

1948, the Arab League launched a separate office to enforce an economic boycott of the State of Israel that functioned upon three levels, by targeting Israeli companies, foreign companies working in Israel, and foreign companies conducting business with other companies with an operational base in Israel. Given these parameters, it was inevitable that the application of the boycott would blur the line between Israel as a state and Jews as a people. That point was cogently grasped by Mark Green and Steven Solow, the authors of the 1981 *Nation* piece. "There is nothing necessarily objectionable in economic boycotts of one country or community by another," they wrote. Yet, they added, "the Arab embargo of Israel can be distinguished from other boycotts by the way it discriminated not only against a country but against an entire religious group. Thus American Jews were sometimes penalized by their employers simply because they were Jews."

However much BDS advocates insist otherwise, that observation remains true today. Unlike, say, the African-American boycott of segregated buses, which aimed to change a racist policy and did not apply to whites in general, the boycott of Israel reaches much wider. Any Israeli who does not explicitly disavow his or her country is fair game – and those who declare their solidarity with Israelis are, as a consequence, equally suspect. Crucially, the "United Call for BDS," which Horowitz and Weiss approvingly link to, dates the Israeli occupation as beginning not in 1967, following the Six Day War, but in 1948, when Israel was created. This is no accident, for the aim of the BDS movement is not to effect a change in Israeli policy, but to dismantle the state which makes those policies. Diehard anti-Zionists won't be bothered by that, of course. Still, there is a much larger group of people within the orbit of the BDS movement – like the U.S. Presbyterian Church, which gathers in a few days time to discuss a report which includes a comparison of Israel with Nazi Germany – who may wish to consider where the demonizing rhetoric and toxic origins of the boycott campaign might lead them.

In addition, as the Presbyterians deliberate on a resolution to divest from Caterpillar Inc., the bete noire of BDS advocates, they might ponder the following. In their *Nation* article from 1981, Caterpillar was named by Green and Solow as one of those corporations complying with the Arab boycott. They quoted a Caterpillar spokesman confirming that the company would cooperate with Arab requests for information about such vital operational matters as whether there were any Jews on the payroll ("If somebody wanted to do business with us and wanted to confirm a fact, we did it," the spokesman said). Isn't it ironic? Caterpillar abandoned those racist practices. Now, the BDS movement wants Caterpillar to readopt them – and is telling the public to scorn the company until it does so. No doubt, the Mufti of Jerusalem would approve.

Another Israel Divestment Hoax

The Huffington Post, November 19, 2010

When I read this report on the *Electronic Intifada* website claiming that the largest pension fund in The Netherlands had divested from the Israeli companies in its portfolio, it struck me that the campaign to subject Israel to a regime of Boycotts, Divestment and Sanctions – BDS for short – had hit a milestone. No longer, I said to myself, is this a matter of campus gesture politics. The long-awaited South Africa effect is finally manifesting. Then it occurred to me that the story might not be true. I contacted the fund's managers, the Dutch company PGGM, and they confirmed my suspicions.

Back in May, Israel's economic vibrancy secured its admission into the Organization for Economic Cooperation and Development (OECD), which gathers together the world's developed countries. As a result, funds focused upon emerging markets were obliged to withdraw their investments from Israeli companies, who'd moved to the different benchmark for developed markets. Bottom line: this had absolutely nothing to do with politically-motivated divestment. If you read the *Electronic Intifada* piece closely, you'll notice the giveaway line "...divested from *almost all* the Israeli companies in its portfolio," begging the question of why, if you've embraced the BDS gospel, would you not divest from every single one? Again, the answer is that the Dutch fund didn't divest in the first place. That is why, in its portfolios that deal with developed markets, you will find two Israeli companies – the software developer *Checkpoint* (now there's a line for all you budding comedians) and the supermarket chain *SuperSol*. This isn't the first time that BDS advocates have clumsily spun purely financial decisions as divestment. As Jon Haber, a particularly tenacious critic of the BDS movement, has observed, a pattern of hoaxes is clearly visible. In February 2009, Hampshire College officially denied the claim of a pro-Palestinian student group that it had divested from Israel. Up next was investment giant Blackrock, whose Vice President informed pro-BDS activists that its decisions regarding investments in Israel had nothing to do with political considerations. Then it was the turn of academic retirement fund TIAA-CREF to depress the mood at the BDS party by denying that it, too, had divested. We're not done yet. There was the Motorola hoax. And perhaps most famously, Harvard University, which found itself thrust into the public eye as the latest champion of BDS this past summer. "The University has not divested from Israel," a spokesman calmly explained. "Israel was moved from the MSCI, our benchmark in emerging markets, to the EAFE index in May due to its successful growth. Our emerging markets holdings were rebalanced accordingly."

Harvard worked with the same set of considerations which informed the Dutch pension fund's decision – maybe, when the BDS campaigners failed to co-opt the jewel in the Ivy League's crown, they resolved to try their luck in Holland. To anyone encountering the BDS issue for the first time, it must seem odd that a campaign that touts its moral integrity resorts to wilful dishonesty as a strategy. If anything, the BDS movement's reliance on lying is a reflection of its manifest failure. Over a year ago, Jon Haber reached a conclusion which is just as insightful now:

Having failed to get a single college or university to divest in the Jewish state, having lost their few attempts to win a divestment victory with municipalities and unions, and now having lost the support of the Mainline Protestant community (once the flagship for the BDS enterprise), "Team Divestment" has been reduced to manufacturing pretend victories where none exist. The strategy seems to be to anticipate likely financial decisions (such as companies trying to get rid of their Israel-Africa shares as fast as possible, given the company's huge losses and exposure in the real estate markets,) send out press releases claiming that these normal business transactions actually represent political choices on the part of large institutions, and hope someone in the media takes the bait. But none is taking the bait. In part, that's because the lies are so downright amateurish. Yet a no less important factor is the widespread understanding that BDS is not merely a tactical choice, but a tangible expression of an ideology which holds that Israel must be quarantined until it ceases to exist. And as anyone with the slightest shred of moral intelligence understands, such a ghastly outcome will be arrived at not through a peace process, but through a genocidal war. Expect, therefore, more spectacular BDS failures in the coming months.

Burns Night for Israel: Scotland's Literary Shame

Pajamas Media, May 26, 2011

Heinrich Heine's maxim about people being burned where books are also burned conjures up some of the most hellish images of Nazi rule. Raging bonfires devouring page after page of literature deemed toxic, their flames growing higher with each volume thrown onto the pile. There goes Freud, now it's Hemingway, next up is Proust, until finally you reach the gates of Auschwitz.

By contrast, a book boycott seems a rather dour affair. Brownshirted thugs burning armfuls of books while surrounded by screaming onlookers is one thing. A bespectacled librarian removing books from the shelves to the warehouse is something else. No? Actually, no. In the case that I have in mind, concerning a provincial Scottish council's decision to deprive its library users of books by Israeli authors, the underlying impulse is pretty much the same. And I'm not the only person to say so. Israel's ambassador to the United Kingdom, Ron Prosor, a man not normally given to bombast, declared: "A place that boycotts books is not far from a place that burns them." No doubt, those council bureaucrats implementing the boycott will be incensed by his statement. After all, while every Nazi supports a boycott of Israel, not every supporter of a boycott of Israel is a Nazi. Most boycott advocates, sensitive souls that they are, would be sorely wounded by such a suggestion. Ergo, all the mealy-mouthed qualifications that follow. This is about solidarity with the Palestinians, not hatred of the Jews and their works; it's *progressive*, y'see. It's not a blanket ban, but something that will be decided on a book-by-book basis. And oh yes, according to West Dunbartonshire Regional Council Spokesperson Malcolm Bennie, the boycott doesn't apply to Israeli books printed *outside* Israel, just those printed in Israel. In other words, the Harcourt edition I have of Amos Oz's *A Tale of Love and Darkness* is OK. My prized English edition of Ahad Ha'am's *Selected Essays*, published by *Sefer ve Sefel* of Jerusalem, is not OK.

The Scots have, ironically, a rather Yiddish-sounding verb for this kind of thing: to "haiver," roughly translated as talking nonsense, or "bollocks," as it's more commonly known throughout the British Isles. It is "haivering" because all the excuses and rationalizations cannot camouflage one basic truth. Just as the German book-burnings aimed at obliterating ideas deemed repellent to Nazi ideology, so its sanitized adaptation, in the form of a book boycott, seeks to quarantine those ideas on the wrong side of anti-Zionist ideology. West Dunbartonshire's decision to boycott Israeli books stems from a 2009 resolution, in the wake of Israel's defensive "Cast Lead" operation in Gaza, to prohibit the council from purchasing and selling goods produced in Israel. In that sense, the council is merely part of a growing pattern of labor unions, academic institutions, and regional authorities signing up to the international campaign to subject Israel to Boycotts, Divestment, and Sanctions (BDS). While such efforts have been rather flaccid here in America – so much so that some U.S. boycott activists feel they have to lie about their alleged successes – in Europe, South Africa, and Australia, gaining traction has been far easier. The long-established ideological obsessions about Jews underlying these activities puncture the misconception that a boycott of Israel, whether generalized or targeted, is simply a tactic to change Israeli policy.

Boycotting is the tangible expression of a visceral opposition to Jewish empowerment that, as the antisemitism scholar Robert Wistrich observed back in 1990, observes in Zionism a "code word for the forces of reaction in general." West Dunbartonshire, in fact, was an early adopter of this outlook. The area is home to the city of Dundee which, back in 1980, flew a Palestinian flag from the parapet of its town hall after being twinned with the West Bank town of Nablus. The prime mover behind that particular gesture was a local Labor Party organizer named George Galloway, later to become a member of the British parliament, an ally and confidante of British Islamists, a drooler in the presence of Saddam Hussein, and, most recently, a craven apologist for the Ba'athist regime of Bashar al Assad in Syria.

Anti-Zionism belongs to the Galloways of this world, those for whom the original sin of Israel's creation is the basic condition for understanding and responding to the push and pull of global events. Charles Maurras, a nineteenth century French rabble-rouser, rejoiced in antisemitism's ability to "enable everything to be arranged, smoothed over and simplified." Anti-Zionism functions in much the same way. As I've discovered over the years, there is little point in debating with people who regard the world in this manner. I've discovered, too, that they thrive when their ideas gain mainstream acceptance, and they shrink when these same ideas are marginalized. A shove to the margins is what will happen if Britain's literary class, painfully silent thus far, elects to confront the rot in West Dunbartonshire's libraries. Sure, some of its leading lights do regard Israel, in the words of a former French ambassador to London, as a "shitty little country" that invites harsh treatment, even if they'd concede that a literary boycott is a tad on the crude side. Yet this is not a uniform view.

The novelist Ian McEwan, for example, was recently awarded the Jerusalem Prize, inadvertantly becoming a poster child for Israel's political tolerance when he slammed its policies in his acceptance speech. Other writers, notably Martin Amis, Zadie Smith, and Salman Rushdie, hardly seem amenable to anti-Zionist witch-hunts. And what about Irvine Welsh, whose drug-soaked fables from bleak Scottish streets have been translated "into 20 different languages, including Hebrew"? He, surely, is exquisitely positioned to demand an about-turn in West Dunbartonshire.

Ben Cohen

Let us, therefore, keep an ear out for the outrage of the British literati. And let's remember that, as long as they remain mute, there's a danger that Burns Night will adopt an altogether more sinister meaning.

Criticizing BDS is Not Enough; Jello Biafra Should Play Tel Aviv

Pajamas Media, July 1, 2011

In 2009, about one month after the end of the IDF's military operation against Hamas, I wrote and produced a short film for online viewing, titled *Vilified: Telling Lies About Israel*. Within a day of being uploaded, the film had registered an audience of thousands. Over the following week, the viewer numbers continued to climb impressively. And then the film got pulled by YouTube.

I'd dearly like to report this as a case of political censorship, but the sad truth is that copyright violation was the reason. At the beginning of the film, over a sequence that detailed the gruesome loss of life in those conflicts routinely ignored because Gaza hogs the media limelight, we used the opening bars of a song called "Holiday in Cambodia," by the Dead Kennedys. With its sinister flashes of echoing guitar set against an ominous, cascading riff, the music was perfect, and certainly helped our film on its viral odyssey. Only we didn't clear the rights – mea culpa – and that silly error meant that all those views were obliterated at the touch of a button. At the time, I did wonder if an anti-Zionist sensibility had played a role in the complaint to YouTube from the Dead Kennedys' publishers. Hence, I took a great deal of pleasure when I learned, this week, that none other than Jello Biafra, the lead singer of the Dead Kennedys, had become the latest member of the club of performing artists whose decision to play in Israel attracted the venom of the BDS lobby, whose initials stand for the boycott, divestment, and sanctions against Israel. But does that mean I was wrong about him entirely? Biafra and his band, which rejoices in the name Guantanamo School of Medicine, had been due to play at Tel Aviv's Barby club on July 2. The news of this engagement left the BDS movement aghast and angry. Biafra is not Justin Bieber, after all; given his status as a demi-god in the anarcholeftist universe of punk rock's West Coast incarnation, the Tel Aviv concert represented a wounding betrayal. "We implore you to cancel your 'Holiday in Tel Aviv!'" begged a petition sponsored by a group called Punks Against Apartheid, in an allusion to the Dead Kennedy's Cambodian ditty. After a bitter back and forth between Biafra and his detractors, the singer finally relented. There would be no concert in Tel Aviv, he told his followers, although he would still visit "Israel and Palestine to check things out myself." At the same time, he did not hide his contempt for the BDS movement:

Jello Biafra and the Guantanamo School of Medicine are not going through with the July 2 date in Tel Aviv. This does not mean I or anyone else in the band are endorsing or joining lockstep with the boycott of all things Israel. ... I know far more about this issue than some people think I do, and I am not a poodle for Hasbara, Peace Now, BDS or anyone else. ... Calling anyone speaking up for Palestinian rights a "terrorist" is dumb. So are the blanket condemnations of everyone who happens to be Israeli that seem to be coming from the "drive all the Jews into the sea" crowd. ... I can't back anyone whose real goal or fantasy is a country ethnically cleansed of Jews or anyone else. If you read Biafra's statement in its entirety, you will notice that its utter confusion is what makes it fascinating. On the one hand, Biafra repeats the standard formulae of the extreme left. On the other, he grasps a critical reality that eludes most of the apparently informed commentators on the Middle East: Israel's enemies include a sizeable chunk of folk who want the country and its people to meet a violent demise. Remember, this isn't ZOA speaking, but a snarling punk whose song "Moral Majority" ended with the observation, "God must be dead/If you're alive." Still, there are words and there are deeds, and Biafra's decision to cancel the Tel Aviv concert is what matters. Already, his about-turn has been seized upon by BDS activists as a victory. Biafra's wobbling in the face of the BDS onslaught neatly captures the slippery nature of punk rock's political interventions. On the surface as with the root causes of anarchy itself, the genre seems uncomplicatedly leftist. Examined more closely, the narratives – there's that word again! – are more complex.

The Sex Pistols came across as boneheaded nihilists ("Don't know what I want/But I know how to get it," they spat, in their legendary "Anarchy in the UK."). The Clash seemed virtually schizophrenic: they paid homage to the terrorist chic of armed European leftists like the Red Brigades ("I wanna get a jacket/Just like yours," they sang in "Tommy Gun"), yet their celebrated 1978 documentary, *Rude Boy*, included a delightful scene in which their drunken roadie, Ray Gange, tussled with a long-haired devotee of Britain's Socialist Workers Party, who'd refused to let his beloved employers play an encore at an anti-fascist music festival. Insofar as The Clash clearly didn't want to belong to a club that would have them as members, this was the Marxism of Groucho, not Karl.

What was true of these punk originators was also true of Biafra and the Dead Kennedys. Indeed, "Holiday in Cambodia" was a sublimely witty take-down of privileged American liberals ("Bragging that you know/how the ni**ers feel cold/And the slums got so much soul," the song taunts a liberal college student). It was a parody directed at precisely the type of dunder-headedness, exemplified by "Punks Against Apartheid," that posits a moral parallel between Israel's policies in the disputed territories and the hellish slaughter of Pol Pot's Cambodia. Nonetheless, for all his lyrical bombast, Biafra – by reneging on his pledge to play that citadel of "apartheid," Tel Aviv – has now revealed a surprising wimpishness. Is this a consequence of the "stress" he described in his statement? From the man who revised the words of "I Fought the Law," so that they end with "And I won"? Surely not!

In determining what to do – as distinct from what to say – Biafra would have been well-advised to consult the emperor of punk, John Lydon, or Johnny Rotten, as he was known during his days as the Sex Pistols' front man. Al-most a year ago, Lydon found himself in exactly the same position as Biafra does now. Like Biafra, he gave his BDS critics short shrift. "Until I see an Arab country, a Muslim country, with a democracy, I won't understand how anyone can have a problem with how [the Palestinians] are treated," he admonished them.

Unlike Biafra, Lydon honored his Tel Aviv appointment. An honorable precedent, then, for Biafra – the artist who insisted, in his joyfully unambi-guous track, "Nazi Punks, F–k Off!," that "punk means thinking for yourself" – to reverse his reversal, and do the same.

Pinkwashing? Try 'Progwashing'

JointMedia News Service, March 25, 2012

Last November, the *New York Times* published an op-ed that took the demo-nization of Israel to another, more insidious level. The attack, authored by Sarah Schulman, a professor at the City University of New York and a lesbian and gay civil rights activist, introduced a new word into the anti-Israel lex-icon: "pinkwashing." "Pinkwashing" is Schulman's spin on a bald fact that has always made liberal pro-Palestinian advocates uncomfortable; namely, that Israel is the only country in the Middle East where lesbians and gay men can openly and safely engage with their sexuality. These rights are now standard in most democracies, but when they appear in the Israeli context, the Israel-bashers start searching for an ulterior motive. Hence, "pinkwashing" is the act of using gay politics and culture to disguise the ongoing oppression of the Palestinians.

It seems incredible that the one Middle Eastern country to rouse anger among a certain coterie of gay activists is Israel – but then the same could be said of church activists who round upon the Jewish homeland while ignoring the vicious subjugation of Christians in Muslim countries. Moreover, the impact of these toxic ideas leads this very same group of activists – who would understandably claim to be victims of discrimination – to practice discrimination themselves. Earlier this month, an organization called "A Wider Bridge," which fosters connections between the gay communities of America and Israel, brought a delegation of lesbian and gay activists from Israel to the west coast. The Israelis weren't here to discuss Middle Eastern politics, but to exchange ideas on how to best manage issues like teenage suicides and HIV prevention. But thanks to the actions of a handful of Boycott, Divestment and Sanctions (BDS) activists, those conversations were not held in Seattle. The Israeli group was to have been hosted by the Seattle LGBT Commission – the acronym stands for Lesbian, Gay, Bisexual, Transgendered – an official body that advises the city's mayor and council on the gay community's concerns. However, the commission caved in the face of protests led by Dean Spade, a local academic who participated in a recent delegation of American gay activists to the Palestinian territories. (A source familiar with this delegation's agenda told me that they did not bill themselves as representing the gay community. They made this decision, they subsequently explained, to protect themselves not from the murderers of Hamas, but from the "Israeli authorities!").

Arthur Slepian, the executive director of A Wider Bridge, was rightly outraged by the commission's cowardly behavior. The Israeli lesbian and gay leaders brought by his group to this country were, he said, "silenced in Seattle by those who seek to demonize and delegitimize Israel. We were dismayed that the commission gave in to objections raised by a small number of activists." Slepian went on to point out that the work of the Israeli group "deserves to be supported, and their stories deserve to be told. It is not 'pinkwashing' to tell the truth." Given that the entire BDS campaign is predicated on lies about Israel, one can safely assume that its supporters have no idea how to distinguish truth from falsehood. BDS campaigners are also disturbingly single-minded: their crusade against Israel blinds them to the positive social outcomes that working with Israelis can bring. Assisting gay teenagers fearful of declaring their sexual orientation, providing humanitarian aid and expertise in the world's disaster zones, developing alternative energy technologies – none of these noble goals matter if Israelis are involved. On March 20, four days after canceling its meeting with the Israeli delegation, the commission issued a simpering statement that was billed as an apology. There was no acknowledgement of the damage that had already been done, nor was there any recognition of the groupthink that leads many on the left to uncritically embrace boycotts of Israel in the name of the supposedly progressive cause of "Palestine."

"The Seattle LGBT Commission sincerely apologizes for the pain, offense and embarrassment that we caused by canceling our scheduled event with leaders from Israel's LGBT community who were visiting U.S. cities," the statement waffled. "It is important for us to learn from this experience and to create a deeper conversation." That "deeper conversation" will only be of value if it confronts the true nature of the BDS movement. Whatever lip service it pays to "nonviolence," the principal aim of BDS is the destruction of the state of Israel – an outcome that can only be achieved by slaughtering the vast majority of Jews currently living there. Most progressives would recoil from an association with a genocidal project, but that is precisely what drives the BDS campaign. Yet, its advocates have managed to present their barbaric, antisemitic agenda as being progressive. What we are dealing with, therefore, is not the smear of "pinkwashing," but the ugly reality of what I call "progwashing."

Happily, within the gay community, pro-Israel activists have launched a counter-offensive, arguing that "progwashing" draws a veil over the repression of gay communities in Arab and Muslim countries. Jayson Littman, founder of the gay pro-Israel organization "Out! for Israel," has no doubts about the challenges this entails. "Gay advocates of BDS are a small minority, but they have a pulpit because a lot of them have academic posts and they speak as Jews," Littman told me. Nonetheless, Littman believes that the vast majority of the gay community has no patience for the BDS campaign's exhortations. In that regard, he points to a recent poll conducted by American Airlines in which 43 per cent of gay respondents named Tel Aviv as the one city where they feel welcome and safe. Inside and outside the gay community, the real danger of BDS lies not in its material impact on Israel's economy, which has so far been negligible, but in its promotion of a discourse that positions Israel as the only rogue state in the world. Eleven years after the UN-sponsored Durban conference legitimized the BDS movement, the time has come to bury its deceits once and for all.

Boycott Israel, the Movie – Starring Emma Thompson

The Algemeiner, April 10, 2012

If Hollywood ever makes a movie about the movement to boycott Israel, I can think of no one better suited to the starring role than Emma Thompson. I imagine Thompson's character as a schoolteacher or a librarian, dowdy looking with just a hint of prettiness. She lives alone in a cozy apartment filled with potted plants and books on personal growth, third-world politics and vegetarian cookery. Her significant other is a fluffy cat that nestles in her lap every night as she sits in front of her computer reading the latest dispatches from occupied "Palestine," her face etched with righteous disbelief. She doesn't have time for a boyfriend, but that won't stop her would-be suitor, an equally self-righteous, mildly kooky Jewish writer – think Peter Beinart – from trying to win her heart.

By the time we're halfway through the film, Emma will have decided that she simply *must* visit the West Bank, despite the enormous dangers posed by the Israeli occupation forces. She comes to this awareness while attending a Passover seder hosted by her aspiring boyfriend, during which he pulls out a fading photograph of his great-grandmother who was murdered during the Holocaust. Fighting back the tears, he confides that, "If she could see what Israel has become, she'd die all over again from the shame." The two fall into each other's arms, waking the next morning to a breakfast of *matzo brei* – as Emma tries to pronounce the name of the dish she's eating, we giggle through the obligatory moment of light relief – before she's whisked away in a taxi to the airport, and thence to the beautiful-yet-tragic land of Palestine. In the West Bank, she cavorts with cute little kids – "just like the ones I teach back home" – drinks mint tea with effusive women who bear the daily humiliation of occupation with a smile and a shrug, and admires the steely-eyed men who stand up to the nasty Israelis with all the conviction of a Gandhi or a Martin Luther King. Emma embraces their anger but concludes that violence is not the answer. Just before she leaves the Palestinian village that now feels like home, she regales the enthusiastically nodding villagers with a speech – tearful, of course – expounding on the importance of non-violence. "Don't use bombs," she exhorts. "Use boycotts." Their applause can be heard all the way to the adjacent Israeli army base, where the commander is suddenly struck by the realization that the Palestinian aspiration for freedom can never be crushed. Roll the credits. And don't call it a chick flick.

With a movie like this one, art would be imitating life – to be precise, Emma Thompson's life. Recently, the Oscar-winning actress joined with other darlings of stage and screen to protest the participation of Tel Aviv's venerable Habimah Theater in a London festival that is performing the plays of William Shakespeare in 37 different languages.

In a letter published by *The Guardian* – a liberal newspaper with a long track record of publishing antisemitic material – Thompson and her cohorts slammed "Habima" [sic] for its "shameful record of involvement with illegal Israeli settlements in Occupied Palestinian Territory." They ended with a demand to exclude the theater from the festival. No such objections were voiced concerning the participation of a Palestinian theater troupe, nor the involvement of the National Theater of China, which is directly funded by one of the world's most repressive regimes. In fact, there are many good reasons to ditch political objections and keep the festival open to all – which its organizers, to their credit, have done, in spite of Thompson's fulminations. To perform Shakespeare is in itself a celebration of artistic freedom. Habimah's version of "The Merchant of Venice," the play that gave us the figure of Shylock, the Jewish moneylender who embodies antisemitic canards even as he challenges them, is sure to be enticing. And I would genuinely love to see how actors from communist China interpret the story of "Richard III." For those like Emma Thompson, though, boycotts are predicated on supposedly universal principles and then applied to only one target – Israel. To understand the strategy here, it's worth recalling the campaign in the UK for a boycott of Israeli academic institutions. Ten years ago, an article in The Guardian noted that Israel's universities are victims of their own success: "The nature of Israel's academic pre-eminence," the article explained, "makes it vulnerable to a boycott." The same logic applies to the flourishing arts scene in Israel. The excellence of a theater like Habimah, along with its enthusiasm to perform outside Israel's borders, renders it a sitting duck for boycott campaigners. In their warped view of the world, Palestinian freedom can only be achieved by quarantining Israelis on the basis of their nationality. Thus do apparently free-spirited artists echo the racist policies of the Arab League, which began its boycott of the Jewish community in Eretz Israel in 1945, three years before the state of Israel was born.

What, then, is the appropriate response to Emma Thompson and those like her? Certainly not to make the movie I described earlier. Instead, they should be given a taste of their own medicine. We are often told that Jews run Hollywood – the same Hollywood that carried on casting Vanessa Redgrave, Emma Thompson's fellow Brit, in leading roles *after* she denounced so-called "Zionist hoodlums" in an Oscar acceptance speech in 1978. Will the studio moguls continue to indulge Thompson as they indulged Redgrave? Or will they show some gumption, and tell her that, for as long as she seeks to discriminate against Israeli artists, she will be banished from our screens? I think I know, sadly, what the answer is. But I'd love to be proved wrong.

South Africa's Rulers Line Up Behind BDS

"Contentions" @ Commentary Magazine, October 30, 2012

To the cheers of assembled delegates, the Third International Solidarity Conference of South Africa's ruling African National Congress, which met in Pretoria earlier this week, endorsed the call for a campaign of Boycotts, Divestment and Sanctions (BDS) targeting the Israel. A lone German representative who stood up and challenged the prevailing wisdom that Israel is the reincarnation of South Africa's apartheid regime was roundly dismissed by the chairman of the ANC, Baleka Mbete, who said that she herself had visited "Palestine," where she'd discovered that the situation is "far worse than apartheid South Africa."

This is not the first time that a senior member of South Africa's leftist political establishment has made that exact point. In a particularly noxious speech delivered last May, the Anglican Archbishop Desmond Tutu asserted that the Palestinians were "being oppressed more than the apartheid ideologues could ever dream about in South Africa." Tutu's co-thinker, the Reverend Allan Boesak – best known for his conviction for defrauding charitable donations from the singer Paul Simon and others – has also declared that Israel "is worse, not in the sense that apartheid was not an absolutely terrifying system in South Africa, but in the ways in which the Israelis have taken the apartheid system and perfected it." And in an interview earlier this year, John Dugard, a South African law professor and former UN Rapporteur, approvingly referred to "black South Africans like Archbishop [Desmond] Tutu and others who have repeatedly stated that, in their opinion, the situation in the Palestinian territory is in many respects worse than it was under apartheid."

At times, these thunderous denunciations from ANC figures have descended into open antisemitism. In 2009, Bongani Masuku, a mid-level ANC operative, was found guilty by South Africa's Human Rights Commission of deploying "hate speech" after he announced that any South African Jew who did not support the Palestinian cause "must not just be encouraged but forced to leave." In his defense, Masuku might have pointed out that he was merely echoing similar sentiments to those expressed by Fatima Hajaig, the former deputy minister of foreign affairs, who claimed that "the control of America, just like the control of most Western countries, is in the hands of Jewish money, and if Jewish money controls their country then you cannot expect anything else." In common with other countries where anti-Zionists angrily deny that their views are founded upon classical antisemitism, South Africa's powerful anti-Israel lobby has a number of tame Jews at its disposal to serve as alibis. Foremost among them is Ronnie Kasrils, a former ANC minister who now devotes his time to the Russell Tribunal on Palestine, elegantly described by my fellow *Commentary* contributor Sohrab Ahmari as "a self-appointed people's court that has met periodically since 2009 to sit in judgment of Israel." In a recent interview with *al-Jazeera*, Kasrils laid out the South African anti-Zionist's credo:

"...what is taking place in Palestine reminds us, South African freedom fighters, of what we suffered from. We are the beneficiaries of international solidarity and need to make a similar payback to others still struggling for liberation. Palestine is an example of a people who were dispossessed of land and birthright just like the indigenous people of South Africa. As a Jew, I abhor the fact that the Zionist rulers of Israel/Palestine claim they are acting in the name of Jews everywhere. I am one of many Jews internationally, and in Israel itself, who declare 'Not in my name.'"

Note the veneer of altruism in these comments, along with the insinuation that, as the first victims of an apartheid form of government, South Africans enjoy special privileges when it comes to franchising the term. But what Kasrils pointedly does not mention is that the ANC's receptiveness to the apartheid analogy was established long before Nelson Mandela presided over the country's transition to majority rule. It was, in fact, the Soviet Union that established the analogy, by linking the Palestinian and black South African struggles in its propaganda. Those readers who can bear to revisit UN General Assembly Resolution 3379, which equated Zionism with racism, should note the awkwardly-worded observation that,

"...the racist regime in occupied Palestine and the racist regime in Zimbabwe and South Africa have a common imperialist origin, forming a whole and having the same racist structure and being organically linked in their policy aimed at repression of the dignity and integrity of the human being." The ANC, which always oriented itself to the Soviet bloc and still maintains a close relationship with the unapologetically Stalinist South African Communist Party, has not discarded this Soviet ideological baggage. That commitment, far more than any distinctive insights generated by the experience of living with apartheid in its South African homeland, explains why the country's leaders are so willing to downplay the historic sufferings of their own people in order to batter Israel with the language of racism. And it perhaps also explains why the BDS movement has failed in its bid to become a mass campaign with real impact. Instead, it has resigned itself to being a forum for assorted extreme leftists to pile moral opprobrium on Zionism and Israel. That is, when they are not paying tribute to Fidel Castro as a "revolutionary icon in the fight for freedom and equality."

Stephen Hawking Signs Up to the Academic Boycott of Israel

"Contentions" @ Commentary Magazine, May 8, 2013

There was much relief when, earlier today, a spokesman for Cambridge University in England released a statement denying that Stephen Hawking, the renowned British physicist, had invoked the academic boycott of Israel as the reason for his decision to withdraw from the "Facing Tomorrow" conference, which will be hosted by Israeli President Shimon Peres in Jerusalem in June. As it turns out, Cambridge spoke too soon. Tim Holt, the spokesman who said that Hawking had backed out for health reasons, was compelled to issue the following clarification:

"We have now received confirmation from Professor Hawking's office that a letter was sent on Friday to the Israeli President's office regarding his decision not to attend the Presidential Conference, based on advice from Palestinian academics that he should respect the boycott."

"We had understood previously that his decision was based purely on health grounds having been advised by doctors not to fly."

The initial doubt over the whether the Hawking story was true is easy to understand. The Boycott, Divestment and Sanctions (BDS) movement has a track record of lying about its successes. Over the last few years, many of their claims about individuals and companies endorsing the boycott – including PGGM, the largest pension fund in the Netherlands, Hampshire College, Harvard University, the academic retirement fund TIAA-CREF, and telecoms giant Motorola – were quickly exposed as false. Additionally, the signal failure of the movement's academic arm to enlist any prominent, respected scholar to its cause naturally sowed doubts about Hawking's apparent endorsement. Finally, it seemed difficult to believe that Hawking, whose own achievements owe a great deal to the Israeli physicist Jacob Bekenstein, would approve something as crude and as ugly as a boycott.

What, exactly, has Hawking signed up to? At the outset, the idea that his decision is related to discomfort with Israel's settlement policies should be dispensed with. The Palestinian Call for an Academic and Cultural Boycott of Israel is refreshingly clear that Israel's presence in the West Bank is simply one element of a much more comprehensive assault upon Israel's legitimacy:

...Israel's colonial oppression of the Palestinian people, which is based on Zionist ideology, comprises the following:

Denial of its responsibility for the Nakba – in particular the waves of ethnic cleansing and dispossession that created the Palestinian refugee problem – and therefore refusal to accept the inalienable rights of the refugees and displaced stipulated in and protected by international law;

Military occupation and colonization of the West Bank (including East Jerusalem) and Gaza since 1967, in violation of international law and UN resolutions;

The entrenched system of racial discrimination and segregation against the Palestinian citizens of Israel, which resembles the defunct apartheid system in South Africa.

In plain speaking, then, the ultimate aim of the boycott movement is to dismantle the State of Israel in its entirety, not simply to secure its withdrawal from disputed territories. We are not talking here about, in the words of the Associated Press, a strategy "designed to bring pressure on the Israeli government," but the wholesale rejection of anything or anyone associated with Israel. It is for this reason, and rightly, that the boycott movement can credibly be described as antisemitic, for it seeks to deny only the Jewish people the right of self-determination, and viciously caricatures the Jewish state as a carbon copy of the old apartheid regime in South Africa. I make this point in anticipation of the coming tussle over whether Stephen Hawking is or isn't antisemitic. His supporters will certainly portray him as a fearless opponent of colonialism, a man who nobly condemned the war that ousted Saddam Hussein's regime in Iraq as a war crime, and who is now being "smeared" – the favored word of anti-Zionists everywhere – as a Jew-hater. Detractors will doubtless point out that Hawking's thinking is riddled with moral idiocy (why pick on Israel while remaining silent on serial human rights violators like North Korea and Iran?) and hypocrisy (major advances in combating Lou Gehrig's disease, which Hawking has suffered from for more than 40 years, have been made in Israel). The overriding consideration is that, regardless of Hawking's personal attitudes toward Jews – which no one bar his closest confidantes could credibly claim knowledge of – he has associated himself with a movement that seeks to eliminate, in the form of the State of Israel, the one guarantee Jews have against a repeat of the genocidal persecutions of the last century. That same consideration should govern any assessment of his decision to withdraw from the Jerusalem conference.

It's also worth noting that while Hawking's trophy cabinet doesn't contain a Nobel Prize, it does include the Presidential Medal of Freedom, awarded to him by President Obama in 2009. One might reasonably ask whether such an award was appropriate, given Hawking's affinity with political movements that are antithetical to the very idea of freedom. And one might also ask whether Hawking, for the sake of consistency, will now return the medal, in protest against Obama's decision to bestow the same honor, last year, upon none other than Shimon Peres.

Tennis Deals a Blow to the Boycott of Israel

Commentary Magazine, November 4, 2013

Malik Jaziri, the top-ranked tennis player in Tunisia who has an impressive record of representing his country in international tournaments, was about to play a quarterfinal match at the ATP Challenger Tournament in Uzbekistan last October. Moments before stepping onto the court, he received a career-shattering email from his bosses at the tennis federation back in Tunis. Jaziri had been drawn against an Israeli professional, Amir Weintraub; the Tunisian tennis federation, which continues to follow the Arab League boycott of the State of Israel to the letter, declared this to be a red line that Jaziri was not permitted to cross. "Following a meeting this afternoon with the Ministry of Youth and Sports, I have the immense regret to inform you that you are ordered not to play against the Israeli player," read the email. Jaziri had no choice but to withdraw and Weintraub went through to the semi-final on a forfeit.

It goes without saying that Jaziri himself was blameless in the matter. Interviewed after being forced to withdraw, he expressed the fear that the decision would badly damage his career. His brother and manager, Amir Jaziri, slammed the decision as "shocking, because it brings politics into sport." Meanwhile, Amir Weintraub himself described Jaziri as "a good friend," adding wistfully that the Tunisian had "really wanted to play." That in of itself is not a surprise; after all, athletes live for competition, not political strife. But what is noteworthy is that the International Tennis Federation (ITF), mindful that this was not the first time that Israeli players had been subjected to a boycott, and anxious to bring the practice to an end, took unprecedented action. Hence this statement released yesterday by the ITF's Board of Directors at their meeting in Cagliari, Italy, confirming that Tunisia has been suspended from next year's Davis Cup:

The Board was not satisfied with the case put forward by the Tunisian Tennis Federation and voted to suspend Tunisia from the 2014 Davis Cup by BNP Paribas competition. The decision of the ITF Board was unanimous although ITF Board Member from Tunisia, Tarak Cherif, recused himself from the discussion and the vote. The 2013 ITF Constitution states the ITF and its members must preserve the integrity and independence of Tennis as a sport and must carry out their objects and purposes without unfair discrimination on grounds of colour, race, nationality, ethnic or national origin, age, sex or religion. "There is no room for prejudice of any kind in sport or in society," said ITF President Francesco Ricci Bitti. "The ITF Board decided to send a strong message to the Tunisian Tennis Federation that this kind of action will not be tolerated by any of our members. The Board felt that suspension from Davis Cup, a competition that was founded 113 years ago to encourage better understanding through sport, would provide a good lesson for the Federation and a fitting penalty for their unfortunate action." The decision of the ITF Board of Directors is final.

The ITF's announcement is a welcome and courageous one for three reasons. Firstly, by correctly depicting the Tunisian decision as based upon "prejudice," it rejects wholesale all the justifications and rationalizations for the boycott of Israel and Israelis advanced by the Arab League Central Boycott Office and its contemporary echo, the antisemitic "Boycott, Divestment and Sanctions" (BDS) movement, which portrays the boycott of Israel as the twenty-first century incarnation of the movement to boycott apartheid South Africa. Secondly, the announcement shifts the costs of a boycott away from the Israelis onto the boycotting countries themselves. Those countries that continue insisting on a boycott of Israeli athletes now have a choice: either drop this primitive bigotry, or accept that through your actions, it is your own professional sports representatives that will be punished.

Lastly, the ITF decision should properly be read as establishing a precedent that can equally apply in other sports. At an international swimming competition in Dubai last month, the Israeli team was grudgingly allowed to participate, but scoreboards at the event, as well as television broadcasts, were banned from mentioning the word "Israel." Gratifyingly, the success of the Israeli swimmers at the tournament meant that the policy of pretending that the team was not present became untenable.

Nonetheless, there should be consequences to these actions. As well as ejecting boycotting countries from competitions, international sporting authorities should also ban countries that still advocate the boycott of Israel – like Qatar, which will host the 2022 soccer World Cup – from hosting such prestigious events. Thanks to the ITF, that outcome is now one step closer.

Chapter Four: Antisemitism and anti-Judaism

What Antisemitism Is (And Isn't)

The Huffington Post, July 30, 2010

This morning, I received an email from a reader informing me that I was "a chicken hawk Jew." For good measure, I was then urged to perform an act with my yarmulke which doesn't bear repeating in polite company. What roused this person's ire was a short post of mine earlier this week about Oliver Stone. Evidently, my correspondent's opinions about Jews are little different from those expressed by Stone in his interview with the Sunday Times. I therefore concluded that the author of the email deserves the label "anti-Semite" just as much as Stone does. Except that unlike my detractor, Stone quickly apologized for his remarks, prompting the question of whether it is fair to call him an antisemite. The answer lies in understanding what antisemitism is – and what it isn't.

Instances of celebrity Jew-baiting, whether Stone sounding off to a journalist or Mel Gibson drunkenly assailing a police officer, encourage the mistaken view that antisemitism is a particularly vicarious type of rudeness that can be overcome through the exercise of self-control. Particularly after the Holocaust, the wisdom goes, ranting about Jews is decidedly inappropriate behavior. Should one's worst instincts win out, will a subsequent, timely apology annul the offense? If antisemitism is boiled down to a matter of insult, then yes, it probably will. But the problem here, as Marx might have said, is the confusion of appearance with essence. What makes antisemitism distinctive is that it's a worldview, a means of explaining why there is injustice and unfairness and conflict in our societies. In his recent epic study, the scholar Robert Wistrich cited the French monarchist Charles Maurras' admiration for the succinctness of antisemitism. "It enables everything to be arranged, smoothed over and simplified," Maurras said.

In the nineteenth century, Maurras and his cohorts wore the antisemite's button with pride. So did Wilhelm Marr, the German rabble-rouser widely credited with coining the term antisemitism, who went on to found The League of Antisemites in 1879. For these men and their followers, antisemitism was not so much an attitude as an ideology. When it comes to Oliver Stone's comments, it's precisely that ideology which is visible. Stone, it's important to recall, diminished the significance of the Holocaust and revived the hoary claim of Jewish media control in order to make his ultimate point: that "Israel has f***** up United States foreign policy for years." Such views are increasingly current among the Chavistas with whom he is so starstruck. In keeping with its politically and theologically promiscuous history, antisemitism is again perfectly compatible with what would commonly, if incorrectly, be regarded as a progressive outlook, especially if the focus is upon the State of Israel. That is why antisemitism remains one of the most furiously contested terms in political debate today. Invariably, those accused of it angrily reject the charge, retorting that they have been unfairly maligned by a crude tactic designed to muzzle what they insist is the horrible reality of Israel.

These are people who would have you believe that the victims of antisemitism today are no longer Jews, but those who are labeled antisemitic. Such sophistry, however, was not available to Oliver Stone, because of his candor in talking about Jews, and not "Zionists" or "The Israel Lobby." In recent memory, only Helen Thomas has displayed an equivalent frankness.

There is a deeper point about those who recycle the favorite themes of antisemitism, yet are careful not to do what Stone and Thomas did, and speak about Jews *qua* Jews. In *Tablet* this week, Lee Smith, who has been valiantly grappling with a cast of characters including Stephen Walt, Glenn Greenwald and Andrew Sullivan, argued that the matter at hand is not the "indiscernible beliefs of individuals," but the way in which these writers, when they write about Israel, are "complicit in the common work of mainstreaming the kind of antisemitic language, ideas, and discourse that were once confined to extremist hate sites on the far right." It's unlikely that Lee Smith's opponents will engage in any critical reflection, perhaps because the truth is too painful to bear. For many of the grand myths of our own time – Israel as the ultimate rogue state, U.S. policy as a hostage of the "Israel Lobby," the Palestinians as the iconic symbol of human suffering – draw on a much older tradition that, just twenty years ago, most people regarded as a matter for historians, not chroniclers of the present. It was these myths which effectively licensed Oliver Stone's remarks. If there is a lesson to be drawn from *L'Affaire* Stone, it is that he did not – and this is why his apology is really by the by – act alone.

Yale Downgrades Antisemitism Scholarship

Pajamas Media, June 8, 2011

Here, in essence, is what Yale University told me on June 7, after I contacted its communications office to ask why an institute dedicated to the study of antisemitism had been shut down: some of our best friends are Jews. "As you may be aware," Yale spokesman Thomas Conroy wrote in an email, "Yale has long been a leader in Judaic research, teaching and collections. Yale's Judaic Studies program has outstanding faculty members who conduct path-breaking research and inspire graduate and undergraduate students who choose from scores of courses and may earn degrees. The University library's Judaica Collection is one of the strongest in the Western Hemisphere. The Fortunoff Video Archive for Holocaust Testimonies is a historic treasure and exceptional scholarly resource."

All well and good. But why, I asked Conroy, was this information pertinent to the closure of the Yale Interdisciplinary Initiative for the Study of Antisemitism (YIISA), just five years after it opened its doors? "Yale has certainly made, and is making a contribution...through scholarly endeavors related to Jewish civilization, history and contemporary thought and issues," he replied. "I point it out to add context." I have no doubt that Conroy made this statement with the best of intentions. However, his words reveal a fundamental misunderstanding of the very phenomenon which YIISA will no longer be able to probe. For any institution that invokes its munificence towards Jewish civilization, in answer to a question about its commitment to scholarly research on antisemitism, clearly doesn't grasp what antisemitism is and what it represents. One of the pitfalls of the contemporary antisemitism debate is that there is too much focus on intent. In the furore surrounding their sordid book, *The Israel Lobby*, John Mearsheimer and Stephen Walt frequently complained that they were being accused of antisemitism, when neither entertained hateful feelings towards Jews on a personal level. Now, if we accept the Mearsheimer-Walt definition of the antisemite as someone who consciously and brazenly loathes Jews, then there is indeed little point in studying contemporary antisemitism, since, in western countries at any rate, few people of any consequence would openly admit to hating Jews *qua* Jews.

On the basis of this definition, it follows that someone accused of antisemitism must be the target of a rhetorical trick designed to derail honest debate about, invariably, Israel and its supporters. It's all very post-modern: the victims of antisemitism today are not Jews, but those tarred as antisemites. When mounting their defense, all such people have to do is point to the bevy of Jewish friends and colleagues in their rolodexes. This silly distortion of antisemitism's meaning is precisely why Yale's 2006 decision to house YIISA, which began life as an independent research institution, was such a welcome milestone. One of the world's finest universities was effectively saying that antisemitism, the hallmark of the two great totalitarian regimes of the twentieth century, cannot be reduced to a matter of personal opinion. In that regard, the fact that the Soviet Union coded its persecution of Jews with terms like "Zionists" and "rootless cosmopolitans" provides a historical foundation to examine the linguistic slipperiness of antisemitism in our own time.

If scholarly enquiry into antisemitism is, then, a legitimate pursuit, what was the problem with YIISA? According to Yale, YIISA was an academic dud. Professor Donald Green, the director of Yale's Institute for Social and Policy Studies (ISPS), said that YIISA's papers failed to excite the interest of "top-tier journals in behavioral science, comparative politics, or history." Students were not attracted to its programs. Contrast that, Green went on, with another ISPS program "that straddles social science and humanities, Agrarian Studies, [and] has produced dozens of path-breaking scholarly books and essays." This is an unfair comparison. Few scholars will bat an eyelid at the mention of Agrarian Studies, whereas the idea of studying contemporary antisemitism – the "historical" kind is a little more acceptable – will meet with howls of disapproval in countless political science departments. Just by existing, YIISA was going against the grain. In that kind of environment, getting your papers published was never going to be easy. YIISA, in point of fact, did produce some important scholarly work during its short life-span, including three outstanding papers by David Hirsh (on anti-Zionism and antisemitism), Bassam Tibi (on the Islamization of antisemitism), and Yaakov Kirschen, aka the cartoonist "Dry Bones" (on antisemitism and 'coded images'). Its regular seminars featured some of the leading thinkers on the subject, like Moishe Postone and Gregory Stanton. Those in the YIISA community with whom I spoke emphasized that they wanted to do even more, citing lack of resources as the main reason why they didn't. Even so, let's concede for a moment that YIISA's work, in the words of Professor Green, "failed to meet high standards for research and instruction." Surely YIISA was a candidate ripe for intervention, not closure? By closing YIISA, isn't Yale telling those who argue that contemporary antisemitism is the equivalent of a reputational smear campaign that they are right? This is where the politics comes in. In my correspondence with Thomas Conroy, I pointed out that YIISA's 2010 conference, which extensively examined antisemitic manifestations in Iran and in the wider Arab/Muslim world, had provoked angry responses from, among others, Maen Areikat, the PLO's Washington representative, who ranted about "anti-Arab extremism and hate-mongering." "Yale doesn't make decisions about programs (or individual scholars) based on outside criticism," Conroy told me. Even if Conroy is correct here, Yale's decisions resonate far beyond its ivory towers. It beggars belief that Yale's academics did not pause to consider that closing YIISA would be interpreted by Areikat – a man who recycles the idiocy that Arabs cannot be antisemites because they are "Semites" – as a vindication of his attack. Moreover, Areikat was not alone. Among those joining the anti-YIISA clamor were Philip Weiss, the pea-brained anti-Zionist blogger sponsored by *The Nation* magazine, and his sidekick Ben White, a frankly creepy figure who couches his antisemitism in the language of Christian liberation theology. After the YIISA conference, this duo – of all people!! – whined about the "besmirching of Yale University by the presence of this festival of propaganda."

Of course, were Yale to organize an academic conference on the subject of "Israeli apartheid," Weiss, White et al. would be salivating at the prospect. For critics like these, academic integrity is only relevant when it boosts their argument. Any dispassionate survey of the social sciences reveals that there is precious little "value-free" research going on anywhere. I only have to look at my own alma mater, the London School of Economics, which, *inter alia*, has accepted funding from the murderous Gaddafi regime, and gave the clownish Naomi Klein a fellowship. Or I could venture into upper Manhattan, where Joseph Massad's Columbia University classes on Middle East politics are their own "festival of propaganda." The point is, why pick on YIISA alone? One of the most influential critiques of current social science in recent years, "The Flight from Reality in the Human Sciences," was written by Ian Shapiro, himself a professor at Yale. In it, Shapiro draws on work conducted with his colleague, Donald Green, to advocate for "problem-driven" scholarship (writes Shapiro: "...the problem-driven scholar asks, 'Why are constitutions enacted?' or 'Why do they survive?' and 'Why do ideologies develop?' or 'Why do people adhere to them?'"). I would venture that antisemitism is an ideal subject for such a method ("What is antisemitism now? How is it different? Why does it persist?"). Let us hope that YIISA finds a new home to continue this research. Admiration for Jewish achievements is not a necessary condition for an offer; a genuine commitment to the subject absolutely is.

Ben Cohen

Can Academia Ever Ignore Politics?

The Forward, June 21, 2011

Can a clear line be drawn between academic scholarship and political imperatives? Of all the questions raised by Yale University's recent closure of the Yale Initiative for the Interdisciplinary Study of Antisemitism (YIISA), this one is the most acute. Even with the news that Yale is going to replace YIISA with a new program for the study of antisemitism, it is still instructive to think about what brought YIISA down. The institute's detractors essentially fell into two categories. Some, like the bloggers Philip Weiss and Antony Lerman, marked its demise with displays of *schadenfreude*, having long caricatured YIISA as a Zionist advocacy organization masquerading as an academic institute.

A second group, represented by professor Deborah Lipstadt who wrote last week, was sympathetic to YIISA in its conception, yet critical of its execution. According to this view, YIISA spent too much time agitating against antisemitism, especially as manifested in the Muslim world, and not enough time studying the phenomenon dispassionately. Both these perspectives shared the same assumption. YIISA's tone, focus, and – as Lerman described it – "politicized approach" toward contemporary antisemitism fatally compromised its academic integrity in favor of strident advocacy. Is that a fair assessment? Take the oft-cited example of YIISA's bias, the paper delivered to its 2010 conference by Itamar Marcus, the director of the Israeli monitoring organization "Palestinian Media Watch." Entitled "The Central Role of Palestinian Antisemitism in Creating the Palestinian Identity," the paper propelled YIISA into the headlines after it sent Maen Areikat, the PLO's Washington representative, into an apoplectic rage. Arabs were being "demonized" by YIISA, declared Areikat in a letter to Yale President Richard Levin. Since Arabs are "Semites," he insisted, they cannot be antisemitic. Ironically, Areikat's reaction underlined just why Marcus's contribution was supremely pertinent to a conference on antisemitism. The "but-we-are-Semites" rationalization frequently heard from Palestinian leaders resonates with ignorant contempt for Jewish history.

The very label 'anti-Semite' was coined not by Jews, but by non-Jewish demagogues, who used it to construct an ideology and a political program with mass appeal. When a nation becomes gripped by antisemitism, its character changes. Its national identity, malleable by nature, embraces opposition to the Jews as one if its main components: Think of France during Dreyfus, or Germany under the Nazis.

Yet an academic conference which asks whether this is also true of the Palestinian Arabs – whose distinctive identity only crystallized in the context of a violent response to the arrival of the Jewish pioneers – finds itself accused of engaging in political advocacy. The sad truth is that dead Jews – victims of crusades, pogroms, the Shoah – are safe terrain for academia. Live Jews, however, are a much more daunting proposition. As anyone connected with YIISA will tell you, the institute's academic challenge was never about maintaining a studied neutrality. Rather, its staff and fellows had to operate in an academic culture openly in thrall to a set of values that, from the outset, promised confrontation: Hostility toward the idea of Jewish national self-determination, receptiveness toward "Israel Lobby" theories of U.S. Middle East policy, the conceit that antisemitism is merely a tool to smear Israel's opponents.

For that reason, YIISA had to reclaim the antisemitism debate. Ultimately, the institute was forced to defend the contention that contemporary antisemitism is not a phantom, but a very real social problem. In that regard, Professor Lipstadt's own work on Holocaust denial is salient here. In her book on the subject, she argues that her research was essential to prevent deniers from gaining influence as the immediate memory of the Shoah began to fade. In academic parlance, this point of departure would be described as "normative" – we should do x to prevent y – and is no less legitimate because of it. How was YIISA's work any different? Its sole offense, I would assert, lay in its determination to go against the grain. Yale may couch its justification for YIISA's closure in terms of academic standards, but that does nothing to explain the undercurrent of hostility from others on the Yale faculty like Jeffrey Alexander, a professor of sociology, who told NPR: "...it would be as if you had a center for the study of, let's say, racism, organized by, let's say, the Black Panther movement." If former YIISA director Charles Small is the equivalent of Stokely Carmichael, heaven knows where that leaves Columbia's tenured anti-Zionist, Joseph Massad, or the London School of Economics, which carried out research funded by the Gaddafi Foundation. By closing YIISA after only five years, Yale has effectively sided with those voices that demean contemporary antisemitism as the fantasy of overzealous Israel advocates. It remains to be seen if the university's new antisemitism program takes up the charge, analyzing antisemitism's all-too-real manifestations, whether in Iran's state doctrine or on the streets of European cities like Malmo, Leicester and Antwerp. If it doesn't, we can only hope that Yale's loss will be another university's gain.

Ben Cohen

Hungary's Antisemitic Double Standard

Radio Free Europe/Radio Liberty, July 25, 2011

Hungary's new media law, which went into effect on July 1, carries a distinctly unpleasant whiff of the country's fascist and communist past. Under its provisions, all media outlets are required to register with a body called the Media Council. The council is empowered to impose fines of nearly $1 million upon those publications and broadcasters deemed to have "insulted" a particular group, along with an amorphous entity defined as "the majority." If a publication violates "public morality," it faces a fine. If its news coverage is judged "imbalanced," ditto. And woe betide any journalist who refuses an order from the council to disclose his sources.

With this one measure, Hungary has unraveled an emblematic achievement of those largely peaceful 1989–90 revolutions that brought communism crashing down across Eastern Europe – namely, the freedom of the press. Instead of nurturing an environment conducive to free inquiry, the law creates a climate of fear and distrust, one of the hallmarks of totalitarian rule. To add insult to injury, two recent cases have emerged that demonstrate that the media law is being applied with a scandalous double standard. In the first case, "Nepszava," a liberal daily, is under investigation by Media Council commissioners over "insulting" reader comments that appeared in the online version of an article criticizing Pal Schmitt, Hungary's president. The comments were pretty mild by the coarse standards of online debate – for example, Schmitt was called a "clown" – but that is besides the point: the wrong political leaders were offended, so the media law was brought into play. In the second case, by contrast, reader comments on an article in the pro-government newspaper "Magyar Hirlap" were riddled with antisemitic slurs of jaw-dropping foulness, yet not a peep has been heard from the Media Council.

Raging Antisemitism

The "Magyar Hirlap" article reported on an opinion piece penned earlier this year by Karl Pfeifer, the veteran Austrian Jewish journalist, in the Vienna daily "Die Presse." In that piece, Pfeifer relayed the contents of an article by Zsolt Bayer, a Hungarian rabble-rouser with close ties to the ruling Fidesz party who passes himself off as a journalist. Bayer's style mirrors the screeching, obscene rants of Julius Streicher, the editor of the Nazi rag "Der Stürmer." His inchoate tirade included a reference to "a stinking excrement called something like Cohen," followed by an expression of regret "that they"

– meaning the Jews – "were not all buried up to their necks in the forest of Orgovany," the site of a pogrom during the Hungarian "White Terror" of 1919–20. Pfeifer's apt description of Bayer as a "fecal anti-Semite" for his obsessive linkage of Jews with human waste was interpreted by "Magyar Hirlap" as an attack on Fidesz. Hence, the online reader comments on its coverage of Pfeifer's piece didn't hold back. Pfeifer, a Holocaust survivor, was called a "gas-chamber deserter." Contributors invoked the imagery of classic antisemitism – "Jewish scabs," "Jewish lice" – along with its contemporary variants, including this choice line: "The Israeli Jewish occupiers...bring only conflict and ruin, while sucking our blood like parasites and draining our vigor." Unlike "Nepszava," which has been victimized solely for hosting comments that discreetly poked fun at the Hungarian president, "Magyar Hirlap" has continued as if there were no media law, and the scurrilous attacks on Pfeifer remain online. The noted Hungarian-American scholar Eva Balogh offered the following explanation as to why that is:

"Despite his venomous writing, the old Fidesz leadership never disassociated itself from Bayer. Yearly there is a Fidesz birthday bash which is proudly attended by the founders, among them Zsolt Bayer. A few years ago after a particularly outrageous antisemitic attack, [Hungarian Prime Minister] Viktor Orban made a special effort to be photographed with Bayer as they were amiably enjoying some private jokes. It was Orban's way of saying, 'Bayer is our boy, we stand by him.'"

More generally, as Balogh, Pfeifer, and other commentators have noted, Hungary is rapidly becoming one of the most xenophobic countries in Europe. Roma ('Gypsies') face regular attack, and those who expose these crimes find themselves on the receiving end of nationalist opprobrium ("Gypsies are killing Hungarians every week," one commenter lectured Pfeifer). The neo-fascist Jobbik party, which sports its own militia, has emerged as Hungary's third-largest, combining an extreme right-wing loathing of Jews and other minorities with anti-Zionist rhetoric more commonly found on the extreme left. And just this month, Hungary made the headlines when a court acquitted 97-year-old Sandor Kepiro, accused of participating in a brutal massacre of Hungarian Jews and Serbian nationals during World War II. Fully cognizant of these toxic conditions, Pfeifer nonetheless sent a letter to Jeno Bodonovich, head of the Media Council, asking him how the new media law is going to be implemented against "antisemitic, racist, and homophobic hate speech." Thus far, he has not received a reply. Such silent expression of contempt is yet another sign that the bad old days are returning.

Ben Cohen

Roger Cohen Discovers Antisemitism

Pajamas Media, August 24, 2011

For some years, the *New York Times* columnist Roger Cohen thrived in his role as a bete noire of pro-Israel advocates in the United States. In his writings on Iran, especially, Cohen attracted considerable ire for discounting Israel's anxieties about the nuclear ambitions of the ruling mullahs, and for generally pushing the idea that the unresolved Palestinian question lies at the heart of the myriad conflicts in the Middle East and wider Islamic world. And then he moved to London. Back in the city where he grew up, Cohen has now – as his latest column announces – discovered that antisemitism is not some dastardly fabrication of the Israel lobby, but a real phenomenon experienced on many levels by many Jews. Off the back of that revelation, Cohen declares himself nostalgic for those same assertive Jews with whom he tussled back in the States. Here, in brief, is what lay behind this sudden transformation. Visiting his sister's house, he ran into her lodger, who, having noticed Cohen fiddling with his BlackBerry, referred to it as a "JewBerry." Cohen didn't follow. The lodger then explained that the free messaging services that come with the device make it a "JewBerry," because Jews are always on the lookout for something free.

Cohen correctly diagnoses this remark as representing the casual antisemitism that has left a lasting imprint on the English, much as it has upon other European nations. He is probably right that someone who makes such remarks isn't necessarily a violent antisemite. I grew up in London too, where I attended a private school with a large number of Jewish boys; all in all, our lot was a happy one, and if we got into the occasional scrap because one of the non-Jewish boys threw a penny coin at us – picking it up marked you as a money-grubbing "yid" – we didn't conclude that another Holocaust was around the corner. What bothers Cohen is that British Jews are, in the title of his piece, "Jews in a whisper." The Jews of Albion do not, Cohen believes, have the gumption of the American brethren. His "inner voice" implores them to "get some pride...speak up!" Why Cohen has arrived at this conclusion isn't clear, because he does not seem to have spoken to any actual British Jews in the course of gathering his thoughts. Had he, for example, consulted with Anthony Julius, the author of a monumental history of English antisemitism, Cohen would have understood that the genteel barbs against Jews he mentions rest on far uglier foundations. This was a land from which the Jews were formally expelled in 1290, and one which pioneered the infamous blood libel through the martyrdom tales of William of

Norwich and Hugh of Lincoln. Fascism did not triumph, but neither was this a country free of its influence; in the 1930s, at a time when some of Britain's most senior leaders were contemplating a deal with Hitler, Jews in the streets of east London faced a mortal threat from the Blackshirts who swore their allegiance to Sir Oswald Mosley. And, of course, as the former mandatory power in Palestine, Britain provided favorable conditions for the vicious anti-Zionism that was to emerge in the decades following the Second World War.

This anti-Zionism certainly bothers Cohen, to the extent that he even mentions its critical component: Muslim antisemitism. But again, he reports no conversations with those who might have educated him on the subject. A conversation with Howard Jacobson, the leading British writer whose recent novel, *The Finkler Question*, is a witty journey through the minds of anti-Zionist Jews, would have yielded valuable insights. The same can be said of the Community Security Trust, a communal defense organization run by individuals who are the very opposite of the supine Jews of Cohen's imagination. One can add, too, the bloggers of Harry's Place, who diligently monitor and attack extremists of all varieties – left, right, and Islamist – as well as the activists of Engage, who combat the academic boycott of Israel. I could go on. The point, though, is that Cohen does not seem willing to connect with anyone who might shake his convictions (a pronounced trait among New York liberals that he must have picked up during his years over here). He is determined to drive home his fundamental argument, and no-one will stop him. Above all else, it is a bizarre argument and it goes something like this. Jews have a duty to combat prejudice against them boldly and bravely. Yet their history compels them to resist the entreaties of those Cohen labels as "Islamophobes," since these folks have simply adapted the discourse of anti-semitism to Europe's Muslims. For Cohen, if no-one else, "the lesson is clear":

Jews, with their history, cannot become the systematic oppressors of another people. They must be vociferous in their insistence that continued colonization of Palestinians in the West Bank will increase Israel's isolation and ultimately its vulnerability. Got that? When someone makes a bone-headed joke about a "JewBerry," the proper response is to denounce the Israeli occupation. The *Times*, frankly, should be embarassed about publishing this type of nonsense. Moreover, it's not the first time; in another recent column from London on the Oslo massacre, Cohen excoriated "Islamophobes" by tying in the death of singer Amy Winehouse, "a Jewish girl from East London whose artistry would once have been dismissed by a racist and murderous European right as degenerate 'cosmopolitan' trash."

Underpinning Cohen's inchoate offerings is a notion that many would reasonably regard as antisemitic: that Jews are collectively responsible for Israel's actions unless they explicitly declare otherwise. Yet if someone was to argue that European Muslims were similarly obliged to condemn each and every Islamist atrocity, Cohen would no doubt declare them "Islamophobic."

Most insidious of all is Cohen's use of antisemitism as a gateway to bash Israel. Like Peter Beinart, he is profoundly troubled by the image of the empowered Jew. Essentially, he believes that the historical mission of Jews is to be without power, even as the antisemites accuse them of being all-powerful. With friends like these, eh?

The Big Lie Returns

Commentary, 23 January, 2012

A blurb on a book jacket would seem an unlikely vehicle for the introduction of a new and sinister tactic in the promotion of an ancient prejudice. But in September 2011, a word of appreciation on the cover of *The Wandering Who* launched a fresh chapter in the modern history of antisemitism. And when the dust had settled – what little dust there was – on the events surrounding the blurb, it had become horrifyingly clear that the role of defining the meaning of the term *antisemitism* did not belong to the Jews. It may, in fact, belong to anti-Semites.

The flattering quotation came from John Mearsheimer, the University of Chicago professor and co-author, with Harvard's Stephen Walt, of *The Israel Lobby and U.S. Foreign Policy*. Mearsheimer's 2007 bestseller, which contends that Israel's American supporters are powerful enough to subvert the U.S. national interest, has been controversial for its adoption of antisemitic tropes – tropes Mearsheimer danced around cleverly. But in endorsing *The Wandering Who* and its Israeli-born author, Gilad Atzmon, Mearsheimer crossed the boundary. The man whose book Mearsheimer called "fascinating and provocative," a work that "should be widely read by Jews and non-Jews alike," is an anti-Semite, pure and simple. A saxophone player by trade, Atzmon was born and raised in Israel but subsequently moved to London. He proclaims himself either an "ex-Jew" or a "proud self-hating Jew" and was quoted approvingly by Turkey's Islamist prime minister, Recep Tayyip Erdogan, at the Davos conference in 2009: Denouncing Israel in vociferous terms before a horrified Shimon Peres, Erdogan quoted Atzmon as saying, "Israeli barbarity is far beyond even ordinary cruelty." Atzmon fixates upon

the irredeemably tribal and racist identity he calls "Jewishness." The anti-
Gentile separatism that compels Jews to amass greater power and influence
is manifested, he preaches, in any context where Jews come together as a
group. *The Wandering Who* finds Atzmon on territory well-trodden by anti-
Semites past and present: Holocaust revisionism (one chapter is entitled
"Swindler's List"), the rehabilitation of Hitler (he argues that Israel's behavior makes all the more tempting the conclusion that the Führer was right
about the Jews), the separation of Jesus from Judaism (Christ was the original proud, self-hating Jew, whose example Spinoza, Marx, and now, Atzmon
himself, have followed). One would think this was categorically indefensible
stuff. Yet, when the blogger Adam Holland e-mailed Mearsheimer to ask
whether he was aware of Atzmon's flirtation with Holocaust denial, as well
as his recital of telltale antisemitic provocations, Mearsheimer stood by his
endorsement of the book. Holland duly published Mearsheimer's response:
"The blurb below is the one I wrote for *The Wandering Who* and I have no
reason to amend it or embellish it, as it accurately reflects my view of the
book." A number of prominent commentators – among them Jeffrey Goldberg, Walter Russell Mead, and even Andrew Sullivan, up to that point a
dependable supporter of Mearsheimer – rushed to confront and condemn
the professor. But Mearsheimer maintained in various blog posts that Atzmon was no anti-Semite and those who said otherwise were guilty of vicious
smear jobs. He wrote on the Foreign Policy magazine blog of his co-author,
Stephen Walt: "[Jeffrey Goldberg's] insinuation that I have any sympathy for
Holocaust denial and am an anti-Semite . . . is just another attempt in his
longstanding effort to smear Steve Walt and me."

And that was that. No affaire Mearsheimer unfolded. The fact that a controversy did not erupt, that the endorsement of a Holocaust revisionist by a
prominent professor at a major university did not lead to calls for his dismissal or resignation or even a chin-pulling symposium in the pages of the
New York Times's "Sunday Review," represents an important shift in the
privileges that anti-Semites and their sympathizers enjoy. Now, it appears,
anti-Semites are being given additional power to define antisemitism by
stating that it is something other than what they themselves represent –
before rising in moral outrage to denounce anyone who might say different.
Their views are not offensive, not antisemitic; no, it is the opinions of those
who object to their views that should be considered beyond the pale. This is
more than a change in the dynamics of antisemitism; it is an inversion of the
accepted logic of minorities and bigots altogether. Unlike blacks, Muslims,
Hispanics, or any other religious or ethnic group, Jews alone are now to be

told by their enemies who does and who does not hate them. The list of flagrant Jew-baiters is growing; those with Jewish names provide an additional frisson. In America, M.J. Rosenberg – a one-time employee of the American Israel Public Affairs Committee (AIPAC) and now called a "foreign policy fellow" at the leftist organization Media Matters – refers to supporters of Israel as "Israel Firsters," recycling the notion that Jewish political loyalties gravitate toward other Jews first and last. There is Max Blumenthal, whose enraged salvos against Jewish chauvinism earned him a flattering profile on the Iranian regime-financed Press TV, the most repulsive of all the English-language satellite broadcasters currently on the market. There is Philip Weiss, a blogger whose bitterly personal reflections on Jewish influence were, until quite recently, underwritten by the Nation magazine's Nation Institute ("I felt that the form demanded transparency about what I cared about, Jewish identity," Weiss wrote about his blog in the American Conservative). What Weiss means by "Jewish identity" was laid bare in a 2007 posting on his Mondoweiss blog, concerning journalist Seymour Hersh's contention that "Jewish money" was driving a new war fervor against Iran. Crowed Weiss: "This is a beautiful moment, too. Hersh is a progressive Jew. Now he is turning on other Jews. 'New York Jewish money,' he says. The soul-searching that I have called for within the Jewish community has begun!!!!"

To understand why such blatant expressions of antisemitism are no longer a cause for moral opprobrium, we have to examine the sociology that determines that Jews, in contrast to nearly every other minority group, sit squarely on the wrong side of the oppressor/oppressed dynamic and thereby make any Jewish complaints about bigotry inherently suspect. The origin of this warped thinking lies in the left's commitment to anticolonialism following the Second World War.[1] Frustrated by Marxist orthodoxies about class, and contemptuous of such bourgeois frivolities as individual rights, writers Frantz Fanon, Regis Debray, and others laid the foundations for a new politics based on identity. Native populations would never see the world clearly until they were liberated from the neuroses imposed on them by their white, Western colonizers. Through the revolutionary process, the colonized would become the masters of theircountries, their cultures, and – above all – their discourse. As it turned out, it was in the colonizing nations, among the disaffected students and intellectuals who swelled the ranks of the New Left, that the politics of identity were embraced most fervently. As Western progressives reassessed their own societies through the filter of identity, matters of sex and race were pushed to the fore. And when it came to defining and identifying racism and sexism, the inner logic of identity politics dictated that these words were the property of the victims. In our own time, these ownership rights have become largely uncontroversial, insofar as most minorities can expect a respectful hearing when it comes to claims of racism. With the Jews, however, the reverse is now true: Claims of antisemitism are so often disputed, scorned, and denied outright. This state of affairs faithfully reflects the perception of the Jews as socially privileged, disproportionately represented in the fields of glamour, intellect, and finance, and – crucially – as the agency behind the dispossession of Palestine's native Arab inhabitants.

This perception is not limited to the extreme left (nor, for that matter, to the far right, which thinks in near-identical terms). It now sits as comfortably with a traditional conservative realist like Mearsheimer as it does with many others who have had little interaction with the New Left or the Chomskyite school of international relations. It leads, furthermore, to a conclusion with a distinctly postmodern twist: Those who truly suffer from antisemitism today are not Jews, but those who are accused of being antisemitic. Those mere speakers of truth, so the thinking goes, are being made to pay for centuries of hateful prejudice. Adherents of anti-Zionism have traditionally avoided speaking about Jews *qua* Jews to dodge the antisemitism bullet. Atzmon observes no such niceties, happily telling an Israeli journalist in a recent interview that he "hates" Judaism, that neoconservative Jews are responsible for the global financial crisis, and – for good measure – that the death marches the Nazis forced the last remnants of concentration camp inmates to go on should properly be seen as a Jewish attempt to escape the advancing Red Army. That Erdogan, Mearsheimer, and numerous others – ranging from Tony Blair's estranged sister-in-law to a prominent Anglican Bishop – do not think the person who speaks such bile is to be avoided, lest his inarguable Jew-hatred be seen as infecting their own views, suggests the degree to which antisemitism has been normalized in the current political culture. Antisemitism's newfound respectability is not unprecedented. Indeed, the fact that anti-Semites have been given power over the definition of antisemitism reflects the very origins of the term. Coined in late 19-century Germany, *antisemitism* was not intended as a descriptor for a troubling social trend – like *racism*, or the more recent *Islamophobia* – but as the positive organizing principle of an emancipatory political movement. While the Jews and their allies regard anti-Semites as propelled by hatred, anti-Semites regard themselves as a fraternity bound by a message of universalist love. "This book is above all a book for friends, a book that is written for those who love us," wrote Edouard Drumont, one of the founders of

France's Ligue Antisemitique, and an especially shrill voice behind the false allegations of treason against Alfred Dreyfus, in his *Le Testament d'un Anti-semite*. Atzmon expresses himself with similar pretensions: "When you talk about humanity, you talk about a universal system of values promoting love for one another." Rather than being anti-moral, the moral sensibility of anti-semitism resides in its presentation of the Jews (or "Jewishness" or "Judaism") as the barrier to a society founded upon love. What seems at first glance to be a material battle is really a spiritual one. With this understanding, we can better appreciate a rare modification in the nature of antisemitism in our own time. I say rare, because, as a framework for interpreting the world, antisemitism resists innovation. Charles Maurras, another French anti-Semite, took great delight in hawking a worldview that "enables everything to be arranged, smoothed over, and simplified."

The modification rests upon a distinction between what I call *bierkeller* and *bistro* antisemitism. Bierkeller antisemitism – named for the beer halls frequented by the German Nazis – employs such means as violence, verbal abuse, commercial harassment, and advocacy of anti-Jewish legal measures. Certainly, the first and second generations of modern antisemitic publicists and intellectuals had no qualms about this sort of thuggery. Since the Second World War, though, this mode of antisemitism has waned sharply, along with the tendency to use the word *anti-Semite* as a positive means of political identification.

Bistro antisemitism, on the other hand, sits in a higher and outwardly more civilized realm, providing what left-wing activists would call a "safe space" to critically assess the global impact of Jewish cabals from Washington, D.C., to Jerusalem. Anyone who enters the bistro will encounter common themes. These include the depiction of Palestinians as the victims of a second Holocaust, the breaking of the silence supposedly imposed upon honest discussions of Jewish political and economic power, and the contention – offered by, among others, Mearsheimer's co-author, Stephen Walt, of Harvard – that American Jewish government officials are more suspect than others because of a potential second loyalty to Israel.

To this list we can now add the assault upon what Atzmon calls the "Holocaust narrative." This type of revisionism doesn't deny that the Nazis killed Jews, but it redistributes a good deal of the blame among the victims. Additionally, it disputes the conclusion of mainstream Holocaust historians that total elimination was the goal of the Third Reich's Jewish policy. All in all, then, the bistro satisfies admirably: Its denizens can confront the cabals of Jewish power unencumbered by the vulgar anti-Semite label, and, freed from the Judeocentrism the word Holocaust reinforces, they can also reevaluate the experience of Jews under Nazi rule. The prevalence of bistro antisemitism, which deals its blows through words rather than fists, is the clearest indicator of the Jewish failure to take ownership of the term originally invented by the enemies of the Jewish people. True, for a long period after 1945, there were hopeful signs that the tide was turning. Lifted by Israel's creation and its military prowess, Jewish communities in the Diaspora spoke and acted with an assertiveness unseen during the Holocaust. Notably, their campaign in behalf of the persecuted Jews of the Soviet Union was an unashamedly public one. The charge of Soviet antisemitism was leveled with confidence, and – outside the circles of Western Communists and their fellow-travelers – registered in the wider public domain with few objections, bolstering the conclusion that in free societies, antisemitism had at last been dealt a death blow. But that was then. Imagine, for a moment, that the Soviet Union was still in existence, still forbidding its Jews to emigrate, still barring them from sensitive jobs and higher education opportunities. Imagine, too, that the Soviets were still pumping out the propaganda of pamphleteers like Trofim Kichko – a clear precursor to Atzmon – who wrote, in Judaism and Zionism, of the connection between the Torah, the "morality of Judaism," and Israeli "aggression." Would a Jewish advocate, standing before a learned liberal audience, be able to categorize these as instances of antisemitism with the same ease that a Muslim civil-rights advocate could expect in an equivalent circumstance?

No, of course not. Actually, were he still alive, it would be entirely plausible that Kichko would be on a speaking tour of North American and European campuses. An army of professors, commentators, and student activists would line up to shield this progressive intellectual from the smear of antisemitism – aided, no doubt, by those self-consciously Jewish leftists whom Kichko reviled, just as Gilad Atzmon does. The use of antisemitism denial as a technique of antisemitism comes to the Western bistros in part from the Arab and Muslim worlds, where rampant antisemitism resulted in the wholesale expulsion of Jewish communities from Arab countries in the latter half of the 20th century. We have all heard the ludicrous platitude that the Arabs, as "Semites," can't possibly be antisemitic. We have heard – endlessly – about the unparalleled tolerance of the Islamic world. And we have grimaced before those spokesmen who whisper that the Arabs of Palestine "are the Jews of the Jews," the final victims of the Holocaust and the most tragic of all. All these lines of argument reject the very possibility of Arab antisemitism, deflecting any moral censure onto those who argue otherwise.

In America, too, the practice of antisemitism denial is older than one might believe. In his fascinating study, The Third Reich in the Ivory Tower, Stephen H. Norwood reveals the wide-ranging sympathy for Nazi Germany on American campuses. Norwood offers an especially relevant account of how the president of Columbia University at the time, Nicholas Murray Butler, dismissed the campus demonstrations that greeted Hans Luther, Nazi Germany's ambassador to the United States, as an uncouth smear campaign.

When it comes to antisemitism, American universities have too often found that there is honor not in opposing it, but in fawning before it or "speaking truth to power" by denying it. The realization that Harvard's Alan Dershowitz is the only famous academic to have confronted Mearsheimer says more about his peers than anything else could. Similar trends are evident in liberal and leftist media and policy circles. As in the ivory tower, in the field of policy debate these skirmishes conform to a pattern: First, make a wildly hyperbolic statement about Israel or the "Israel Lobby." Second, prepare to be denounced as an anti-Semite. Third, assume the role of the victim – one more example proving yet again that the Jews can't be trusted to diagnose what constitutes antisemitism. Time and again, this strategy of deflecting and denying antisemitism has proved reliable. Following the recent controversy over claims by Josh Block, a former AIPAC spokesman, that left-wing outfits like Media Matters and the Center for American Progress are pushing the dual-loyalty canard with growing brashness, the commentator David Frum wondered "whether it is more unacceptable inside today's liberal Washington to use the language of antisemitism – or to protest the language of antisemitism." Frum got his answer when Block was relieved of his title at the progressive Truman National Security project for issuing group e-mails citing Jew-baiters in the left-wing media. The vilification of Block leaves little doubt about the answer. In the eyes of liberal pundits, his deception was unmasked the moment he introduced the charge of antisemitism. Only a few days after Block raised his concerns, the New York Times columnist Thomas Friedman asserted that the standing ovation that Israeli Prime Minister Benjamin Netanyahu received from Congress was "bought and paid for by the Israel lobby." Not to be outdone, Time columnist Joe Klein, in a sympathetic nod to isolationist Republican Presidential candidate Ron Paul, weighed in against sending "American kids off to war, yet again, to fight for Israel's national security." Although Friedman later regretted his phrasing – it would have been better to have said the ovation was "engineered," he said – neither he nor Klein faced the kind of deafening censure that would have greeted similar barbs directed at another minority. That these two barometers of accepted center-left rhetoric felt safe writing such things shows just how effective the work of the bistro has been.

In the face of the unfolding reality I have outlined, the scholars, journalists, and Jewish community officials who track the troughs and peaks of antisemitism have not been impassive. In 2004, their efforts culminated in a noteworthy milestone. The European Union Monitoring Center (EUMC) published its "working definition" of antisemitism, thereby launching a counteroffensive against the antisemitic revival that was found in distilled form at the UN's 2001 "anti-racism" conference in the South African city of Durban. At the heart of the definition lay this statement: "Antisemitism is a certain perception of Jews, which may be expressed as hatred toward Jews. Rhetorical and physical manifestations of antisemitism are directed toward Jewish or non-Jewish individuals and/or their property, toward Jewish community institutions and religious facilities." The declaration is imperfectly worded: To the uninitiated, there is a head-scratching fogginess in the sentence, later on, that "antisemitism...is often used to blame Jews for 'why things go wrong.'" Nonetheless, the definition was a valiant attempt, early on in the fight, to reestablish antisemitism as the oldest and most enduring of bigotries. Many of the favored themes of bistro antisemitism – Jewish power, Holocaust analogies, the denial of Israel's legal and historical legitimacy – were purposefully included in the definition as illustrations of how contemporary antisemitic discourse operates.

Not long after the working definition began percolating, Yale upped the stakes by announcing the Yale Interdisciplinary Initiative for the Study of Antisemitism (YIISA). Through a series of papers, seminars, and conferences, YIISA tackled the problems identified in the EUMC working definition with gusto. One publication laid bare the antisemitic provenance of the campaign among British academics to boycott Israeli universities. Several more focused on the woefully under-researched subject of antisemitism in Palestinian and wider Arab society. Taken together, the EUMC definition and the research carried out by YIISA indicated that at least one antisemitic fantasy – that Jews and their allies control, as Mearsheimer and Walt put it, the "public discourse" about U.S. Middle East policy and the antisemitism charge – might just become reality. At minimum, the imprimatur of both the European Union and an Ivy League school would underline that antisemitism, whether in the academy, in international affairs, or on the streets of a Parisian banlieue, is a genuine presence and not another nefarious Jewish hoax. The grand scale of these ambitions only magnifies their eventual defeat. Who talks about the EUMC "working definition" of antisemitism? Virtually no one. And Yale closed down its antisemitism initiative in the early summer of 2011. The previous year, the initiative had staged a conference that featured a presentation on antisemitism's role in shaping Palestinian identity. The PLO representative in Washington, Ma'en Areikat, accused Yale of having been hijacked by pro-Israel lobbyists masquerading as academics. Areikat's ire encouraged those Yale social scientists who resented the new initiative's existence to speak their minds. It was hit with the charge that its true allegiance was to the state of Israel, instead of its sponsoring university. Having been turned into its own case study of dual loyalty, the Yale initiative was then reproached for treating the ideal of academic rigor with cavalier disregard. Donald Green, the director of Yale's Institute for Social and Policy Studies, deemed that the initiative had "failed to meet high standards for research and instruction," sealing its fate. There is, of course, no disputing that the Yale initiative's scholarship was informed by certain basic arguments: that antisemitism is a social curse; that its reliably consistent content is perpetuated in an array of more or less obvious forms; and that, in the present climate, the Muslim world offers it an environment more hospitable and promising than any other. In that sense, the Yale initiative was little different from other academic exercises in social inquiry, particularly those concerned with matters of racial prejudice and colonial history.

Good social scientists understand that neutrality is an unattainable state. It is perfectly acceptable for social enquiry to carry value-based assumptions, so long as its propositions are sufficiently credible to be tested. That includes those propositions that disturb the unspoken biases that become entrenched in academic research. By tossing this consideration aside in its evaluation of the Yale Interdisciplinary Initiative for the Study of Antisemitism, Yale undercut the very academic standards it was supposedly protecting. Almost 70 years after the Holocaust, the prospect that a definition of antisemitism, as understood by its victims, might one day emerge uncontested seems as remote as ever. In his notorious peroration on "the big lie" in 1925, Adolf Hitler wrote: "From time immemorial...the Jews have known better than any others how falsehood and calumny can be exploited. Is not their very existence founded on one great lie?" In discussing the use of deceit as an element of statecraft, Hitler was actually describing the methods he would use to achieve power and maintain his stranglehold on it. Today's anti-Semites deploy similar logic in asserting their authority to choke off discussions of their own infamy.

The truth is that the rising fixation with Jewish power in our time has unwittingly revealed Jewish emasculation instead. Jews do not control the discourse; rather, the discourse controls them. Nonetheless, if we accept that antisemitism has, by exchanging violence for discourse, also been emasculated, does its persistence matter, particularly during a period of history that stands out through the presence of a Jewish state and the absence of antisemitic legislation in nearly all the countries where Jews live? That question can be posed in another way: Do we need to sink to the depths of the 1930s in order for antisemitism to be taken seriously? Furthermore, we must ask, do Jews need to be subjected to acts of violence and discrimination in order to remind the wider world who the true victims of antisemitism are? And even then, can we be confident that the blame for physical manifestations of antisemitism will be placed upon the anti-Semites and not the Jews? The answer, judged on today's trends, is sadly negative. The anti-Semite who avoids violence has no reservations about enabling, excusing, and rationalizing it. Israel, the supreme embodiment of Jewishness, would ultimately be held culpable for a pogrom in Istanbul, or, for that matter, in Tehran or Caracas, in which the protagonists carried signs and chanted slogans about the suffering of the Palestinians. By the same token, should the Holocaust-deniers and conspiracy theorists massed along Israel's borders launch a war of extermination against it, we can be assured that this same theory of culpability would be articulated even more brazenly. Since the Holocaust, Jewish communities have mistakenly concluded that the relative absence of antisemitism reflects a greater awareness that antisemitism, as understood and experienced by Jews themselves, is a grave social ill. There is no basis to think that anymore. As long as the adversaries and enemies of the Jews control the meaning of the term antisemitism, Jews will remain vulnerable to that most sacred of antisemitic calumnies: that they alone are the authors of their own misfortune.

Footnotes

1 Leftist support for the establishment of Israel in the 1930s and 1940s was itself a species of anticolonialism; Jews were seen as staging an assault on British colonialism and were therefore to be encouraged.

Scholarship and Antisemitism at Yale

Jewish Ideas Daily, March 26, 2012

Almost a year has passed since Yale University shuttered the five-year-old Yale Interdisciplinary Initiative for the Study of Antisemitism, known by the unwieldy acronym "YIISA," and replaced it with the Yale Program for the

Study of Antisemitism, or "YPSA." The organizational shuffle produced a torrent of criticism in the Jewish and general press. But nine months later, there is virtual radio silence about the new YPSA program. So, how is it doing? And how does its approach differ from that of YIISA? Yale asserted that it closed the old YIISA because the program paid too much attention to political advocacy and not enough to rigorous scholarship. Yet, as Alex Joffe noted in these pages at the time, YIISA's scholarly product differed little from the output of other Yale programs that continue to flourish. Others said that YIISA signed its own death warrant by staging a 2010 conference focused on Muslim antisemitism. James Kirchick related an anecdote told to him by YIISA's director, Charles Small, who delivered the keynote. Small's mother was there, beaming with pride. As Small left his seat for the podium, he whispered to her, "Ma, this is the beginning of the end."

Sure enough, the PLO's Washington representative complained about the conference's depiction of Palestinian antisemitism. The PLO protest was widely viewed as a factor in YIISA's demise. Critics also linked Yale's anxieties about YIISA to its efforts to raise its profile in the Middle East, and its regret at losing out to Harvard and Georgetown on a $20 million gift from Saudi Prince Alwaleed Bin Talal for an Islamic studies center. Against this background, dead Jews – victims of crusades, pogroms, the Shoah – were safer objects of study than live ones. Maurice Samuels, the director of the replacement program, YPSA, specializes in 19th-century French literary and cultural history. When Samuels was appointed, some asked whether he had the right academic background for the job. "Modern antisemitism was arguably born in 19th-century France," he told me recently. "Today, France is on the front lines of the 'new antisemitism.'" A few days after Samuels made this observation, the al-Qaeda terrorist Mohamed Merah gunned down a teacher and three children at a Jewish school in Toulouse. I asked Samuels about a comment by Yale's Jewish chaplain, James Ponet, in which he emphasized that the study of antisemitism has particular value for the light it sheds upon "other hatreds and prejudices that are operative in the world now." Samuels did not disavow Ponet's position: "What he says is true and admirable, in its belief that the study of antisemitism has broad humanistic appeal." But Samuels was firm that antisemitism is not just another hatred: "The religious and economic dimensions of Jew-hatred are pretty unique, as are the current ideological dimensions. Antisemitism has provided a total worldview in a way that other racisms have not." When asked about YPSA's research focus, Samuels cited his own work on "the interplay of philo-Semitism and antisemitism in France from the French Revolution to the present," as well as work by YPSA scholars on the Eastern European Holocaust, the association of Jews "with myths about the origin of credit in the early modern period," and the psychology of antisemitism and racism.

"I don't want to make comparisons with YIISA," Samuels told me. However, his YPSA colleague, Yale sociologist Jeffrey Alexander, who once compared YIISA to a center for the study of racism that was run by Black Panthers, continues to stress the difference between YPSA and its predecessor. For instance, Alexander told me, while the mullahs' antisemitism plays a critical role in Iran's attitude toward Israel, YIISA's emphasis on Iran reflected Israel's foreign policy imperatives. YIISA's consorting with scholars who ascribed the worst intentions to Iran "just pushes people away," he said. "When you get someone talking like that, it becomes a political talk about mobilizing the Left against Iran. It's not an academic analysis of antisemitism."

Alexander also distinguished YPSA from YIISA on the question of antisemitism in Western politics. When I asked him whether YPSA was in a position to bring clarity to the current controversy around the term "Israel-Firster," he replied, "YPSA as a corporate entity would not speak in that way, that's a difference with YIISA. There are many groups that need to monitor these controversies, but YPSA isn't doing that right now." Both Samuels and Alexander insisted that YPSA is engaged with current issues – for example, "the first systematic study," as Samuels described it, "of the representation of the 'other' in Palestinian and Israeli textbooks." I asked Alexander whether he saw parity between representations of Arabs in Israeli textbooks and the bloodcurdling portraits of Jews in textbooks across the Middle East. "I wouldn't say there's parity," he answered, but "there's a mutually-reinforcing circle of distrust. Everything seems to be a self-fulfilling prophecy." Samuels and Alexander reject the idea that they are shying away from Muslim antisemitism. Both share the conviction that YPSA must eschew political partisanship in its investigations of such issues. Nonetheless, their stance raises questions: Is YPSA a neutered version of YIISA, filtering the virulence of Islamic antisemitism through the prevailing sensibilities of current Western social science? Can one properly study prejudice without adopting certain normative assumptions? Walter Reich – psychiatrist, George Washington University professor, former Holocaust Museum director, and a member of the former YIISA board of advisers – acknowledges the value of YPSA's scholarly concerns but sounds a warning: "A university program on antisemitism that does not pay due scholarly attention to the origins, nature, purposes, and goals of today's antisemitism would not be a serious undertaking," even if paying such attention "provokes criticism from, say, the political Left, or from those who oppose Israel." Reich thinks "perhaps two or three years must pass before we can judge whether or not YPSA has struck a fair scholarly balance between the antisemitism of the past and the antisemitism of the present and the future." Were the old YIISA still in existence, there would be no doubt about the passionate tone of its future work. The new YPSA has yet to prove whether, in assessing antisemitism, calmer is better.

U.S. academic controversy could shed light on future of antisemitism studies

Ha'aretz, May 14, 2012

How should the study of prejudice, including antisemitism, be approached in an academic setting? American universities have traditionally shed more heat than light on this knotty question, as an ongoing and bitter controversy involving the field of black studies demonstrates. A couple of weeks ago, Naomi Schaefer Riley, a prominent writer on education, posted a spirited and provocatively-worded critique of black studies on the website of the Chronicle of Higher Education, the leading U.S. publication covering the university sector. Highlighting the loaded claims of certain black studies scholars, Riley lambasted the discipline for its in-built political bias. "Let some legitimate scholars find solutions to the problems of blacks in America," she concluded. "Solutions that don't begin and end with 'blame the white man.'" As one might expect, Riley's article caused an uproar, not just in black studies departments, but among liberal academics and commentators more generally. Less anticipated was the subsequent decision of the Chronicle to expel Riley from its pool of writers. Thus far, the clash over Riley's article has not spilled over into the similarly polarizing debate in academic circles over antisemitism. Nonetheless, there are striking parallels between the two.

Riley's fundamental objection to black studies is based, as she put it in a piece for the Wall Street Journal, on her assessment that it "is a cause, not a course of study." Very much the same charge was leveled, in 2011, at Yale University's institute devoted to the study of antisemitism, known as YIISA. In YIISA's case, however, the complaint of political bias compromising academic integrity was principally articulated by liberals. Even more significantly, YIISA was shuttered after only five years of operation, whereas black studies departments remain open for business at several universities across the United States. YIISA's emphasis on the influence of antisemitism on political attitudes in the Muslim world, as well as on the presence of traditional antisemitic themes in the discourse of Western opponents of Zionism, won the institute few friends in the left-leaning universe of American social science (by contrast, the seminars organized by its successor program, known as YPSA, are far less controversial.). And it is certainly true that YIISA's overall tone was highly politicized – its interventions on Iran and its collaboration with Jewish defense organizations breached, in the eyes of many critics, the line between academia and advocacy.

Yet the political convictions that informed YIISA's work were no more pronounced than those prevailing in black studies departments – and, indeed, related disciplines like women's studies, with its emphasis on the negative effects of "patriarchy," and Middle East studies, which has routinized the belief that Israel is a racist, colonial enterprise. Why the apparent double standard? One answer is that YIISA challenged the dominant consensus on antisemitism, just as Riley did with black studies. Both did so in a bold, even aggressive, manner that the ivory tower found unsettling. Both shared the punishment of exclusion as a consequence. Which brings us back to the opening question: what is the role of the university in the study of prejudice? Clearly, neutrality cannot be the point of departure. In recognizing the existence of prejudice, we recognize at the same time that it is a problem which needs to be addressed and managed.

A good example is the work of Professor Deborah Lipstadt on Holocaust denial. In her book on the subject, she argues that her research was essential to prevent deniers from gaining influence as the immediate memory of the Shoah began to fade. In academic parlance, this method would be described as "normative" – we should do x to prevent y – and is no less legitimate because of it. But it is a method that becomes dangerous when the normative assumptions close off potential avenues of inquiry, or when dissenting views are shut down. Israel's opponents are fond of saying that charges of antisemitism are fabricated solely to smear them; in challenging that widely-held view, YIISA went against the grain. Meanwhile, Riley's unorthodox doubts about black studies resulted in a slew of ad hominem attacks on her, some of which were – even in their own words – downright silly. If American universities are to make a serious contribution to the study of prejudice, these censorious antics need to stop. At the moment, we are learning more about the prejudices of academics then we are about prejudice in the wider society. For every minority – African-Americans, Jews, Latinos and others – that's bad news.

Ben Cohen

Antisemitism is toxic, whether intentional or not

Haaretz, August 2, 2012

Barely a week goes by without a fresh controversy involving the word "antisemitism." And every time antisemitism rears its head, it is agonizingly clear that there is little consensus on what this most ancient of prejudices means in our own time. Two articles from the last month illustrate this point. The first, by Amira Hass in Haaretz, argued that the researchers who monitor antisemitic incidents were ignoring assaults by Jewish residents of the West Bank on neighboring Palestinian Arabs, whom she referred to as "Semites," and contended that the assaults could thus be termed "antisemitic". By expanding the definition of who can be a victim of antisemitism, Hass removed, in a single stroke, its historic association with Jews alone.

The second article, by Anna Breslaw in the U.S. Jewish magazine Tablet, centered on the author's disturbing confession of her dislike for, and distrust of, the survivors of the Holocaust. Thanks to Breslaw's unfiltered candor – which included the approving use of the word Judenscheisse, an old German slur linking Jews with excrement – people normally on polar opposite sides of the antisemitism debate found themselves united in condemning her words as brashly and crudely antisemitic. On the right, John Podhoretz, the editor of Commentary magazine, described Breslaw's article as "the most egregious piece of antisemitic filth in years," while on the left, Katha Pollitt of The Nation – a magazine that has not shied away from portraying accusations of antisemitism as cheap, politically-motivated smears – tweeted her regret that she and Podhoretz found themselves in agreement.

So is the meaning of antisemitism as elastic as Hass implies? Or is it simply that we know it when we see it, as the furious reaction to the Breslaw piece suggests? The word itself is the most sensible starting point. "Antisemitism" was not a word coined by Jews, but by anti-Semites in late 19th century Germany. A bizarre assortment of third-rate thinkers, most notably the rabble-rouser Wilhelm Marr, sought to reinvent Christian hostility to Judaism for a secular era as a scientifically valid theory of race.

As the historian Leon Poliakov noted in writing about Marr, there was an air of envy embedded in his 1879 work, "The Victory of Judaism over Germanism," in which an emphasis on supposed Jewish racial characteristics melded with a fantasy about the extraordinary power of the Jews. "You will not be able to stop the great mission of Semitism," Marr wrote bombastically.

By "Semitism," Marr meant not the speakers of Semitic languages, nor the members of the non-existent "Semitic" race. He was speaking specifically of Jews. Why, then, the attempt to expand antisemitism's remit to include Arabs? Why not simply employ the term "racism" in any discussion of discrimination faced by individuals of Arab origin? A generous interpretation would put this down to a misuse of the term "Semitic." However, the historical record demonstrates that the deployment of the word "antisemitism" in an Arab context is a long-established technique aimed at forcing the Jews to share it with another people for whom it was never intended.

Everyone has heard or read some variation of the theme, "We are Semites, so how dare you call us anti-Semites," from Arab sources. The method underlying this protestation is fairly easy to decipher: Firstly, the acknowledgement that, especially since the Holocaust, it is no longer respectable to call oneself an anti-Semite, even while pushing antisemitic ideas; secondly, the insinuation that there is an equivalence between the historic persecution suffered by Jewish communities all over the world and the fate of the Arabs of Palestine in 1948; thirdly, the implication that antisemitism is a smear casually tossed out to strip the harshest critics of Zionism and Israel of their credibility, including "Semites" themselves. One might say that the distinguishing feature of antisemitism in this age of Jewish empowerment – by which I mean that a Jewish state exists, and that the vast majority of Jews live in countries free of discriminatory legislation – is that it is coded. Expressions like "Israel-Firster" (the notion that Jews are more loyal to Israel than to the countries of which they are citizens) have a definitively pejorative feel, but those who deploy them invariably bristle at the charge that they are trafficking in older, more noxious tropes.

Which brings us to Anna Breslaw. Perhaps the greatest disservice her piece performed was that it enabled those pundits who normally sneer at any mention of antisemitism, and who are often accused of antisemitism themselves, an easy opportunity to declare their disgust at what she wrote. This group includes the Jewish blogger, M.J. Rosenberg, who has done more than anyone else in America to popularize the term "Israel-Firster." In a recent blog entry bemoaning the link drawn between antisemitism and anti-Zionism, Rosenberg conceded that the word "antisemitism" is meaningful "...to real victims of antisemitism like those French kids in France who were killed because they are (sic) Jewish." He then went on to declare: "It is not about Israel." Assuming that the "French kids" Rosenberg refers to are the ones slaughtered at a Toulouse Jewish school by a self-professed al-Qaeda terrorist, it is quite absurd to argue that the issue of Israel is unrelated, as even the most superficial understanding of contemporary Islamism would grasp. (Osama Bin Laden himself, in an October 2002 'letter to America,' called Israel's creation a "crime which must be erased," before adding that the "people of Palestine are pure Arabs and original Semites.") But the over-riding point is this: Hatred of Jews qua Jews, particularly in the type of lan-guage used by Anna Breslaw, is the only time when antisemitism can be called by its name. Everything else is an invention. This semantic game has enabled the ugliest themes of traditional antisemitism – notably, the sinister tribal imperatives at work in the activities of the "Israel Lobby" – to estab-lish themselves in apparently respectable discourse. It is a game, moreover, that has worked. Hence the paradox: The more coded the words are, the more dangerous they are. The 2006 book The Israel Lobby by Professors John Mearsheimer and Stephen Walt – slammed by the prominent commen-tator Walter Russel Mead as "a book that anti-Semites will love, but it is not necessarily an antisemitic book" – has been infinitely more influential than Anna Breslaw's article could ever be, and has encouraged readers to think of Jewish power as shadowy and unaccountable.

What all this proves is that a writer can enable antisemitism irrespec-tive of whether that was his or her intention. What this also proves is that, as far as a large swathe of writers and intellectuals are concerned, antisemit-ism can only be identified as such if it comes in the form of a Mein Kampf-like screed against Jews. In 2012, as in 1879, the Jews themselves do not own the word "antisemitism," even as they experience its real-world effects.

Lambs to the Slaughter

Jewish Ideas Daily, August 22, 2012

Last week, the normally cautious Jewish community of Amsterdam took the unusual step of describing a member of the Dutch parliament as a "serious danger to Jews in the Netherlands and consequently Europe as a whole." For anyone who follows the twists and turns of Jewish political fortunes in Eu-rope, such warnings do not come as a huge surprise. From the far-Right Jobbik Party in Hungary to the far-Left Respect Party in Britain, the list of Jew-baiters holding elected office is getting longer and longer. But this time the member of parliament in question belongs to the *Partij voor de Vrijheid* (PVV), or Party for Freedom, which touts itself as the most passionate advo-cate for Israel in Europe. The PVV's flamboyant leader, Geert Wilders, is no stranger to Jewish gatherings in Israel and the United States, where he has succeeded in raising both money and political support. Until now, Wilders has made opposition to what he calls the "Islamization" of the Netherlands the centerpiece of his politics, and his bombastic message about the perils of Muslim immigration into Europe has struck a chord with the less nuanced sectors of the Jewish Right. (The nearest American equivalent to Wilders is his friend Pamela Geller, a blogger and activist who speaks in similarly apocalyptic terms about the "Islamization" of the United States.)

But Wilders's appeal to Jews is on the verge of being irreparably damaged by his continuing endorsement of one of the PVV's parliamentarians, Dion Graus. Two years ago, Graus championed a legal offensive in the Dutch parliament against *sh'hitah*, the Jewish ritual method of slaughtering animals for kosher consumption. While the Dutch Senate threw out that bill, many Dutch Jews fear that a successful turnout for the PVV at next month's general election will enable Graus to move on to his next target: circumcision. The continuing influence of Graus over Wilders motivated Wim Kortenoeven, a Dutch parliamentarian who resigned from the PVV earlier this year, to visit New York at the beginning of August. Kortenoeven believes that the pro-Israel groups and individuals in America who have backed Wilders – he names David Horowitz of *FrontPage* magazine and Professor Daniel Pipes as examples – are not sufficiently aware of the threat that Graus poses to Dutch Jews, largely because they find the PVV's pro-Israel positions so appealing. Though not Jewish himself, Kortenoeven is well-known to Dutch Jews as a Middle East analyst whose sympathies lie solidly with Israel. Between 2000 and 2010, Kortenoeven worked for the Dutch organization CIDI, the main provider of pro-Israel information and analysis in the Netherlands. At the end of 2008, Wilders, keen to burnish his foreign policy credentials, invited Kortenoeven to join the PVV's parliamentary slate. Over coffee at a Manhattan hotel during his visit, Kortenoeven told me that he hesitated for several months before accepting Wilders's offer. The catalyst, he said, was a remark his youngest son made when the two vacationed together in Pennsylvania in the summer of 2009. Hearing his father grumbling about the state of Dutch politics as he read the news on his laptop, the younger Kortenoeven implored him to put up or shut up.

Kortenoeven duly accepted Wilders's offer, entering parliament for the PVV in 2010. At the time, a bill to curb *sh'hitah* had been unveiled in the Dutch parliament, but Kortenoeven never thought that it would be a complicating factor in his relations with his new colleagues, since its sponsors came from a different party (to be specific, the Party for Animal Rights). In the event, Graus turned out to be the most energetic backer of the bill. In a televised debate with Benoit Wesly, the head of the Jewish community in Maastricht, Graus, who became notorious in Holland for allegations that he savagely beat his pregnant wife, accused Jews of engaging in the "ritual torture" of animals. Wesly countered by reminding Graus that his mother had fled Nazi Germany for Holland in order to survive as a Jew, and that one of Hitler's first acts after he became Chancellor in 1933 was to ban *sh'hitah*. Against this background, an open clash between Graus and Kortenoeven was inevitable. During an April 2011 meeting of the PVV's parliamentarians, Kortenoeven challenged Graus on the *sh'hitah* issue, and encountered a furious response. Sitting at the other end of a long table, Graus leapt to his feet, waving a huge sheaf of papers. "I thought he was going to hit me," Kortenoeven recalled. "Graus slammed the papers on the table. 'Here are all the arguments to support the legislation!' he screamed at me, two inches from my face." As Kortenoeven tells the story, neither Wilders nor the other parliamentarians challenged Graus's outburst, shuffling nervously instead. That reaction, Kortenoeven said, was consistent with Wilders's previous refusals to confront Graus. On another occasion in 2011, when Kortenoeven told Wilders that Graus's attacks on *sh'hitah* were endangering relations with Dutch Jews, the PVV leader snapped back, "How can I stop him! He already said this 5 or 6 times!" "He was enraged," Kortenoeven reflected. "He'd lost control over Graus."

The question, therefore, is why Wilders continues to tolerate Graus. Kortenoeven believes that Graus, who produced a television documentary about Wilders, may have come across sensitive information that could compromise the PVV leader. The same blackmail theory is the subject of a forthcoming book by Marcial Hernandez, another PVV parliamentarian who resigned from the party at the same time as Kortenoeven. *Wilders Unmasked: From Messiah to Political Parasite* – Kortenoeven explains that the title refers to Wilders raising money from American Jews while betraying Dutch Jews – will hit the stores a week before the Dutch elections. Beyond Graus himself, how can the apparent crisis of identity within the PVV – supporting Israel on the one hand, backing anti-Jewish measures on the other – be explained? I asked Kortenoeven whether the real targets of the PVV on the issues of ritual slaughter and circumcision were Dutch Muslims, who number one million, rather than Jews, who total just 30,000. Kortenoeven was adamant that Jews were the primary targets, pointing out that Muslims permit the stunning of animals in the production of halal meat, a method that the opponents of *sh'hitah* agree to. On the issue of circumcision, he argued that Muslim males can be circumcised until the age of 13, by which time they are capable of voicing an objection. No such objection is possible when it comes to Jews, because of the halakhic requirement that circumcision be carried out on a male child eight days after his birth.

Kortenoeven believes that the PVV's focus is shifting away from European Muslims toward a rejection of the European Union – a long-favored theme of European nationalists, including Dion Graus. Following 9/11, there was something of a realignment on the European Right. Writers and politicians opposed to Islamism as a political movement found themselves alongside more traditional right-wing nationalists, many of them propagators of anti-semitic credos. That, he concludes, bodes ill for Jews in Holland and elsewhere in Europe, but the message will only register if the American Jews enthused by Wilders and the PVV pay heed.

Europe's Assault on Jewish Ritual

Commentary, November 2012

On July 21, 600 German doctors appended their signatures to a letter in the Frankfurter Allgemeine newspaper calling for the practice of circumcision to be outlawed. In depicting circumcision as a form of bodily harm imposed by adults on powerless children, the doctors asserted that "religious freedom cannot be a blank check for sexual violence against underage boys." The letter was published less than a month after a district court in the city of Cologne ruled that circumcision is a criminal act. Both the small German Jewish community and its much larger Muslim counterpart expressed outrage at the decision. In a rare show of unity, their leaders jointly protested the ruling with a series of statements, interviews, and modestly attended public rallies. German politicians, too, weighed in anxiously, foremost among them Chancellor Angela Merkel, who articulated the fear that Germany risked turning itself into a "laughingstock" by preventing Jews from carrying out this most sacred ritual. Merkel has a point, to say the least: A country that forbids Jews from performing the Brit Milah upon their sons, in accordance with the injunction passed from God to Abraham in Genesis, is a country where Jews cannot live. By August, the circumcision ruling had found its first target for prosecution. Rabbi David Goldberg, a mohel (an individual licensed under Jewish law to perform circumcision) who serves the tiny Jewish community of Hof in northern Bavaria, was charged with causing bodily harm. "This latest development in Hof is yet another grave affront to religious freedom and underlines the urgent need for the German government to expedite the process of ensuring that the fundamental rights of minority communities are protected," declared Rabbi Pinchas Goldschmidt, of the Conference of European Rabbis, in response. "We call upon the minister of the interior to take immediate action to secure those rights in the short term."

The spectacle of anguished German Jews scurrying to protect their religious rights from further encroachment has the flavor of a literary thought experiment, a "Plot Against America" transferred to German soil. The proposition that circumcision might be outlawed in Germany – Germany! – less than a century after the Nuremberg Laws, Kristallnacht, and the mass extermination of Europe's Jews still strikes one as a warped fantasy even after its reality has become clear. And that may explain why Germany's traditionally nuanced and cautious Jews have had to confront their deepest fears. "I seriously have to ask myself whether this country still wants us," wrote Charlotte Knobloch, the former head of the German Central Council of Jews, in a raw commentary for the *Süddeutsche Zeitung*.

"To me, it seems there is clearly a latent desire among parts of the German population to attack the practices of minority religions," Rabbi Walter Rothschild told the *Wall Street Journal*. So panicked was the German government by the thought that circumcision might be outlawed that, in early October, it announced it would push through legislation to protect circumcisions performed by specially trained professionals, including mohels. That such a measure is necessary speaks to the depth of public opposition to circumcision. "The circumcision debate sometimes turned very hostile, which was not rationally explicable," said Dieter Graumann, the president of the Central Council of Jews in Germany. "Nowhere else in the world was this issue debated with such sharpness, coldness and sometimes brutal intolerance." Across Europe, there is a new assault on the legitimacy of Jewish ritual. While the attempt in Germany to turn the legal screws on circumcision is the assault's most historically resonant example, other countries, among them the Netherlands, Norway, and Sweden, have also sought to place Jewish religious customs and traditions – notably *shechita*, the halachically sanctioned method of slaughtering animals for kosher consumption – outside of the laws of the land. When it comes to examining this anti-ritual trend, two interpretations are dominant. First, that the objection to ritual practice is rooted in the so-called culture wars that have played out in the ethnically and religiously diverse societies that emerged in Europe after the Second World War. Writing in the *Washington Post*, Michael Gerson efficiently summarized the elements of this dispute, which places individual rights and communal norms in direct competition. "It is the role of the state to defend individual self-determination against oppressive institutions, including religious institutions," Gerson explained, in an article viscerally objecting to the Cologne court's ruling. "Since circumcision is coerced, it is [deemed] unjust." Second, the attack on ritual is understood as an attack on Jews and Muslims in equal measure. Indeed, a related argument holds that Muslims are the real targets of anti-ritual legislation, in which the Jews represent unfortunate, but unavoidable, collateral damage. On the surface, there is some merit to this last view. Democracies are, in theory, obliged to couch restrictive laws in the most general terms possible, since to mark out a single community amounts to discrimination. The contention that the anti-ritual trend is primarily anti-Islam is strengthened by the demographic statistics: The Jewish population in Europe, including Russia, stands at around 2 million, while the number of Muslims in the European Union alone is estimated to be as high as 25 million. In political terms, Europe's Jewish leaders have always been satisfactorily accommodating, unlike various European Muslim communal groups, many of them ideologically and institutionally tied to the Muslim Brotherhood. In that light, it is surely no accident that the political parties that have sounded the most dire warnings about creeping Sharia law in Europe, such as the Freedom Party in Holland and the Swiss People's Party, have been at the forefront of the surge in anti-ritual sentiment. Yet just as Europe's Muslims cannot be airbrushed out of the anti-ritual narrative, it is a grave error to regard the Jews as its accidental victims, especially against the background of a revival in European antisemitism. Hostility toward Jewish ritual long predates the arrival of a multicultural Europe. Therefore, one must ask a question that is at once sensible and provocative: How, if at all, does the attack on ritual pertain to the common targeting of European Jews for their affiliations with Israel and Zionism? To begin with, the statements made in Germany against circumcision strikingly echo those of left-wing anti-Zionists, particularly when it comes to deflecting the accusation of antisemitism. Consider the words of Holm Putzke, a professor at the law department of the University of Passau, in support of the Cologne court's ruling: "The court has, in contrast to many politicians, not allowed itself to be scared by the fear of being criticized as antisemitic or opposed to religion."

The accusation of antisemitism as an intimidatory tactic has become a commonplace in Germany, much as it has in America and elsewhere in Europe. The German novelist Günter Grass argued much the same thing in his recent poem "What Must Be Said," bemoaning the prospect of an Israeli attack on Iran. Included in one verse of the poem was the clumsily sarcastic phrase, "verdict, 'antisemitism,'" as an explanation for German reluctance to criticize Israel. The core message is unmistakable: Whether the topic at hand is Israeli foreign policy or the ancient religious rites of the Jewish people, critics will invariably be silenced by the invocation of antisemitism. Anticipating this tactic – by portraying it as a red herring designed to turn attention away from the critical imperative of protecting the bodies of defenseless children from the backward customs of their parents – is one means of defeating it. Another is to find an individual of Jewish origin to prop up the anti-ritual position. In their crusade against Israel, anti-Zionists have recognized the importance of praising Jews who damn their brethren, and again, this has not been lost on the anti-ritualists. In the letter to the *Frankfurter Allgemeine* signed by the 600 doctors, special mention was made of an Israeli, Jonathan Enosch, who is opposed to circumcision. Enosch is an activist with a minuscule group in Israel, Ben Shalem (Hebrew for "intact son"), that also characterizes the ritual as a form of abuse. This largely unknown individual the German doctors nonetheless elevated to the status of prophet, in much the same way Palestinian advocates present anti-Zionist Jews as courageous revealers of truth to a stiff-necked people who will not bend. At the same time, it can be countered that however significant these overlaps in argumentation might be, they are not mirrored in organizational terms, as the antiritualists are not exclusively based in the left-wing groups that have pushed anti-Zionism. That, however, is cause for worry, rather than comfort, for it demonstrates that hostility toward Jewish distinctiveness is not confined to a particular political constituency. Indeed, there is bitter irony in the strong crossover between anti-ritualists and non-Jewish supporters of Israel. For the latter group, the Jewish state represents a bulwark against the Islamic barbarism – as they would portray it – on display in Europe's cities. Yet their unwavering secularism means they are uneasy about Jewish identity in a strictly religious sense. A recent article by Clemens Heni, a German who writes extensively about antisemitism, pointed out the anomaly of pro-Israel activists in Germany urging their supporters not to attend a pro-circumcision gathering in Berlin. "They want a fantasy Israel with no Judaism at all," Heni observed. The story is similar in the Netherlands, where the loudest voice in the anti-ritual movement belongs to the Freedom Party of Geert Wilders. Acclaimed in Israel and in sections of the Jewish community in America for his resolute antagonism toward Islamism – though many would argue that his fight is with Islam per se – Wilders has been one of the most outspoken supporters of Israel on a continent that increasingly regards the Jewish state as the reincarnation of apartheid South Africa. Yet that has not stopped his party from backing legal measures to outlaw ritual slaughter. And even though Wilders suffered major losses in September's parliamentary election, some Dutch Jews fear that he has enough parliamentary presence to mount a new offensive against circumcision. The notion that the anti-ritual movement is really focused on Muslims has surfaced not only in Germany but also in Holland. And, as in Germany, the primary focus of the Dutch debate about the Jews has undermined that same claim. In the Dutch case, Muslims were given legal benefits at the expense of Jews. An attempt earlier this year to push a ban on ritual slaughter through the lower house of the Dutch parliament stumbled upon a compromise – that animals be stunned prior to slaughter – that was perfectly acceptable to Muslim tradition. In contrast to the demands of kashruth, the production of halal meat permits stunning in advance. Should the Dutch follow the German route on circumcision, a similar compromise may well arise on this issue, too. While Judaism insists that circumcision be performed on an eight-day-old male infant, provided he is in good health, Muslims permit circumcision up until the age of 13. Hence, at stake in Holland is the possibility that specifically Jewish circumcision may be outlawed – on the grounds that a baby is incapable of voicing an objection to the procedure – while its Muslim variant will be permitted, based on the logic that once a child acquires the power of speech, he acquires as well the power of refusal. The pitfalls here are obvious. In all close-knit communities, a decision to opt out of core rituals carries the attendant threat of excommunication and banishment; in societies governed by Islamic law, there is also the real prospect of a death sentence. If the circumcision of Muslim boys is permitted on the basis that they can refuse the operation, that right to refuse is unlikely to be exercised in many, perhaps most, cases. Moreover, the physical pain associated with circumcision – the most commonly cited moral objection to the practice – is immeasurably worse for a young boy than for a baby.

That Wilders and his party were unperturbed by the adoption of positions specifically targeting Jews tells us a great deal about the current configuration of the nationalist, anti-European Union right in Europe. As the Dutch election approached, Wilders realized that opposing Islam and supporting Israel wasn't going to muster sufficient votes; accordingly, he seized upon the traditional conservative rejection of the European Union as the centerpiece of his platform, extending his reach to people who did not share his opinion of Israel as a privileged ally in the war on Islamism. As the ongoing battles over *shechita* and circumcision in Holland prove, Wilders does not see the need to reflect his foreign-policy values on the domestic front. Perhaps that was why the chief rabbi of Israel, Yona Metzger, felt it necessary, in a letter to Wilders protesting his party's stance on *shechita*, to point out the following: "I am fully aware of your firm support of the Jewish state of Israel and do respect and thank you for this. But one cannot separate between the Jewish state and the Jewish people." Metzger might have sent a similar message to Marine Le Pen, the leader of the extreme right Front National (FN) in France. When Le Pen suggested, in September, that a ban on Muslim women wearing headscarves be extended to Jews wearing kippot, she called on Jews to sacrifice their rights in the name of the wider fight against Sharia ordinances establishing themselves in French public life. In order to avoid being "burned" as a "Muslim-hater," Le Pen explained, she was appealing to "our Jewish compatriots to make this small effort, this little sacrifice probably" in the name of equality. "I'm sure a big part of them are ready to make that little sacrifice," she added, rather disingenuously. The assault on Jewish ritual in Europe has broadened the appeal of antisemitism while retaining the core themes and techniques associated with its most recent, Israel-centered manifestation. At root, both strands of anti- Semitism are motivated by antipathy towards Jewish "tribalism." In stubbornly retaining their differences, Jews wilfully go against the grain of history, whether by insisting on the integrity and security of their nation-state, or by retaining religious practices that are incompatible with enlightened secularism. When it comes to circumcision, the assertion that the removal of the foreskin is an abuse of the individual lacks the basic condition conventionally associated with human-rights violations: namely, the victims' own acknowledgement of having been systematically maltreated.

Millions of male children are circumcised every year, and the vast majority reach adulthood never claiming that their bodies have been damaged without their consent. This, of course, raises the question of how the anti-ritualists can appeal to the language of human rights in the absence of a mass of "victims" who provide the raw material for their case. The answer is plain. Anti-ritualism, like anti-Zionism, uses human-rights concerns as a fig leaf for a much more insidious agenda: namely, the removal of those characteristics that make Jews Jewish. However much the anti-ritualists are in denial, the historical record demonstrates conclusively that opposition to Jewish ritual has always been a central theme of antisemitism, in its premodern and modern forms. For example, the Roman Emperor Hadrian banned circumcision along with other Jewish observances in order to ensure, as the leading scholar of antisemitism Robert Wistrich has argued, that "the Jews had definitively ceased to exist as a nation in their own land." Similar themes are evident in the forelock-tugging letter submitted, in 654 C.E., by a group of lapsed Toledo Jews to the Visigoth king: "We will not practice the operation of circumcision. We will not celebrate the Passover, Sabbath, and other festival days, as enjoined by the Jewish ritual." In modern times, Jewish ritual has been portrayed as an enemy of both Christian and Enlightenment values, with their various emphases on love, the innate equality of human beings, and the duty of care to all God's creatures. The peculiarly European obsession with the flawed idea of "animal rights" – a construct that ignores the fact that rights flow from a social contract with the state, and depend on the ability of their bearers to communicate and reason with each other – is what lay behind the Swiss prohibition of *shechita* at the end of the 19th century, Norway and Sweden in the first half of the 20th century, and New Zealand as recently as 2010. Most famously, Nazi Germany banned *shechita* in 1933, just three months after Hitler seized power. In the notorious anti-semitic film *Der ewige Jude* ("The Eternal Jew"), the Nazis portrayed *shechita* as a gruesome Jewish celebration of animal suffering. The antiritualists think in largely the same terms, even if they prefer to ignore the noxious provenance of their beliefs. Is Charlotte Knobloch, the German Jewish leader, therefore correct in wondering aloud whether there is still a place for Jews in Germany? Antisemitism today lacks the grotesque characteristics of its previous eruptions: mass violence, the triggering of mass flight, the legally enshrined inferior status of the Jews. But the overall trend remains clear. Slowly yet inexorably, the foundations for a separate Jewish existence in Europe are being chipped away. And unlike in America, where the anti-circumcision movement exists only at the margins of political debate, antiritualism in Europe *encompasses* elected politicians, large swathes of the medical profession, and sympathetic voices in the commentariat. We ignore it at our peril.

Self-Hatred or Self-Help?

Jewish Ideas Daily, November 15, 2012

One of the most insightful scenes from Larry David's comedy series, *Curb Your Enthusiasm*, begins with David and his on-air wife, Cheryl, standing at the entrance to a movie theater. As they chatter aimlessly, David starts whistling a tune composed by Richard Wagner. Cheryl's delight at the bewitching melody is offset by the reaction of a bystander, a fellow Jew who rounds on David for whistling a composition written by "one of the great anti-Semites of the world." The two embark upon a furious argument, which culminates in David's adversary slamming him as "a self-loathing Jew." "I do hate myself," David barks in response, "but it has nothing to do with being Jewish."

This splendidly barbed exchange demonstrates the extent to which the accusation of "Jewish self-hatred" has penetrated mainstream culture, particularly in recent years, when disputes over Zionism and Israel among Jews

Ben Cohen

have given the term a fresh lease of life. Yet anyone seeking to understand exactly what a "self-hating Jew" is would be none the wiser having witnessed Larry David's fury. Similarly, the invective around the Middle East conflict serves, as Paul Reitter argues in his slim, intriguing volume, *On the Origins of Jewish Self-Hatred*, to obscure rather than shed light upon this most curious of intellectual labels.

As with its conceptual godparent, the word "antisemitism," the idea of "Jewish self-hatred" is rooted in the frantic, often hostile, debates about the nature of Judaism that sprang forth in Germany in the final decades of the nineteenth century. Reitter, a professor in the German department at Ohio State University, notes that some Orthodox Jewish commentators began damning the Reform movement as "Jewish anti-Semites" in 1882, just three years after the rabble-rouser Wilhelm Marr, popularly credited with having invented the term "*Antisemitismus*," published *The Victory of Jewry over the Germans*. Awareness of Jewish self-contempt also became, Reitter argues, "a kind of metaphor for the more general malaise" that swooped down on a rapidly modernizing, conflict-ridden Europe. One writer, Hermann Bahr, described a Vienna, filled with disaffected individuals shedding old identities and adopting new ones, as "Jewified." Meanwhile, the 1903 suicide of the youthful philosopher Otto Weininger, perhaps the best-known figure to have been afflicted with Jewish self-hatred, and supposedly the only Jew to have drawn Hitler's admiration, is often held up as evidence of how deadly this complex of attitudes and neuroses could be.

Indeed, the writer Theodor Lessing, whose 1930 work *Der Jüdische Selbsthass (Jewish Self-Hatred)* occupies a good deal of Reitter's study, warned that certain manifestations of Jewish self-hatred would "leave you dead." Yet Reitter asserts that Lessing's book was decidedly not a morbid account of the inevitability and inescapability of self-hatred, but rather an early foray into the self-help genre. Many of the aphorisms found in Lessing's book – "be whatever you are, and always try to live up to your best potential" – would not look out of place pinned to an office corkboard in large, bolded letters. Reitter's thesis is that the notion of *Selbsthass* was intended affirmatively, as a prop to the mental and social liberation of the Jews. Before Lessing, Reitter notes, there was Anton Kuh, a German Jewish journalist with a voracious appetite for wordplay, who coined the term in 1921. For Kuh, Jewish self-hatred was both "an affliction and an existential option" – in other words, not a form of Jewish antisemitism imprisoned by self-disgust, but a pathway to achieving harmony and understanding inside and beyond the various Jewish communities. When it came to the key options that faced Jews during the interwar period – assimilationism and Zion-

144

ism – Kuh rejected both. (Reitter cites a gruesomely prescient remark of Kuh's about the pitfalls of assimilation: "In the end, an ax blow will lop off their bowed heads.") Inspired by Nietzsche's revulsion in the face of German nationalism, Kuh contended that the embrace of self-hatred contained a healing power that would result in a new spirit of love throughout the human family. With hindsight, one can read this in several ways, few of them generous: Kuh can seem soppy and shallow, as well as painfully short on actual detail – which makes the relatively benign response he received from several of his fellow Jewish intellectuals that much more fascinating.

It fell to Theodor Lessing to draw the parameters of Jewish self-hatred. Although born into a prosperous and assimilated Jewish family in Hanover, Lessing grew up petrified of his brutal father, neglectful mother, and a school at which the humiliation of under-performing students was routine. As a result, writes Reitter, Lessing was ideally positioned to become the primary theorist of Jewish self-hatred. Before he composed *Der Jüdische Selbsthass*, Lessing had tracked the polemical exchanges on Judaism between Karl Kraus and Heinrich Heine, engaged in his own with the writer Thomas Mann, and written up his thoughts on the *Ostjuden* (Eastern European Jews) during a visit to Galicia. Throughout, Lessing's views are as unsettling as his childhood. At one point, he opined that, although there was no normative basis to the claims of racial anti-Semites, such as Houston Stewart Chamberlain, they may nonetheless have been functionally correct in their diagnosis of the Jewish Question. If the shadow of Gentile antisemitism hung over Lessing's work, then the challenge was to overcome it without succumbing to its prescriptions, as Otto Weininger arguably did. In that regard, Lessing placed enormous stress on the specific historical role of the Jews, as well as on the condition of the Jews as emblematic of a wider psychosocial malaise. "The Jews," he wrote, "had to think through and resolve problems that came about for younger and happier peoples only later."

Quite what all this means for the debate about Jewish self-hatred in our own time Reitter doesn't say. In delving into the archeology of the term, the book locates itself in a comparatively short phase of modern Jewish history, and likewise focuses on individuals who are, for the general reader, a tad obscure. Sometimes it seems as if Reitter is unsure of himself outside of his own detailed framework, such as when he describes "Poale Zionism" – more accurately, *Poale Zion* (Workers of Zion), the Marxist-Zionist party that became a critical political influence in the early years of the State of Israel – as a "maverick" faction. More significantly, the book ends too abruptly, almost as if it is unfinished. True, the book concentrates on the origins of the term "Jewish self-hatred," but that, surely, makes the later mutations of

Jewish self-hatred even more relevant. One wonders, for example, what Kuh and Lessing would have made of the non-Jew Jean-Paul Sartre's characterization of "inauthentic Jews" – offered in his highly influential post-war work, *Anti-Semite and Jew* – as "men whom other men take for Jews and who have decided to run away from this insupportable situation." Nor is there any examination of whether and how the meme of "self-hatred" manifested in studies of other minorities, as it did in various post-war sociological and psychological surveys of African-Americans. Introducing this comparative element might have put the shared insistence of Kuh and Lessing that, since Jews are uniquely possessed of self-hatred, they are uniquely equipped to deal with it, into a more clinical perspective. As for those readers seeking enlightenment about how self-hatred figures into contemporary disputes among Jews over Zionism and Israel, they will be sorely disappointed by Reitter's book. That in itself is no bad thing; not every inquiry into Jewish identity needs to be framed by references to provocateurs or propagandists. But their centrality to current explorations of this phenomenon underlines that, whatever the original positive intent behind the term "Jewish self-hatred," the interpretation of it as a form of Jewish antisemitism will remain dominant.

Morsi's Antisemitism Reveals More About Us Than Him

JNS/The Algemeiner, January 21, 2013

It's a story that began with an eagle-eyed Jewish blogger who writes under the pseudonym "Challah Hu Akbar" and progressed all the way to the White House. In the process, it has reignited the debate as to whether Egypt's Muslim Brotherhood President, Mohamed Morsi, is really the pragmatic moderate that many believe him to be. On Jan. 3, Challah Hu Akbar tweeted an item from the Middle East Media Research Institute (MEMRI) in which Morsi, in a 2010 speech, uttered what is a standard Islamist antisemitic slander, namely that Zionists are descended from "apes and pigs." A little more than a week later, noticing that Morsi's statement had barely registered with the wider media, *The Atlantic* columnist Jeffrey Goldberg wrote a blog post with the entirely apt headline, "Egyptian President Calls Jews 'Sons of Apes and Pigs;' World Yawns." At *Forbes* magazine, Richard Behar made an identical point, adding that in the same set of remarks, Morsi had called for a boycott of the United States – whose taxpayers have provided Egypt with billions of dollars in aid – because of its support for Israel. Eventually, the Morsi story found its way into the *New York Times*, which felt duty-bound to point out that "Mr. Morsi and other political and Brotherhood leaders typically restrict their inflammatory comments to the more ambiguous category of 'Zionists.'" Actually, it's not ambiguous at all. Especially since the Second World War, the word "Zionist" has always been code for "Jew" in the capitals of the Muslim world, as well as in the capitals of the late, unlamented communist bloc of states. And in case there was any lingering doubt, a subsequent Morsi item posted by MEMRI, also from 2010, showed the Muslim Brotherhood leader helpfully urging his people "not forget to nurse our children and grandchildren on hatred towards those Zionists and Jews."

Unusually, given the prevailing view that accusations of antisemitism are a smear cooked up by an unscrupulous Jewish – sorry, I mean Israel – Lobby, condemnation of Morsi did follow. The *New York Times* published an editorial urging President Obama to directly convey to Morsi that such offensive comments ran counter to the goal of peace. White House spokesman Jay Carney also issued a statement, declaring, "President Morsi should make clear that he respects people of all faiths, and that this type of rhetoric is not acceptable or productive in a democratic Egypt." Of course, no apology from the Egyptians was forthcoming. Instead, Yasser Ali, Morsi's spokesman, claimed that his boss's comments had been taken "out of context," and were really directed at Israeli "aggression" in Gaza. In fact, Ali's statement is far less stupid than initially appears; anti-Semites in the Arab world know that there is a strong current of opinion in the west that regards their fulminations against Jews as justified, if unfortunately-worded, anger towards Israel. Ali was playing to that particular gallery. And that leads to a broader, far more important observation. In its editorial, the *New York Times* asked, "Does Mr. Morsi really believe what he said in 2010? Has becoming president made him think differently about the need to respect and work with all people?" Disgracefully, the Times also argued, "Israelis are not immune to responding in kind either" (a sentence that appeared to have been overlooked by establishment Jewish groups like the American Jewish Committee, which rushed to welcome the editorial). As for the White House's Carney, his statement categorized Morsi's remarks as "religious hatred," a term that barely scratches the surface of what is really at issue here. For the Morsi affair tells us much more about how antisemitism is understood in the West than it does about the nature of Islamist antisemitism. If the Times is to be believed, then the episode is merely a depressing example of how both sides dehumanize each other with nasty rhetoric. Similarly, the White House wants us to think that Morsi's offense was religious intolerance.

As I've long argued, antisemitism isn't just another form of bigotry. It is a method of explaining why the world is as it is; incendiary rhetoric against Jews, therefore, isn't just an afterthought, but the natural consequence of the genuinely held belief that our planet is in the grips of a Jewish conspiracy. One has to assume the Times would not have questioned whether the antisemitic outlooks of Hitler and Stalin were genuinely held, so why do so with Morsi? There are two reasons. Firstly, the misguided view that antisemitism is essentially a European phenomenon, and thus an alien import into the Muslim world that will disappear once the Israeli-Palestinian conflict is resolved. That reflects, secondly, an enormous ignorance about the origins of antisemitism in the Muslim world and its centrality to the Muslim Brotherhood's worldview. In his masterpiece "Terror and Liberalism," the scholar Paul Berman quotes Sayid Qutb, the leading theoretician of the Muslim Brotherhood, which was formed in 1928, as writing that "most evil theories which try to destroy all values and all that is sacred to mankind are advocated by Jews." Elsewhere in the book, Berman painstakingly docments Qutb's frankly Hitlerian view of the Jewish role in world history, including his repeated assertions that Jews had conspired against Muslims from the dawn of Islam.

These were the ideological foundations of the Muslim Brotherhood then, and they remain firmly in place now. Any compromise with the Jews, such as a peace treaty with Israel, would therefore be another twist in the same conspiracy. According to Qutb and his followers, the only honorable path is to vanquish the Jews entirely. These are the same beliefs of Mohamed Morsi. They may be insidious, but they are authentically held. Asking him to recant them, as the White House did, is like asking Hitler to apologize for *Mein Kampf*. A far more productive approach would be to integrate the persistence of Islamist antisemitism into policy analysis of our relationship with Egypt. Critically, we need to ask whether someone who really believes that there is a hidden Jewish conspiracy at work – and that, consequently, political relationships are camouflage for that – can be a partner in any sense of that term. Going by their reactions to Morsi's remarks, neither this White House nor its supporters in the commentariat are up to that task.

Will Venezuelan antisemitism die with Hugo Chavez?

Haaretz, March 6, 2013

Over the several months that preceded yesterday's announcement by the Venezuelan government of the death of Hugo Chavez, there was one over-arching theme in the discussion of the country's political future: to what extent will *Chavismo* – a term that encapsulates both Chavez's authoritarian governing style and his radical ideology – survive into the post-Chavez era? It's a question that is especially pertinent for Venezuela's Jewish community as well as the State of Israel. During his fourteen years in power, Chavez's foreign policy was grounded on alliances with some of the world's most bellicosely anti-American states, like Cuba, Iran and Syria. Inevitably, given the close relationship between America and Israel, Venezuela became the source of some of the most incendiary anti-Israel rhetoric heard during the last decade and a half. Just as inevitably, this antagonism towards Israel spilled over into open hostility towards the dwindling Venezuelan Jewish community, which found itself cast in the role of a fifth column seeking to undermine Chavez's Bolivarian revolution. Now that Chavez has departed from this world, will the Jew-baiting tendencies of Chavismo persist or subside? At the moment, sadly, there is little reason for optimism on this front.

Those Jewish organizations in the United States who maintain close contact with the Venezuelan Jewish community point out that, bar some major unforeseen developments, there is unlikely to be a further mass exodus now that Chavez is dead. The current size of the community is estimated at between 7–9,000, an enormous dip from the peak of 30,000 at the start of the Chavez era. The remnant that has stayed put will, for the time being, watch political developments closely, in the hope that Chavez's successors might adopt a more pragmatic and conciliatory approach.

"It's difficult to predict the future of antisemitism in Venezuela," Daniel Duquenal, the author of Venezula's leading dissident blog, told me. Should Nicolas Maduro, the current Vice-President and Chavez's chosen successor, become Venezuela's next leader, Duquenal argues, there is little reason to believe that antisemitism will dissipate. Maduro, a former bus driver, is an orthodox follower of Chavez, but he lacks the late *Comandante*'s charismatic touch. Against that weakness, "the pro-Iran, knee jerk anti-American and anti-Israel currents may want to use antisemitism as an 'argument,'" Duquenal said. Sammy Eppel, a leading Venezuelan Jewish human rights activist, feels similarly. Those state-controlled Venezuelan media outlets that have promoted antisemitism in the past will continue to do so "unless they get a clear directive to the contrary," Eppel said. Eppel is particularly concerned by Maduro's statement that the cancer which claimed Chavez's life was deliberately implanted. In making this bizarre declaration, Maduro, who told reporters that a "scientific commission will prove that Comandante Chavez was attacked with this illness," explicitly invoked the death of the PLO leader Yasser Arafat. Echoing the insistence of many Palestinians that Arafat was poisoned, Maduro said that like Chavez, Arafat was also "inoculated with an illness." Said Sammy Eppel: "The canard that Chavez's cancer was induced by some foreign conspiracy is troubling." Thus far, Maduro has not linked the poisoning allegations to Israel or the local Jewish community. However, fears that he might do so can't simply be dismissed as paranoia. Especially over the last ten years, a clear pattern of anti-Jewish harassment has become visible. In 2004 and again in 2007, Venezuelan security services raided Jewish institutions, among them the Jewish school in Caracas and the Hebraica Jewish Community Center. Just last month, an Argentine website revealed that SEBIN, the Venezuelan intelligence agency, had been spying on the *Espacio Anne Frank*, a non-profit center that uses Anne Frank's experiences under the Nazis as the basis for its human rights and tolerance programs. A SEBIN dossier asserted that the center "operates as a strategic arm of the Israeli intelligence in the country...operating in the field of subversive socio-political influence through representatives of far-right Zionist groups and economic elites." In an email the JTA Jewish news service, Paulina Gamus, the director of *Espacio Anne Frank*, candidly responded that, "[T]hey accuse us of belonging to the Mossad and the Israeli secret services only because we are an institution that promotes respect of different religions and cultures and has a Jewish component, although we are all Venezuelans."

Venezuela's opposition parties, vilified by the regime on a daily basis as agents of foreign powers, could also provide further raw material to sustain the antisemitic trend. At the moment, Henrique Capriles, a devout Catholic who proudly notes his family's Jewish origins, is seen as the likely opposition candidate should elections be called. Capriles, who faced off against Chavez during last October's presidential election, in which he garnered an impressive 44 per cent of the vote, was the subject of a feverish antisemitic whispering campaign throughout the contest. Just last week, while Capriles was visiting relatives in New York, Maduro declared, "I have all the data, exactly where he is in Manhattan, in New York, at this moment." It doesn't take a huge stretch of the imagination to speculate that Maduro will accuse Capriles of having had ulterior motives in traveling to the United States. On the other hand, said blogger Daniel Duquenal, should Maduro's principal rival Diosdado Cabello, a wealthy businessman with strong ties to the Venezuelan military, prevail as the government's preferred candidate, "we may see the end of the formal antisemitism that we see now in some state media." However, any power struggle between Maduro and Cabello is certain to be bitter, and therefore vulnerable to all kinds of conspiracy theories, including antisemitic ones. Most of all, the stoking of antisemitism and anti-Zionism has been a critical element of the Chavez regime's bid to become the ideological center of the world's radical states. With other Latin American countries like Argentina, Ecuador and Bolivia now jockeying for the position of guardian of the continent's revolutionary elements, the Chavistas who have outlived Chavez may decide that lowering the volume on anti-Jewish rhetoric is, for the time being, a compromise too far.

Orban Whitewashes Hungarian Antisemitism

"Contentions" @ Commentary Magazine, May 5, 2013

As I read Hungarian Prime Minister Viktor Orban's speech to the delegates of the World Jewish Congress, who assembled in Budapest this past weekend, I found myself visualizing the furrowed eyebrows and anxious seat shuffling going on in the audience. For not only was Orban's speech a chain of platitudes from beginning to end, it was downright dishonest. The WJC says it held its conference in Budapest as a gesture of solidarity with Hungary's Jews, who are once again the targets of the kind of vicious antisemitism for which Eastern Europe is renowned. The direct source of the poison is the extreme right-wing Jobbik Party, which is these days the third-largest party in the Hungarian parliament, having won 17 per cent of the vote during the April 2010 elections. But several observers of the Hungarian scene have argued that Orban's ruling Fidesz Party variously ignores, plays down or even encourages the antisemitism of Jobbik; Orban's speech to the WJC, therefore, was his opportunity to clearly explain whether he considers Jobbik a threat, as well as his chance to make amends for his close friendship with Zsolt Bayer, an antisemitic writer who has compared Jews to "stinking excrement" and has opined that "a significant part" of the Roma gypsy population are "unfit for existence."

In the event, neither Jobbik nor Bayer even made it into the speech. Instead, Orban declared that the situation in Hungary isn't really that disturbing: I know that Jewish leaders have come here from all over the world. Including from places where antisemitism sometimes claims the lives of schoolchildren. And from places where following the antisemitic murder of children, there is no consensus on whether a minute's silence in memory of the victims may be ordered in state schools. From places where bomb attacks that claim lives are launched against synagogues. Nothing of this nature has so far occurred in Hungary.

Really? Try telling that to Ferenc Orosz, the head of Hungary's Raoul Wallenberg Association. At the end of April, Orosz attended, together with his family, a soccer match at Budapest's Puskas Stadium. A group of spectators sitting nearby were bellowing the Nazi chant, "Sieg Heil," and Orosz courageously demanded that they stop. Of course, the hooligans turned on him, spitting "Jewish communist" and other antisemitic epithets in his direction. When Orosz attempted to leave the stadium at the end of the game, two men blocked him, one of whom punched him in the face, leaving him with a broken nose. Evidently, the WJC wasn't too impressed by Orban's implication that antisemitism shouldn't be taken overly seriously unless bombs are exploding in synagogues. In a statement released after Orban's speech, the WJC expressed its "regret" that the prime minister had not "confronted...the threat posed by the anti-Semites in general and by the extreme-right Jobbik party in particular...Mr. Orban did not address any recent antisemitic or racist incidents in the country, nor did he provide sufficient reassurance that a clear line has been drawn between his government and the far-right fringe." (Having spent several years working for American Jewish advocacy organizations, I know that their desire to maintain access to troubling leaders like Argentine President Christina Kirchner and Turkish Prime Minister Recep Tayyip Erdogan dampens down any criticism they might advance; the WJC statement is thus a notable and welcome departure from that unfortunate habit.)

Ultimately, the WJC wanted something from Orban that he wasn't prepared to give them; not just an abstract statement that "antisemitism is unacceptable and intolerable," but a concrete undertaking to eradicate it from Hungarian politics. Orban's silence on the nature of the threat to Hungary's Jews will, rest assured, be interpreted as a license by the country's anti-Semites (like the Jobbik parliamentarian Marton Gyongyosi, whose idea of solidarity with the population of the Gaza Strip was to publish a list of Jews he considers to be a "national security risk") to continue their agitation. For that reason, a precise understanding of Jobbik's antisemitic worldview becomes all the more important. It is true that Jobbik leaders echo the Nazis in their constant associations of Jews with human waste and sexual mischief, and in that sense, it is correct to classify the party as a part of the extreme right. Yet, as the Gyongyosi episode demonstrated, Jobbik has also imbibed the visceral loathing of Zionism and Israel more commonly associated with the extreme left. Gyongyosi himself told an antisemitic rally staged in Budapest on the eve of the WJC conference that Hungary has "become subjugated to Zionism, it has become a target of colonisation while we, the indigenous people, can play only the role of extras". As James Kirchick has observed, statements like this one explain why Jobbik, with its "virulently anti-Europe rhetoric, anti-Western worldview, and undisguised antisemitism," has "embraced the mullahs" who rule Iran. Nor is the romance with Iran confined to Jobbik. Eleven of the 27 parliamentarians on the executive of the "Hungary-Iran friendship committee," which is chaired by Gyongyosi, belong to Orban's Fidesz Party. And that, incidentally, is another detail that somehow didn't make it into Orban's speech.

The Church of Scotland's War on Judaism

JNS/The Algemeiner, May 13, 2013

In a recent, exhaustive study of antisemitism, the German scholar Clemens Heni explains the significance for Christian theology of the story of Ahasver, a Jewish shoemaker in Jerusalem who, legend has it, refused Jesus a resting place as he made his way to Golgotha bearing the cross on his back. Ahasver's punishment, says Heni, was to wander the world for eternity, an image that formed the basis for what the Nazis famously called "der ewige Jude" – "the eternal Jew." "The attribute 'eternal' cries out for redemption," writes Heni. "For Christianity, it embodies the refusal on the part of the Jewish people to accept the coming of Jesus as the Son of God." Of course, as Heni points out, this was a particularly strong theme throughout the Middle Ages. What's notable, though, is that this same noxious depiction of the Jews is enjoying a new lease of life in certain sections of the Church today.

At the beginning of May, the Church of Scotland published a document entitled "The Inheritance of Abraham? A Report on the 'Promised Land.'" Now, doing what I do, I spend a great deal of time reviewing anti-Zionist and antisemitic literature, and I like to think that I am passed being shocked. Reading the Church of Scotland report, was, therefore, something of a rude awakening; so immersed is the text in antisemitic clichés and malicious distortions of Jewish theology that I wondered whether I had been transported back to a time when people didn't wash or brush their teeth, had a lifespan of 30 years or so, and spent their time on this earth living in fear of Jewish devils. The purpose of the report is to dismiss the claim that the "Hebrew Bible" – heaven forbid that these people should use terms like Torah or Tanakh! – provides grounds for a privileged connection between the Jewish people and the "Promised Land," which we Jews sinfully refer to as "Eretz Israel." What follows is frontal assault on Jewish "exclusivism" that deploys the tired old trick of citing a Jew – in this case, Mark Braverman, an arch opponent of Zionism – in order to protect the text from accusations of antisemitism. But antisemitic it most definitely is. Some choice excerpts:

"Braverman is adamant that Christians must not sacrifice the universalist, inclusive dimension of Christianity and revert to the particular exclusivism of the Jewish faith because we feel guilty about the Holocaust. He is equally clear that the Jewish people have to repent of the ethnic cleansing of the Palestinians between 1947 and 1949. They must be challenged, too, to stop thinking of themselves as victims and special, and recognise that the present immoral, unjust treatment of Palestinian people is unsustainable."

"As long as Zionists think that Jewish people are serving God's special purpose and that abuses by the state of Israel, however wrong and regrettable, don't invalidate the Zionist project, they will believe themselves more entitled to the land than the Palestinian people."

"Jesus offered a radical critique of Jewish specialness and exclusivism, but the people of Nazareth were not ready for it... Jesus' cleansing of the Temple means not just that the Temple needs to be reformed, but that the Temple is finished."

Let's translate the above lines minus the academic, ostensibly reasonable tone in which they are couched: "Jews! Stop whining about the Holocaust. Stop making us feel guilty about the Holocaust. Repent, every single one of you, for the evil you have committed against the Palestinians. And, oh yeah, enough of the 'Chosen People' thing – you people are so arrogant, no wonder nobody likes you. Even Jesus himself ran out of patience with you..."

The moral crime committed by the Church of Scotland – and I use that phrase deliberately – is rooted not just in the trashing of centuries of Jewish learning and scholarship, nor the wholesale fabrication of a Jewish "crime" in the form of the "ethnic cleansing" of the Palestinians. More than all of that, this report is a declaration of war against Judaism itself. If the "Temple is finished," then the only form of Judaism that is acceptable is the one subscribed to by collaborators like Mark Braverman, who want us to adopt an eternal posture of repentance and shame. The report both cites and reflects the poisonous ideology of Sabeel, a Palestinian Christian institute whose mission is to attack both Zionism and Judaism. Note that Sabeel makes no distinction between Zionism and Judaism; just as the ideologues of the now dead Soviet Union insisted there was no difference between the two, so do these radical Christians. And to add grievous insult to heinous injury, Sabeel, as the Israeli organization NGO Monitor has repeatedly pointed out, receives funding from the governments, and thus the taxpayers, of countries like Sweden, The Netherlands and Canada to the tune of hundreds of thousands of dollars. The consequences of all this are clear, at least to my mind. To posit that Jews might engage in constructive dialogue with the Sabeels of this world is utterly ludicrous. They want to destroy us, and their war is a zero-sum game. Our response should be equally harsh: we must seek to destroy them. That means confronting and exposing them every time they raise their heads, whether in the comments section of a blog or at a student meeting on a college campus. It means highlighting their ideological support for the terrorism that targets Jews solely because they are Jews – when it comes to Sabeel's worldview, an outrage like last year's massacre at a Jewish school in the French city of Toulouse should logically be regarded as the natural result of Jewish crimes that go back to the time of Jesus. Above all, it means targeting their funding sources. And rather than just arguing for funding to be cut, let's approach that aim more imaginatively. Many Christians today, most of them in Muslim countries, live with persecution of the most grotesque kind: pastors are locked up in Iran, churches are bombed in Nigeria, Copts are attacked in Egypt. The money that would be otherwise squandered on the irredeemable anti-Semites of Sabeel, along with their global echo chamber, should be transferred into a global fund to help the persecuted Church. In both the Jewish and Christian traditions, such an act would be regarded as both charitable and just.

Poland Bans Kosher Slaughter

"Contentions" @ Commentary Magazine, July 15, 2013

Back in April, when the imposing Museum of the History of the Polish Jews opened its doors in Warsaw, there was much talk of how the relationship between Jews and Poles had been transformed for the better in recent years. The sentiments expressed by Jan Kulczyk, a wealthy Polish businessman who helped finance the museum, seemed to encapsulate a new era: "When the Jewish nation and the Polish nation, when we are together, when we look in the same direction, it is great for us, great for Poland and great for the world."

The news that the Sejm, the Polish parliament, has rejected a government-sponsored bill to protect ritual slaughter, in both its Jewish and Muslim variants, suggests that, sadly, Jews and Poles are facing opposite directions when it comes to religious freedom. As a result of the vote, which comes on the heels of last year's supreme court ruling that ritual slaughter, or shechita, is no longer exempted from requirements to stun animals prior to killing them, the production of kosher meat has effectively been banned in Poland. All the excitement about the revival of Jewish life there now seems rather misplaced, given that, as Poland's American-born Chief Rabbi Michael Shudrich bemoaned on his Facebook page, Poland has become a country "in which the rights of the Jewish religion are curtailed." In any country, such a decision would be strongly protested; in Poland, the weight of history gives objections to the ban an added urgency. During last year's debate over the supreme court ruling, Piotr Kadlcik, head of the Union of Jewish Communities of Poland, opined that "[T]he outrageous atmosphere in the Polish media surrounding shechitah reminds me precisely of the similar situation in Poland and Germany in the 1920s and 1930s." This time around, the historical analogies are no less visible. Kadlick again voiced his warning about the patterns of the last century repeating themselves, adding that "populism, superstition and political interests won out." Israel, whose prime minister, Benjamin Netanyahu, paid an official visit to Poland just last month, was equally sharp in its condemnation. Decrying the "rude blow to the religious tradition of the Jewish people," the Israeli Foreign Ministry asserted that the Sejm's decision "seriously harms the process of restoring Jewish life in Poland." Reacting to the Israeli statement, Poland's centrist prime minister, Donald Tusk, sounded almost wounded. "Especially the historical context is, to put it mildly, off target and is not applicable to the situation," he said. Isn't it? One of the reasons why Jews are especially sensitive to legal measures against ritual slaughter, as Tusk surely knows, is that the Nazis banned it in Germany only three months after they came to power in 1933. And like many of today's animal rights activists, the Nazis depicted the methods of shechita as a gruesome, needless celebration of animal suffering.

Even so, the historical parallels don't overlap completely. The two main Polish political parties that opposed the government bill are not, as might reasonably be expected, populated by snarling right-wing skinheads. One of them, the Democratic Left Party, or SLD, was co-founded by Alexander Kwasniewski, who served as Poland's president from 1995–2005. Throughout his time in office, Kwasniewski was feted by Jewish groups, particularly in the United States, for his strong stand against antisemitism; after leaving office, he was one of the backers of the European Council for Tolerance and Reconciliation, an organization that is unlikely to share the SLD's revulsion for shechita. The other party, the Palikot Movement (named for its founder, Janusz Palikot), is variously described as liberal, even libertarian. The party's support for gay civil unions and the legalization of soft drugs are noteworthy in a country that remains socially conservative and devoutly Catholic. Yet one of Palikot's leaders, Andrzej Rozenek, sounded like a traditional anti-Semite when he declared that "there is no permission for animal cruelty in the name of money" – the implication being that what really worries Jewish defenders of shechita is the loss of a $400 million dollar regional market for kosher goods produced in Poland.

Poland is not the first country to ban shechita – European states from Norway to Switzerland have also prohibited its practice – but its historic position as the cradle of the Holocaust means that extra scrutiny of any legal measures against Jewish rituals is inevitable. Preventing shechita in a country where, as Rabbi Shudrich noted, hunting remains legal, renders the concerns about cruelty to animals laughable. It also opens Poland up to an accusation last leveled against Germany, where an effort to ban circumcision was recently defeated: namely, that for all of its Jewish museums and memorials to the Holocaust, the country finds the task of being nice to dead Jews far more appealing than guaranteeing the rights of living ones.

In Poland, Jews and Muslims Unite – Over Meat

The Wall Street Journal, October 11, 2013

Leave it to Poland to bring together Jews and Muslims. Despite having only 20,000 Jews, the Eastern European country has a booming kosher-slaughter industry worth an annual $350 million, one-third of all of the country's beef exports. Yet the industry has been slowed for a year amid a controversy over the legality of ritual slaughter. Now, a coalition of Jews and Muslims – whose halal meat is slaughtered in a similar fashion to kosher meat – is anxiously awaiting a ruling from the Polish High Court over whether ritual slaughter will remain legal. Since Poland's constitution explicitly guarantees religious freedom, Jews and Muslims should be at liberty to slaughter and consume animals in accordance with their ancient beliefs. But in 2002, parliament passed a law requiring, on humane grounds, that all animals be stunned before slaughter. Given that religious laws governing both kosher and halal slaughter forbid such stunning, the Polish agricultural ministry issued a directive in 2004 exempting the Jewish and Muslim communities.

A drawn-out legal and political battle with animal-rights activists ensued. Among them was the celebrated Polish actress Maja Ostaszewska, who bombastically compared ritual slaughter to performing surgery on a human being without anaesthetic. Last November the High Court ruled that stunning animals before slaughter was necessary – regardless of religious belief. And three months ago, a government-sponsored bill to override the High Court and protect ritual slaughter was defeated in parliament, 222 to 178.

The contradiction between the country's constitution and the parliamentary vote has left the legal status of ritual slaughter in limbo. Absent a definitive High Court ruling about whether animal welfare trumps religious freedom – the 2012 decision only addressed stunning – many of Poland's kosher and halal food manufacturers have erred on the side of caution, halting production after last year's ruling. Michael Shudrich, who has served as Poland's chief rabbi for almost a decade, said that his attempt to slaughter animals for the last Passover holiday in March was prevented by a Warsaw veterinarian, who referred the case to the local prosecutor. (Fortunately for the rabbi, the lack of clarity over the law meant that the prosecutor didn't pursue him.)

The ban also has had significant economic costs. When the government's attempt to rescue ritual slaughter in parliament failed this summer, large abbatoirs, like the Biernacki slaughterhouse in western Poland, cut the prices they were paying for cattle by as much as 13%. Meanwhile, the Polish Meat Association has warned of significant job losses among the country's more than 500,000 livestock producers if ritual slaughter is permanently banned. Given the history of persecution suffered by Jews in Poland, it was inevitable that attempts to curb ritual slaughter would generate charges of antisemitism. Indeed, Jewish leaders inside and outside the country have reminded Poles that the Nazis banned ritual slaughter in Germany three months after Adolf Hitler came to power in 1933.

Still, those leading the battle to protect ritual slaughter don't believe their opponents are driven by anti-Jewish bigotry. "This has more to do with ignorance," said Jonathan Ornstein, a former New Yorker who heads the Jewish Community Center in Krakow. Mr. Ornstein and Rabbi Shudrich both described a relentless campaign by animal-rights activists, inundating members of parliament with dozens of emails and phone calls each day. The protestors regularly make false claims, including that kosher slaughter is outlawed in the U.S. This pressure, along with support from a rebel faction of the ruling Civic Platform party, caused the defeat of the government's pro-ritual slaughter bill in July. With the High Court ruling on the horizon – Rabbi Shudrich expects it to be delivered by the end of this year – advocates for ritual slaughter want to ensure that the decision goes their way. To avoid reducing the controversy to one about antisemitism, Messrs. Shudrich and Ornstein are emphasizing the idea that ritual slaughter is predicated on the importance of animals suffering as little as possible. The message is buttressed by the fact that both men are vegetarians. They've also mobilized Poland's normally reserved community of 30,000 Muslims. "Right now, it's very hard for Muslim people to find halal meat. We have to buy it from Germany, which is very expensive," said Mohammed Munir Hussein, a student from Bangladesh who has been living in Krakow for the past five years. The issue has brought Muslims and Jews together. "I didn't know any Jews before, now I've made Jewish friends," Mr. Hussein told me. Jews and Muslims in Poland – which is 90% Catholic – have found an ally in the Polish Episcopal Conference, the nation's top Catholic body, which last week issued a robust statement in support of ritual slaughter, noting "Poland's long tradition of religious freedom." Poland isn't the only country in Europe where there is hostility toward Jewish and Muslim religious practices. Similar moves against ritual slaughter in the Netherlands and the circumcision of infant boys in Germany attracted strong public support before eventually being defeated.

But earlier this month, the Council of Europe, a 47-nation body that controls the European Court of Human Rights, passed a resolution challenging "traditional methods" in performing circumcision, urging greater state regulation of the practice. What this suggests is that even if Poland's High Court does decide in favor of ritual slaughter, voices in Europe will continue urging restrictions of religious liberty.

Jewish museum's obsolete debate on antisemitism

Haaretz, November 7, 2013

There is a beguiling paradox around the term "antisemitism." Prejudice of varying degrees toward Jews is a centuries-old phenomenon, yet there remains precious little agreement as to what antisemitism involves in our own time. Anyone who has observed the twists of the antisemitism debate during the last decade will know that the quarrel about definition has been extraordinarily polarized. On one side are those who believe that global hostility to Zionism and Israel's existence, frequently based upon sinister theories about Jewish power, represents the most acute form of antisemitism today. On the other is a cluster of Jewish and non-Jewish voices who insist that this "new antisemitism" is a mischievous attempt to conflate legitimate opposition to Zionism as a political movement with that odious, largely defunct bigotry, antisemitism.

As someone who has actively participated in this debate, I'll readily admit that the back and forth has gotten rather stale. However, as the brouhaha over a conference on antisemitism at Berlin's Jewish Museum on Thursday night illustrates, the differences that animated this dispute in the first place aren't likely to disappear anytime soon. To begin with, there is the seemingly unimportant matter of the conference's timing. Organized to coincide with the 75th anniversary of Kristallnacht, when Nazi mobs rampaged through Germany, rounding up and murdering Jews and ransacking Jewish stores and synagogues, it begins on Friday night and ends on Saturday. Critics charge that it is inappropriate to hold a conference on antisemitism over the Jewish Sabbath, since it is almost impossible for observant Jews to attend. In an email to me, one of the conference organizers defended the decision on the grounds that Herbert A. Strauss, a German Jewish intellectual who established the Center for Research on Antisemitism at the Technical University of Berlin in 1980, "always insisted in that it is not forbidden to... learn on Shabbat." As well-intentioned as this response is, the absence of observant Jews from the proceedings – they will be sitting down for Shabbat dinner around about the time of the keynote conference lecture – will actually restrict any number of lived-in-the-skin learning opportunities. Since Jews who are visibly Jewish, by dint of wearing kippot, shopping in kosher stores, or dropping off their children at Jewish schools, are more likely to be targeted in antisemitic attacks than their secular brethren, one can reasonably assume that a conference on antisemitism would be much enhanced by their attendance.

A far bigger controversy revolves around the academic chosen to deliver the keynote lecture, the Oxford University philosopher Brian Klug. Klug famously intervened in the contemporary antisemitism debate with a 2004 article in the left-wing American journal The Nation, in which he argued that the notion of a reignited "war against the Jews" was "as much a figment of the imagination as its mirror image: a Jewish conspiracy against the world." In subsequent writings, Klug has reiterated this core point. As I remarked in a dossier to the Berlin conference that highlighted Klug's problematic statements, I do not object to the invitation per se. Nor do I believe that Klug is a crude chauvinist like, for example, the American political activist Max Blumenthal, whose recent, widely ridiculed book attacking Israel is replete with insultingly antisemitic chapter headings like "The Concentration Camp" and "How to Kill Goyim and Influence People." What alarms me and others is that Klug is being given an unchallenged podium at prestigious venue to restate positions that are frankly worn out (assuming, of course, that he isn't planning to use the occasion to announce a radical change of heart).

The very title of Klug's lecture, "What do we mean when we say 'antisemitism'?" implies that very little has changed since his Nation article nearly a decade ago. Whereas in fact, the parameters of both the antisemitism debate itself, as well as the broader issues with which it intersects, have been dramatically transformed. One of the claims behind the dissociation of anti-Zionism from antisemitism – that the two couldn't be equated – rested upon the supposed global import of the Palestinian conflict with Israel. The argument went like this: Parochial Jewish anxieties about past Jewish suffering should not block efforts to challenge the "Zionist narrative" behind the "the occupation," aka the greatest threat to world peace and justice.
Actually, events in the Middle East over the last three years have underlined the reverse of this occupation-centric view of history. The Israeli-Palestinian

dimension is only one, and certainly not the most significant, aspect of a regional crisis that sweeps up national identities, religious sectarianism, and the persistence of corrupt, undemocratic regimes. The more fitting question to examine, therefore, is why western intellectuals concerned with the Middle East are so preoccupied with Israel alone, and the extent to which this reflects inherited ideas about the dangers of Jewish power.

Then there's the equally discredited assumption that Arab and Muslim antisemitism is principally an outgrowth of enmity to Zionism. In the last decade, a coalition of scholars and activists has made a persuasive case that the mass expulsion of Jewish communities from the Arab world in the 1940s and 1950s would not have been possible without a powerful strand of indigenous antisemitism to build upon. But if the Berlin conference does not deem a largely hidden historic injustice like this one to be worthy of consideration, how can we arrive at a rounded picture of anti-Zionism's relationship to antisemitism? Lastly, there are the perceptions and feelings of Jews in Europe right now. A preview of the forthcoming European Union Fundamental Rights Agency survey on antisemitism reveals that almost 50 per cent of Jews in Belgium, France and Hungary have considered emigrating because of antisemitism. Are we simply to reassure them that the brewing opposition in Europe to ritual slaughter and circumcision is based on human rights concerns, or that anti-Zionism is motivated by aspirations to justice? How do we resolve that with the overwhelming evidence that far-right parties like Jobbik in Hungary and Golden Dawn in Greece oppose Zionism solely because of their loathing of Jews? Indeed, can those American Jews who argue that there is no future for Jews in Europe ever be proved wrong, considering this context?

I won't claim to have a monopoly on the answers to these questions. But I do know that until we acknowledge what we've got profoundly wrong in the current antisemitism debate, there's no scope to make any progress. And despite the forthcoming conference's timeliness and resonant location, there are good reasons to believe that our understanding of antisemitism today will not be refined by its keynote speaker.

Norway Moves Against Circumcision

Commentary Magazine, November 15, 2013

Almost one year after Chancellor Angela Merkel successfully leaned on the German parliament to pass legislation guaranteeing the rights of parents to have their infant boys circumcised, the practice is now under threat in another European country. This week, Norway's health minister, Bent Hoie, announced that new legislation is in the pipeline to "regulate ritual circumcision." Hoie took his cue from Anne Lindboe, Norway's children's ombudsman, who believes that "non-medical circumcision" – in other words, circumcision of boys in accordance with the laws of both Judaism and Islam – is a violation of children's rights. JTA quoted Lindboe as having told the leading Norwegian newspaper, *Aftenposten*: "This is not due to any lack of understanding of minorities or religious traditions, but because the procedure is irreversible, painful and risky."

Lindboe is certainly not a lone voice in this debate. A large number of parliamentarians from the opposition Labor Party have expressed support for a ban, while the Center Party, which controls 10 of the seats in Norway's 169-member legislature, is officially in favor. Small wonder, then, that Ervin Kohn, the head of Norway's tiny Jewish community of 700 souls, has described the issue as an "existential matter." Clearly, the push factors that led nearly 50 percent of Jews in Belgium, Hungary, and France to confess, in a survey on antisemitism conducted by the European Union's Fundamental Rights Agency, that they are considering emigration have manifested in Norway also. The Norwegian developments follow the October vote by the Parliamentary Assembly of the Council of Europe, a 47-member body that is not institutionally linked to the EU, recommending restrictions on ritual circumcision. The ensuing outcry among European Jewish leaders and Israeli politicians led a nervous Thorbjorn Jaglund, the council's secretary-general, to assure the Conference of European Rabbis "that in no way does the Council of Europe want to ban the circumcision of boys." But given that the Council of Europe has no control over national legislatures, that statement is essentially toothless.

The abiding question here is why hostility to ritual circumcision has become such a hot topic in European states. When it comes to circumcision, the kinds of survivors groups that push for tougher legislation on, say, child sexual abuse or violence against women simply don't exist. Hence, if the vast majority of men who have undergone ritual circumcision aren't clamoring for a ban, why the insistence on portraying them as victims?

According to Rabbi Pinchas Goldschmidt, the head of the Conference of European Rabbis, the anti-circumcision campaign is an integral component of a continent-wide "offensive" against Muslim communities, in which Jews represent "collateral damage." There is some merit to this view, yet it ignores the fact that legal measures against Jewish ritual have a long and dishonorable pedigree in Europe. It's widely known that the Nazis banned shechita, or Jewish ritual slaughter, three months after coming to power in 1933, but they were beaten to the punch by Switzerland in 1893 and Norway in 1930 – and you don't need to be an expert on European history to know that there were no Muslim communities of any meaningful size in these countries when these legislative bills were passed. Moreover, it can be argued that by grouping male circumcision with the horrific practice of female genital mutilation, which in Europe mainly afflicts women from Muslim countries, the Council of Europe was going out of its way not to target Muslim communities specifically. In a classic example of the cultural relativism that plagues European institutions, its resolution on the "physical integrity of children" listed as matters of concern, "...female genital mutilation, the circumcision of young boys for religious reasons, early childhood medical interventions in the case of intersex children, and the submission to or coercion of children into piercings, tattoos or plastic surgery."

As this week's edition of the Economist argues, this categorization is nonsensical: Our intuition tells us that the circumcision of baby boys is probably okay, at worst harmless and culturally very important to some religions, while the excision practised on baby girls in some cultures certainly is not okay. The same piece observes that, in any case, the determination of European leaders to prevent a ban on circumcision will likely foil any parliamentary legislation to that end. A similar point was made in a recent *Haaretz* piece by Anshel Pfeffer, who derided fears among Israeli legislators of a ban on circumcision as just so much hyperbole.

However, what's missing here is the understanding that a practice doesn't have to be proscribed for it to be frowned upon. Large numbers of Europeans already regard circumcision as a backward ritual, and the current Norwegian debate is likely to persuade many more that circumcision should be opposed in the name of human rights. Over the last decade, European Jews have watched helplessly as their identification with Israel has been stigmatized: with a similar pattern now emerging over Jewish ritual, an adversarial political climate that falls short of actual legislation may yet be enough to persuade them that their future on the continent remains bleak.

Chapter Five: The US and Israel

Obama Administration Excoriates Israel...Again

JointMedia News Service, December 12, 2011

"Let every eye negotiate for itself and trust no agent," says the deceived Claudio in Shakespeare's *Much Ado About Nothing*. However cynical it sounds, there are times when a maxim like this one rightly guides the affairs of diplomacy, just as it does the affairs of the heart. And if it encapsulates Israel's current attitude to the prospect of peace negotiations, what fair-minded person – after two decades of frustrated exchanges, spurned offers and frequent, blood-curdling denunciations of Zionism across the Arab and Muslim worlds – could find this unreasonable? The Obama Administration, apparently, does. Within the last fortnight, two top-level officials and one ambassador have, on three separate occasions, taken Israel to task for an extraordinary range of alleged misdeeds, including its hardline intransi-gence, its poor record on civil rights, and the way its policies have enabled the spread of antisemitism among Europe's Muslim populations.

Item one: Defense Secretary Leon Panetta repeated the mantra about Israel's increasing isolation in the context of the unprecedented regional upheavals still misleadingly referred to as the "Arab Spring." Panetta's lec-ture ended with a phrase that may well become his epitaph, at once a call to action and an admonition: "Return to the damn table!" That would be the negotiating table, a location that Panetta – in bewildering defiance of the actual record – insists Israel is avoiding like the proverbial plague. Item two: Secretary of State Hillary Clinton lashed out at what she regards as the ero-sion of Israeli democracy. Specifically, she cited a Knesset bill that would limit foreign funding of Israel's NGOs, segregated seating for women on certain buses in Jerusalem, and the decision of a group of male IDF soldiers to leave a ceremony where female soldiers were singing. The analogies which Clinton invoked to frame these issues could have been lifted from a J Street press release, or worse: the segregated seating was "reminiscent of Rosa Parks," while the objection to the female chorus brought to mind no less than Iran.

Item three: The U.S. Ambassador to Belgium, Howard Gutman, told a Jewish conference that a distinction should be made between traditional antisemitism and its contemporary form, acutely visible among European Muslims, in which hatred of Israel transitions into general hatred of Jews. If

Israel were to heed Panetta's demand and return to the "damn table," these malign attitudes would dissipate in the wake of a Middle East peace settlement. There has been much speculation as to whether these statements were coordinated. In my view, it doesn't really matter. The chief consideration is the degree to which they reflect the Obama Administration's general worldview. In distinguishing its Middle East policies from the previous George W. Bush Administration, the Obama White House has stressed its readiness to reach an accommodation with existing realities, rather than transforming them at the point of a gun. The most recent example is Obama's commitment to a historic compromise with the region's dominant current; those political forces who, in the Administration's view, marry the vision of an Islamic state with the trappings of democracy. Islamists they may be, but of the moderate variety.

The problem, of course, is that this assessment is a fantasy. Any differences among Islamists are primarily about tactics, not ideas. When it comes to that old bugbear of the Jews, how does al-Qaeda differ meaningfully from the Muslim Brotherhood-affiliated parties grabbing the reins of power in Tunisia, Morocco and Egypt? Both are committed to wiping out the Jewish state, which essentially means, for al-Qaeda, wiping out all the Jews, and for the Muslim Brotherhood, all the Jews except for a small remnant of compliant anti-Zionist haredim. What the Obama Administration refuses to even see, never mind take seriously, is the eliminationist project which lies at the core of the Islamist position towards Israel. To do so would undermine the image of these people as driven by a happy combination of legitimate grievances and limited expectations, thus making them eminently reasonable partners for dialogue.

It is these parameters that permit Hillary Clinton to traffic in the moral relativism that obscenely compares illiberal attitudes among one of Israel's many demographics with the policies of Iran, a state in which Muslims who convert to Christianity face the death penalty. They permit Leon Panetta to defy established truths in a manner that would be instantly recognizable to the conspiracy-mongers in the Arab media. And they permit Howard Gutman to ignore centuries of homegrown Muslim antisemitism – one consequence of which was the wholesale expulsion of Jewish communities from Arab countries in the latter half of the last century – in order to push the falsehood that Israel lies at the beginning and the end of these myriad conflicts. After years of endless barbs against the supposed myths and lies underlying the foreign policy of the Bush Administration, it's time to train the spotlight on Obama.

This Administration's policies in the Middle East should not just be of concern to Jews – although Jewish voters should be urged to express their disapproval at next year's election. They should be a source of worry to anyone who understands that the spread of democratic values and practices is critical to America's security and wellbeing. For too long, we have endured these spiteful swipes against America's most loyal ally in the Middle East, while elsewhere in the world, the Administration touches its forelock before some truly nasty regimes. Forget the Middle East – where was the Obama Administration this past weekend, as thousands of Russians protested Vladimir Putin's rigging of this month's elections? Why does Obama continue to pussyfoot around the Pakistani government, offering condolences for the deaths of Pakistani soldiers killed in a NATO airstrike who were openly assisting Taliban forces attacking American troops?

For all of its rhetorical attacks against Israel and its government, one truth will outlast this Administration. No matter who is in power in Israel – Labor, Kadima, Likud or some other permutation – that country's foreign policy will *always* be anchored in loyalty to the United States. There are few other countries, whether inside or outside the Middle East, about which a similar judgment can be made.

Attacking Israel Online

Commentary, July 1, 2012

Throughout the greater Middle East, opposition to the concept and existence of a Jewish state is an idée fixe for hundreds of millions of Arab and non-Arab Muslims. A hatred of Jewish political sovereignty that frequently dovetails with more traditional antisemitism animates café discussions and street protests as surely as it prohibits regional political progress. Yet the strand of anti-Zionism that has lately come to attract the most attention in the West is the one articulated by a tiny minority of left-wing Jews at a handful of websites. Full-time antagonists of Israel such as M.J. Rosenberg, Max Blumenthal, Philip Weiss, and Peter Beinart have accumulated an influence that vastly exceeds their single-digit numbers. This is in part due to the financial sponsorship of successful and well-established media institutions. Until March 2012, Rosenberg was employed by Media Matters for America (MMfA) at a salary of some $130,000 per annum. Weiss was supported for years by the Nation magazine's Nation Institute. Peter Beinart's new Open Zion blog is hosted by the Daily Beast, an online publication jointly owned by the Harman family and the Internet media giant IAC.

But Rosenberg, Weiss, and Beinart take a different view of their place in the media conversation. They believe themselves to be fearless truth-tellers who actively resist a censorious tribal culture that bulldozes any hint of discord. Rosenberg offered a pithy insight into this in an April 2012 opinion piece for the website of al-Jazeera. After claiming that pro-Israel advocacy organizations were hindering efforts to secure a peaceful resolution of the conflict between Israel and the Palestinians, he concluded with an exhortation. "Being pro-Israel means caring about Israel," wrote Rosenberg, whose career has been built on the fact that he briefly worked for the American Israel Public Affairs Committee three decades ago. "It does not mean using it as an excuse for power brokering and suppressing dissident voices."

Dissident voices? Properly understood, the word dissident describes intellectuals and activists operating in oppressive societies. What they do frequently results in imprisonment, torture, and even death. The dissidents of whom Rosenberg speaks so modestly, since they include himself, are not silenced, but rather celebrated, by media establishments ranging from the Huffington Post to the BBC. The persistent inclusion of these "dissident voices" in discussions of America, Jews, and Israel has proven very useful indeed, since their membership in the tribe is deemed to give them special standing in presenting their indictment of Israel – and, somewhat more subtly, inoculates Gentile critics of the Jewish state against the charge that their attacks on Israel might be antisemitic. How can they be if they are merely echoing the arguments made by such passionate, such moral, such fearless, such dissident Jews? In an Internet age characterized by instant, rolling comment, they have helped to reactivate a set of ideas that many thought had perished with the grubby pamphlets published in the old Soviet Union, screeds that bore titles such as "Zionism: A Tool of Reaction." Whereas the true dissidents of the Cold War era introduced words such as samizdat into the vocabulary of the West, the ersatz dissidents of the Jewish left have popularized a host of expressions – Judaization, Israel-firster, Zionist apartheid, and so forth – that were once relegated almost entirely to the openly antisemitic fringe. What an accomplishment.

As Rosenberg's remark makes plain, the common point of departure for online Jewish anti-Zionists is the unaccountable, transcendent power of disparate pro-Israel organizations lumped together under the umbrella term the Israel lobby. The determination of this lobby to muzzle "dissenting" voices inside the Jewish community is the favored theme of writers such as Michael Lerner, the Berkeley-based progressive rabbi and founder of Tikkun magazine, and Richard Silverstein, a Seattle-based blogger with a penchant for seeing Mossad plots behind every Middle East news story. Similarly, the explicitly anti-Zionist Jewish Voice for Peace (JVP) operates a blog, appropriately entitled Muzzlewatch, that purports to monitor "efforts to stifle open debate about U.S.-Israeli foreign policy."

Such paranoid theories take their expositors into deep – arguably clinical – eccentricity. In an April 2012 blog entry, Rosenberg opined that the availability of kosher food at a White House reception was just another display of forelock-tugging by an administration that lives in fear of the Israel lobby's wrath. The post's title ("Obama: Stop Pandering to the Jewish Right Already") was meant to be read in the folksy cadence of an offended American Jew. "The same exact impulse that causes the Obamas to blowtorch their ovens to Hassidic standards," he wrote, "also leads the administration to be in perpetual suck-up mode to Prime Minister Netanyahu on matters like Iran and the Israeli occupation, matters of life and death." In addition to being uncommonly powerful, the Israel lobby is supposedly made up of U.S. citizens whose primary loyalty is to Israel, and who will choose the Jewish state over the United States should circumstances demand. It is Rosenberg who is credited with having spread the term Israelfirster in the online columns he wrote in his capacity as a "foreign-policy fellow" at Media Matters. And with the New York Times columnist Thomas Friedman asserting, in December 2011, that the standing ovation for Israeli Prime Minister Benjamin Netanyahu at the U.S. Congress "was bought and paid for by the Israel lobby," it is no wonder that Rosenberg expressed great authorial pride as a result – or that Media Matters might initially have felt great pride that it had come to exert such influence on the most "mainstream" of mainstream commentators on the Middle East. Almost immediately, however, Jewish groups and pro-Israel commentators charged that the term Israel-firster, as deployed by Rosenberg, was inherently antisemitic – and presented indubitable evidence that the term was a favored epithet of neo-Nazi groups. Rosenberg was compelled to announce that he would cease abusing his opponents in this way, and within three months, he and Media Matters parted company. Rosenberg indignantly denied that he had been fired, claiming on the Huffington Post that he made the magnanimous decision "to leave to protect an organization I love from people who, in their single-minded devotion to the Israeli government, will go after anyone and anything who stands in their way." So much for taking responsibility for making rhetorical common cause with Hitler-lovers. In any case, his Israelfirster charge is neither clever, nor daring, nor new. It is, rather, a shopworn offense to common decency. The notion that Jewish officials are more loyal to their own kind than to the state or the institutions they serve goes back at least to 1894 and the false conviction of the French army captain Alfred

Dreyfus. George Orwell, writing about antisemitism in the immediate after-math of World War II, noted similar sentiments in the grumblings about a "Jewish war" in which the fighting and the dying was principally done by Gentiles. "To publicize the exploits of Jewish soldiers, or even to admit the existence of a considerable Jewish army in the Middle East, rouses hostility in South Africa, the Arab countries, and elsewhere," Orwell wrote. "It is easi-er to ignore the whole subject and allow the man in the street to go on think-ing that Jews are exceptionally clever at dodging military service." It is exact-ly this kind of lazy, conspiracy-laden thinking that informs the Israel-firster smear.

Philip Weiss, editor of the Middle East–focused website Mondoweiss, takes a more personal approach to his anti-Zionism. He writes often about his psychic struggles with his own Jewish identity – not surprising, since what he most hates about himself is also the source of his reputation. Inter-viewed by the antisemitic ex-Israeli writer Gilad Atzmon, Weiss reflected that Jewish identity imparts "a sense of difference, yes, inevitably of elite identity, that's part of Jewish history and one I struggle with." He also de-lights in stoking the notion that he traffics in antisemitism. "I can justly be accused of being a conspiracy theorist because I believe in the Israel lobby theory," he wrote in a recent blog entry. "I quoted seven Jewish writers on this point, including [Harvard Professor Alan] Dershowitz: 'The recent neo-conservative movement in America has also been dominated by Jews.'" The practice of selectively quoting Jewish advocates against themselves is asso-ciated most of all with neo-Nazi propaganda outfits such as the website Jew Watch, so Weiss is in exactly the kind of company he deserves. In 2009, the Web provocateur Max Blumenthal posted a video on YouTube called "Feel-ing the Hate in Jerusalem." In it he talks to drunk American Jewish students in downtown Jerusalem and elicits grotesque statements about how much they hate Arabs. On the Huffington Post, Blumenthal went on to defend the stunt as an example of in vino veritas. "The notion that the racist diatribes in my video emerged spontaneously from a beery void is a delusion, but for some, it is a necessary one," he wrote. "It allows them to erect a psychologi-cal barrier against acknowledging the painful consequences of prolonged Zionist indoctrination."

Blumenthal has a knack for uncovering the influence of Zionism in the most unlikely places. Writing on the Web-only English-language version of the Lebanese newspaper al-Akhbar in November 2011, he noted that the "Israelification of America's security apparatus, recently unleashed in full force against the Occupy Wall Street Movement, has taken place at every level of law enforcement, and in areas that have yet to be exposed." It was a fitting observation for the readership of al-Akhbar, which has made a hero of the late Hezbollah terrorist Imad Mughniyeh and whose editor believes that Jews in Israel should return en masse to the more comfortable "capitalist environment" of Europe. In another al-Akhbar piece, Blumenthal asked, "When have Zionists ever let historical nuance get in the way of a campaign to muzzle critics of Israeli policy?"

Compared with such explicit ugliness, Peter Beinart's blog, Open Zion, seems mild and contemplative – an impression that appears very much to be Beinart's goal, given the radicalism of his own policy suggestions. He recently proposed that the United States pursue a targeted boycott of Jewish communities in the West Bank. He did so as part of the promotional drive for his latest book, The Crisis of Zionism. Beinart's account of Israel's failures and liabilities earned him praise in the Atlantic and the New Yorker for his "courage" in taking on the Israel lobby, which posed such a threat to him and his career that, after the publication of the article from which his book would spring, Beinart reportedly received a courageous advance of several hundred thousand dissenting dollars. Open Zion, in its name and design, seems intended to herald some supposedly long-neglected flowering of unapologetically diverse opinion on Zionism. There is Beinart himself, supporting a boycott of Jewish businesses, musing endlessly about the pitfalls of Jewish power, along with a host of lesser impersonators who write articles with titles such as "How I Lost My Zionism" and "Can You Be a Zionist If No-One Thinks You Are?" (Answering his own question, the author of this last piece, Jay Michaelson, writes, "I hesitate to claim the label because I don't want to be associated with those who wear it proudly.")

Then there are the pro-Israel loyalists: the forceful Israeli historian Benny Morris, the Judaism scholar Yehuda Mirsky, the Knesset Member Einat Wilf. One gets the distinct sense that these writers are intended to function as a permanent opposition. A third category is composed of think-tank analysts and nonprofit advocates who are ostensibly focused on the iniquities of Israeli policy but who willingly deploy the stock-in-trade dogmas of anti-Zionist ideology. Jewish critics of Israel, such as Daniel Levy of the New America Foundation and Lara Friedman of American Friends of Peace Now, play a key role in undermining the influence of Open Zion's pro-Israel contributors. Responding to a piece by Morris on Palestinian rejectionism, Levy argued that the real obstacle to a negotiated settlement is the naqba – the Arabic word for "catastrophe," used by Palestinians and their supporters to describe the creation of Israel – and "the second-class status of Palestinian citizens within the Jewish state." These words are an uncomplicated reflection of the basic stance of anti-Zionism, which holds that Jewish sovereignty is the diseased heart of the Middle East's discontents.

Finally, there is the category of Open Zion writers for whom the very existence of Israel is at best an irritant, at worse an offense. Members of this clan include Trita Parsi, the president of the National Iranian American Council (NIAC), whose mandate is to encourage an empathetic American engagement with the current Iranian regime, and Yousef Munayyer, a Palestinian activist who pushes the insidious line that Israel is an apartheid state that must yield in favor of a single Palestinian entity between the Mediterranean Sea and the Jordan River. But for all its strenuous posturing about "open" discussion, Open Zion is most notable for its silences. Readers will search the blog in vain for analysis of the recent events that have spread extraordinary discomfort throughout the Jewish world. When Günter Grass, the former Waffen-SS recruit who later became one of Germany's literary celebrities, penned the turgid poem "What Must Be Said," in which he laments that Holocaust guilt was propelling his country to support an Israeli war against Iran, Open Zion did not deem these verses worthy of even a paragraph. The question of why a man who was personally involved in the slaughter of the Jews felt confident enough to repackage his antisemitism as hostility to Israel was left to other outlets to consider – few of which are explicitly concerned with the "Jewish future," as Open Zion declares itself to be.

Similarly, the website barely mentioned the March 2012 assault by an al-Qaeda gunman upon a Jewish school in Toulouse, France, which resulted in the murders of a rabbi and three small children. Again, there are a number of apposite questions about the Jewish future arising from this atrocity, ranging from the appropriate level of security at Jewish institutions to the denial by Tariq Ramadan, a European Islamist much admired by Western intellectuals, that the gunman was motivated by antisemitism. On these and related matters, Open Zion had nothing meaningful to say. By contrast, it is safe to assume that had a lone Israeli extremist entered a Jerusalem mosque and sprayed worshippers with bullets, the blog would have gone into overdrive. Why? Because the paradigm of Jewish power to which Beinart subscribes does not allow for Jewish vulnerability, only Jewish aggression. Moreover, according to prevailing liberal sensibilities, when Jews do suffer, it is because the iniquities of the state of Israel brought such an outcome upon them. That, perhaps, is why Open Zion has a subject tag that reads "Real Antisemitism," to be employed on those rare occasions when Jews face hatred as a reality, and not as the invention of some unscrupulous AIPAC staffer.

Such willful myopia is not without precedent. Prior to the Holocaust and the Arab war of annihilation against the nascent state of Israel in 1948, Zionism coexisted in an uneasy equilibrium with non-Zionist and anti-Zionist currents among American Jews. A marked distaste for Jewish national aspirations was shared by many liberal, assimilationist Jews. It is this tradition, more than any other, that finds its contemporary resonance in projects such as Open Zion. In 1885, a gathering of Reform rabbis in Pittsburgh issued a statement on Jewish identity that eventually became known as the "Pittsburgh Platform." More than a decade before the First Zionist Congress met in Basel, Switzerland, the Pittsburgh rabbis rejected the core philosophical foundations of Zionism: "We consider ourselves no longer a nation, but a religious community, and therefore, expect neither a return to Palestine, nor a sacrificial worship under the sons of Aaron, nor the restoration of any laws concerning the Jewish state."

The principles behind the Pittsburgh Platform found organizational expression in the work of the American Council for Judaism (ACJ). Now a shadow of its former self, the ACJ once enjoyed access to the highest levels of the American government. In 1954, a speech on the Middle East delivered in Dayton, Ohio, by then assistant secretary of state Henry Byroade drew heavily on the influence of Rabbi Elmer Berger, the ACJ's founder, in urging that Jews in Palestine effectively surrender their national ambitions. Both Berger and his colleague Alfred Lilienthal, a former State Department lawyer, became progressively more shrill in their denunciations of Zionism as the years wore on. Barely remembered now, Lilienthal was something of an innovator. Although Beinart might think it rather novel and provocative to write about the "hoarding" of the Holocaust by Jewish organizations, it was Lilienthal who coined the inelegantly offensive term Holocaustomania as the prime motivator behind what he called "Washington's Israel-first" Middle East policy. "I sincerely resented the Zionist propaganda which wanted to make my Christian fellow citizens believe that all American Jews, in a fictitious 'unity,' desire a political separation of 'the Jewish people,'" he wrote in a memoir.

Excoriated by their fellow Jews decades before an omnipotent Israel lobby could be fashionably blamed, Berger and Lilienthal would find their most sympathetic audience in the Arab world. In 1978 Lilienthal wrote a tome called The Zionist Connection: What Price Peace? It was published by the firm Dodd Mead. Three years later, Lilienthal was presenting smaller publishing houses with a letter guaranteeing the purchase of 10,000 copies of a paperback version of The Zionist Connection – a letter issued by the interior ministry of the government of Saudi Arabia.

In 1977, Lilienthal had turned up in the Libyan capital, Tripoli, for a confe-rence on "Zionism and racism" organized by EAFORD, a nongovernmental organization financed by the regime of Muammar al-Gaddafi. "What we today know in the West as antisemitism has never existed in the Arab world," he assured the assembled delegates. In 1987, Lilienthal and Berger were the star attractions at an EAFORD-sponsored symposium in Washing-ton, D.C., on Zionism and Judaism. "Free, responsible, informed political debate about the policies of the Zionist state is impossible," Berger snarled before his audience. Might Berger and Lilienthal's ideological heirs soon find themselves the exclusive darlings of Middle Eastern anti-Semites? There is already some indication fate is moving in this direction. M.J. Rosenberg's troubles with Media Matters certainly indicate some institutional reticence in the United States with anti-Zionist punditry. Max Blumenthal, in addition to being a frequent contributor to al-Akhbar, was also the subject of a fawn-ing profile on Press TV, an English-language satellite broadcaster financed entirely by the Iranian regime. In receiving this dubious honor, he won the seal of approval from a state that has turned the denial of the Holocaust into an official doctrine.

Mass-movement anti-Zionism will be happy to incorporate Jewish anti-Zionists and march onward. Hatred of Israel is a malleable doctrine of false justice that welcomes all comers and provides for unlikely bedfellows. These days, the burden of proof is increasingly, and perversely, placed on those arguing in Zionism's behalf. But, ironically, charting both the writings and the career trajectories of devoted anti-Zionists makes a uniquely strong case for the continued existence and protection of the Jewish state.

Obama and Israel: Degrees of Separation

JNS/Jewish Journal Los Angeles, August 1, 2012

American foreign policy, and specifically its Middle Eastern dimension, came back into play last week in a presidential election campaign that has largely focused on domestic issues. The big dispute centered around which candi-date had outflanked the other in reaching out to Israel – as Mitt Romney prepared for his arrival in Israel, President Obama announced that he would sign a bill enhancing cooperation between the United States and Israel. Con-gress already passed that bill, the U.S.-Israel Enhanced Security Cooperation Act, with strong bipartisan support. As an expression of policy, it is a wel-come reaffirmation of American objectives with regard to a final settlement between Israel and the Palestinians. That there needs to be a two-state solution is pretty much the global consensus, but the bill places strong emphasis on the requirement that Israel's neighbors recognize its right "to exist as a Jewish state," an inflection that, with the exception of Canada, most of the other parties with regional influence tend to downplay. The bill also quotes former President George W. Bush's elegant 2008 summation of what makes the U.S.-Israel relationship distinctive: "The alliance between our governments is unbreakable, yet the source of our friendship runs deeper than any treaty."

Most importantly of all, the bill commits the U.S. to preserving Israel's "qualitative military edge," the one factor that has prevented the Middle East from collapsing into an all-out, genocidal war of elimination since the Jewish state's creation in 1948. That means speeding up the delivery of F-35 fighter aircraft to Israel and improving cooperation in all areas of security, from counterterrorism to cyberspace. So is everything now a bed of roses in a bilateral relationship that has been through distinctly sour moments since Obama's election four years ago? There was never, of course, any question that the U.S.-Israel relationship would be ruptured; the issue has been the degree of separation between the two countries on key political and military challenges. Obama famously believes that there needs to be, as he told U.S. Jewish leaders gathered at the White House in July 2009, more "daylight" between the U.S. and Israel. Obama said this in order to contrast his approach with that of his predecessor; yet, three years later, we are no closer to a meaningful deal between Israel and the Palestinians.

In the meantime, the dynamics of the region have changed radically. The notion, beloved of the United Nations and European governments, that the road to a peaceful, prosperous Middle East runs through Jerusalem was always a dubious one; now, following the regime changes in Egypt, Tunisia and Libya, and the ongoing bloodshed in Syria, the idea that the Palestinians hold the keys to peace seems almost laughable. Israel's greatest concerns revolve around the region as a whole, of which the Palestinian aspect is merely one part, and not the most important. Foremost is Iran's nuclear program, and not far behind is what the U.S.-Israel Enhanced Security Cooperation Act terms "a rise in the influence of radical Islamists," most obviously the new Muslim Brotherhood administration of Mohamed Morsi in Egypt, and the unmitigated hostility of Prime Minister Erdogan's Islamist government in Turkey.

All of these governments are supportive, to varying degrees, of the Islamist narrative on Zionism and Israel; at best, they will grudgingly accept Israel as a temporary fact, but they are millions of miles from acknowledging its historic, legal and moral legitimacy. Israelis are all too aware of this new reality, in which the predictable behavior associated with the old regimes, like that of Hosni Mubarak in Egypt, has vanished. And that is why what might seem to be minor slights – I'm thinking of exclusion of Israel from the counterterrorism forum convened by Secretary of State Hillary Clinton in Istanbul in June – can be interpreted as an alarming abandonment of Israel at a time when its regional standing is about where it was in 1967.

Even more significantly, as the veteran diplomat Aaron David Miller argued in a recent piece for Foreign Policy magazine, "unlike Clinton and George W. Bush, Obama isn't in love with the idea of Israel." This lack of emotional identification is the main theme of a new advertising campaign launched by the Emergency Committee for Israel, which, in highlighting Obama's comparative coldness towards Israel, quotes a Palestinian official who observed the absence of an "emotion-based relationship" between Obama and Israel. That's a major reason behind Miller's conclusion that more turbulence is inevitable should Obama win in November and should Benjamin Netanyahu remain Israel's Prime Minister. As he writes, "on the issue of a peace settlement, Obama's views are much closer to the Palestinians than to Israel." That is not the case with Mitt Romney, who has been stepping up the pro-Israel rhetoric of late. In an otherwise bland interview with Ha'aretz as he departed for Israel, Romney made the telling point that "the question is not whether the people of the region believe that there should be a Palestinian state. The question is if they believe there should be an Israeli state, a Jewish state." At the moment, by and large, they don't. Hence the justified concern at the prospect of a second term with a president who has no patience with Israel's deepest worry of all – that its neighbors don't think it has a right to be there in the first place. I once had a fascinating conversation with a former senior official of the Clinton Administration, in which he related a discussion he'd had with a leader of the Palestinian Authority. Asked why the Palestinians had bailed out at the 11th hour on the final peace deal put forward by Clinton in 2000, the PA leader replied that he and his colleagues were expecting a Republican president to take the reins at the White House, and that they would get a more favorable deal under those circumstances. The Clinton official responded that if the Palestinians understood anything about George W. Bush, they would realize that such a waiting game was futile. In that event, he turned out to be right. Yet, more than a decade later, the Palestinians are still playing the waiting game. Only this time, their calculations might be closer to the mark. A second Obama administration could provide with the Palestinians with, to adapt a well-worn saying, an opportunity not to miss an opportunity. What isn't clear is whether the Palestinian leadership is smart enough to take advantage of that, and push themselves back to the center of Middle East politics.

The Changing Middle East as seen from AIPAC 2013

JNS/The Algemeiner, March 4, 2013

WASHINGTON, DC – From the second one arrives at the Washington Convention Center, the AIPAC spectacle is all-encompassing. From the anti-Israel demonstrators clustering around the entrance to the sparkling, multi-screen plenaries in the main hall, there is a both a sense of showmanship and a sense that this is, for two days, the only show in town.

Even so, the razzmatazz at this year's AIPAC policy conference couldn't quite mute the background murmurs about the organization's declining influence. There was Chuck Hagel's confirmation as Defense Secretary, and there is the ongoing debate about the impact of sequestration on Israel's defensive capabilities. When Senator John Cornyn (R-TX) complained that the Obama Administration still had not delivered advanced F-35 fighter aircraft to Israel, he inadvertently invited his audience to ponder, "All powerful Israel Lobby? What all powerful Israel Lobby?" Away from the podium speeches that restated, to standing ovations and thunderous applause, the critical talking points of Israel advocacy – "Israel is the only democracy in the Middle East," "all options must remain on the table concerning Iran," "there is no genuine Palestinian peace partner," and so forth – there was serious reconsideration of Israel's current strategic position in the Middle East. Senator John McCain (R-AZ) memorably summarized the stakes involved when he told the AIPAC crowd, "I have not seen the Middle East and the world in a more dangerous situation in my lifetime."

What, perhaps, is distinctive about this "dangerous situation" is that it contains a complex of conflicts in which Israel is not an active participant, but a nervous bystander waiting on a series of uncertain outcomes. The much-vaunted Arab Spring, more accurately described by the Israeli journalist Amos Harel as "the Arab upheaval," has taken different forms in different countries, but the common denominator is that, in not a single instance, has a democratic, open society emerged at the other end. In the Arab Gulf region in particular, long-established repressive and corrupt regimes, most obviously in Saudi Arabia, remain in place; as the American columnist Bret Stephens pointed out, much as we might wish for an end to the Saudi monarchy, in all likelihood what follows them will be worse.

Old certainties – like the position of Turkey as a friend of both Israel and the western powers – have been dramatically undercut, as demonstrated by Prime Minister Erdogan's vicious assault on Zionism as a "crime against humanity." Most of all, there is Iran. While there was little discussion of the one conflict in which Israel is directly involved, that with the Palestinians, the AIPAC parley was dominated by anxiety that Iran is on the cusp of acquiring a nuclear weapon. Speaking at the main plenary, Vice-President Joe Biden accentuated a significant, if subtle, shift in the Administration's articulation of its Iran policy. America's goal, Biden said, "is to prevent Iran from acquiring a nuclear weapon, period." Then, for added effect, Biden repeated: "Prevent, *not* contain, prevent." The picture that has emerged at AIPAC, then, is of an Israel facing unknown, indeterminate threats that are far greater than the known threats it has encountered in the past. As a consequence, detailed policy prescriptions were hard to come by. Absent from the policy conference were recommendations as to how Israel should proceed in negotiations with the Palestinians (because there aren't any) or maintain its historic 1979 peace treaty with Egypt (because there's not much it can do should that country's Muslim Brotherhood leaders decide to tear it up.) Instead, the focus was on Israel as frontline member of the community of democratic nations, the terrain where the cultural, political and perhaps military struggles between western openness and Islamists strictures will be played out.

That was certainly the subtext of one of the more interesting, if sparsely attended, breakout sessions at AIPAC, on Canada's relationship with Israel. All the Canadian politicians who spoke stressed that the reason Canada goes to bat for Israel so energetically in international forums is based on Prime Minister Stephen Harper's dictum that "we're going to support what's right, not what's politically expedient." Canadian parliamentarian Robert Dochert pointed out that the Toronto riding he represents contains 25,000 Palestinians and 500 Jews, but even so, his support for Israel won't waiver. What AIPAC this year proves is that there is considerable mileage in the values Israel shares not just with the U.S., but with other western states like Canada. And while enlightened values in themselves don't win wars, it's equally true that without enlightened values, wars cannot be won.

Do We Still Need a Special Envoy on Antisemitism?

"Contentions" @ Commentary Magazine, June 8, 2013

Reading the remarks of Ira Forman, the State Department's newly-appointed special envoy to monitor and combat antisemitism, to a Washington D.C. gathering of the American Jewish Committee, I was seized by one heretical thought that was quickly followed by another. Are there any real benefits to be gained from the existence of this position? And does the special envoy help to clarify or obscure the reasons behind the persistence of antisemitism in our own time? The position was created by the Global Antisemitism Review Act that was signed into law by President Bush in 2004. The act was authored by the late Democratic congressman Tom Lantos, a Holocaust survivor whose horror at the global upsurge in antisemitic beliefs and violence that accompanied the outbreak, in 2000, of the second Palestinian intifada led him to campaign for a dedicated State Department official to stay on top of the problem.

Bush was receptive because he regarded the fight against antisemitism as an essential component of promoting the values of liberty around the world. Announcing the act's passage, Bush declared that "extending freedom also means confronting the evil of antisemitism." The first special envoy, Gregg Rickman, did an admirable job of setting the tone, particularly in explaining the intimate connections between anti-Zionism and antisemitism. That cannot have been an easy task, especially as Rickman's main interlocutors were European diplomats, most of whom shudder at the idea that distaste for Israel can be motivated by distaste for Jews. When Rickman left government following President Obama's election in 2008, the post remained vacant for more than a year before Hannah Rosenthal, a former Clinton administration official, was appointed. With Rosenthal's arrival, there was a notable shift in emphasis: whereas the Bush administration framed the fight against antisemitism as integral to the broader struggle for political liberty, under Obama it was repositioned as one of several components of a tolerance agenda. The excessive attention Rosenthal gave to prejudice against Muslims provoked her predecessor, Rickman, into advocating that she be rebranded as the "special envoy to monitor Islamophobia," in order that "someone else who cares more about the fate and welfare of Jews" be appointed in her stead. It's too early to predict whether Forman will attract the same controversy that Rosenthal did. Given his previous role as CEO of the National Jewish Democratic Council, expectations that he will stick his neck out on an issue that adds an unwelcome layer of complexity to the administration's Middle East policies will be low to begin with. Nonetheless, several clues to his approach can be found in his Washington speech. In broad terms, Forman made the right noises. His account of recent antisemitic outrages from Hungary to Iran was certainly accurate, if pedestrian. But what was absent was any understanding of what makes antisemitism unique.

Charles Maurras, a notorious French anti-Semite of the 19th century, once observed that the great strength of Jew-hatred is that it "enables everything to be arranged, smoothed over, and simplified." This, in turn, helps explain why antisemitism finds fertile ground in such culturally diverse locations as Venezuela and Egypt, as well as why it wins adherents on both left and right. Burying this distinctiveness in the name of a multi-ethnic coalition that regards all prejudices as equally toxic, as Rosenthal surely did during her time as special envoy, necessarily blunts an effective response. A related criticism is that too much of the Special Envoy's time is spent on commemorating past atrocities against Jews, at the expense of current problems. In his speech to the AJC, Forman urged his audience "not to think that the picture is all bleak. There has been good news as well as bad." However, the "good" news he related was exclusively concerned with Holocaust commemoration in Europe and the United States. What that ignores, of course, is the painful truth that it is much easier for a country like Belgium to commit itself to educating school kids about the Holocaust than it is to clamp down on the various Islamist groups agitating against Jews within its own borders. A related passage of Forman's speech was even more striking. He described a recent visit to Auschwitz with an unnamed "Palestinian imam" who left the extermination camp carrying the following conclusion:

"Because the people here in Europe, with what they have faced in the past, they have overcome the discrimination, all the terrible things. And now they live with peace...with safety. This means we can, in the Holy Land, do the same thing. We can overcome our conflict, our wars, our people who were killed, and we can talk together to reach a peace."

There is nothing wrong with talking about peace. But is gushing over the invocation of the Holocaust in a Palestinian appeal for peace in the "Holy Land" what a special envoy on antisemitism should be doing? Wouldn't it be preferable to highlight the manner in which the hardwired antisemitism of groups like the Muslim Brotherhood both confounds the peace process and contributes to the insecurity of Diaspora Jewish communities? And if we are going to educate about the Holocaust, shouldn't the stress be on how the mass genocide of the Jews was the culmination of centuries of antisemitism, rather than an abstract illustration of the inhumanity which human beings are capable of? Finally, isn't the Holocaust the best illustration of just how exposed and vulnerable Jews are when they don't have their own state? It may be that articulating these arguments would push the special envoy into politically and diplomatically difficult terrain. If that's the case, then arguably we'd better off if his position didn't exist in the first place.

J Street and the Decline of American Power

JNS/The Algemeiner, October 1, 2013

A few weeks ago, I ventured the theory that rather than the so-called "Israel Lobby" controlling the administration, it's the administration that controls the Israel Lobby. As evidence, I cited two recent episodes. Firstly, Secretary of State John Kerry's much-vaunted effort to revive Israeli-Palestinian conflict negotiations, which, to this date, have gone nowhere for much the same reason that past efforts have failed: the Palestinian refusal to recognize Israel's historic legitimacy by abandoning the so-called "right of return." Nonetheless, American Jewish organizations faithfully broadcast Kerry's message.

Secondly, the Obama Administration's mobilization of the American Israel Public Affairs Committee (AIPAC) to garner support on Capitol Hill for limited air strikes against the Syrian regime. That also came to naught, largely because Obama himself was seduced by the Russian President Vladimir Putin's offer to cajole Syrian President Bashar al-Assad into giving up his chemical weapons. Both the "Lobby" and the administration would likely reject the charge that one controls the other. Instead, they would portray the relationship as a two-way street, with lots of mutual backscratching going on. But outside the fevered minds of Israel Lobby conspiracy theorists, it's clear that the administration holds the cards. Consequently, an otherwise spectacularly unsuccessful president has pulled off one small achievement, by closing off any prospects for sustained opposition to his Middle East policies from the mainstream Jewish organizations. And in exchange, the White House will provide its leading lights, like Kerry and Vice President Joe Biden, to speak at events sponsored by these same organizations in order to demonstrate to well-heeled donors that their influence remains intact.

From the White House's standpoint, that's a pretty good deal. Which brings me to J Street, the leftist lobbying group that claims to be pro-Israel, and which has just held its annual policy conference. J Street wants to be seen as part of the Jewish mainstream, and its roster of speakers this year – among them Biden, Israeli Justice Minister Tzipi Livni, and Middle East negotiator Martin Indyk – certainly undermines the assertions of Jews on the right that its influence is marginal. Nonetheless, J Street's moment in the sun is the result of fortuitous political circumstances, rather than any ingenious strategy on its part. As the *Washington Free Beacon*'s Adam Kredo reported last week, the group has spent $100,000 reaching out to lawmakers to look kindly upon both Iranian diplomatic entreaties and Palestinian efforts to secure unilateral recognition – a stance that directly contradicts the administration's commitment to direct talks.

As we are now at a juncture where the administration is attempting to engage Iran on a level not seen since the Islamic revolution of 1979, J Street's willingness to persuade American Jews that the mullahs can be trusted comes in very handy. Leave aside, for the moment, the abysmal spectacle of a Jewish organization prettifying the outreach of Hassan Rouhani, Iran's new president, who is as much of a Holocaust denier as his predecessor, Mahmoud Ahmadinejad, just not as bombastic. J Street has always had tin ear when it comes to antisemitism, as its dogma determines that Jew-hatred, along with Iran's nukes and the Arab refusal to normalize relations with Israel, will disappear if only Israel would make territorial concessions to the Palestinian authority. There are more important reasons for alarm at the administration's alignment with J Street. One, there's the pettiness: AI-PAC's efforts on Syria have been hung out to dry, while the White House is apparently unconcerned at J Street's refusal to back Obama when he was dangling the prospect of air strikes against Assad. Two, it's emblematic of the Obama administration's approach to foreign policy. Rather than maintaining our status as an unchallenged superpower, the emphasis is instead upon persuading nervous Americans that, unlike the evil George W. Bush administration, we are not going to go to war, and we are not going to tell foreigners what to do, even if their leaders are human rights abusing tyrants.

In other words, what we've seen over the last month is the rapid decline of American power. In this drama, J Street, much like other left-wing groups, is an enthusiastic cheerleader, nothing more. The rest of us will have to calculate what that means for U.S. allies in the Middle East, not just Israel but the conservative Sunni regimes too. Their distrust of any deal with Iran will not be assuaged by Obama – and if they decide to take unilateral action without American support, we really will be saying, "Welcome to the New World Order."

America's Two-State Solution Fixation Pushing Israel Back to the 'Iron Wall'?

JNS/The Algemeiner, October 9, 2013

A hint of frustration flashed across Israeli Deputy Defense Minister Danny Danon's face when I asked him about the criticism he has received from American Jewish establishment organizations concerning his rejection of the two-state solution.

"If American Jewish organizations will call upon the Israeli prime minister to fire me because of my opinion on the two-state solution, it's crossing the line," Danon told me on his recent visit to New York, referring to recent statements issued by both the Anti-Defamation League and the American Jewish Committee that charged him, as well as his ministerial colleague Naftali Bennett, with damaging Israel's image because of their forthright views. "I can't imagine that the same Jewish organizations would have called upon [the late Israeli Prime Minister Yitzhak] Shamir to fire Shimon Peres when he was promoting one of his peace plans," Danon added, invoking the uneasy left-right coalition government that ruled Israel for much of the 1980s. "When the government leans to the left, they will support it 'unconditionally.' If the government is positioned to the right, you start to see maneuvering not to support it."

My purpose in relating this conversation is not to trigger yet another debate about the role of American Jewish organizations in dutifully restating the positions of the White House in their dealings with Israeli officials. Danon's comments are instructive because they demonstrate that influential Israelis are reconsidering what has become, for both American Jewish leaders and the American administration, an article of faith: namely, that the two-state solution is the only show in town. There is an understandable reluctance to question both the wisdom and the viability of a two-state outcome to the Israeli-Palestinian conflict. Traditionally, this has been the preserve of Palestinian extremists, like the Hamas regime in Gaza, who reject Israel's very identity as a Jewish state. Equally, there is no reason to allow those who would happily annihilate Israel to frame the terms of the discussion. Israel has to make its calculations based upon its own interests. As far as Danon is concerned, Palestinian intransigence has left the case for the two-state solution looking flimsy. As he argued in a recent *New York Times* op-ed, Israel would be better off annulling the Oslo Accords and seeking a solution to the Palestinian issue that places more responsibility upon Egypt for the Gaza Strip, and more responsibility on Jordan for the West Bank.

Such a stance is radically removed from the official American position, which continues to pursue the two-state solution, most recently through Secretary of State John Kerry's initiative, which has been heavy on PR and light on impact. It suggests – as the Israeli political analyst Yossi Klein Halevi observed last week in the *Wall Street Journal* in a piece highlighting Prime Minister Benjamin Netanyahu's pledge that Israel "will not allow Iran to get nuclear weapons" – that on both the Palestinian and Iranian fronts, Israel might decide that a "strained relationship with the White House" is a less risky option.

Of course, no one wants that scenario to become reality – Danon, for one, genuinely believes that there is a special relationship between the U.S. and Israel that needs to be preserved – but at the same time, Israel cannot allow vital security decisions to be determined by whatever ideas happen to be in vogue in Washington. And looking at the Kerry initiative, the holes are painfully visible. Indeed, we talk about a two-state solution as if the very real split between the Fatah-ruled West Bank and Hamas-ruled Gaza were taking place in a parallel universe, rather than being a powerful reason why the two-state solution is looking rather haggard. During our talk, Danon mentioned the "Iron Wall," a concept that originated with the great Revisionist Zionist leader Ze'ev Jabotinsky who described it, in a 1923 essay, as a "strong power in Palestine that is not amenable to any Arab pressure." Jabotinsky did not argue that an agreement with the Arabs is eternally doomed – his point, which remains valid today, was that a sovereign Jewish state must approach the issue from a position of confident strength.

That doesn't mean just military strength. It also means, I'd venture, alliances with other peoples in the region, like the Kurds, who have suffered from both Arab chauvinism and Islamist extremism. Above all, it means having the courage, as Danny Danon does, to start thinking alternatively.

Chapter Six: On Islamism and Iran

Iran is an Enemy. That Doesn't Mean Turkey is a Friend

JointMedia News Service, January 17, 2012

N inety years after the Ottoman Empire gasped its final breath, Turkey is again rising to a position of dominance. For the discontented masses in the Middle East and beyond, non-Arab yet Muslim Turkey has become a rallying point, thanks to its government's strident defense of the Palestinians and, after decades of enforced secularism, its pious embrace of Islam as a foundation for Turkish society. As a result, Turkey's Islamist Prime Minister, Reccep Tayyip Erdogan, has assumed a status much coveted by Middle Eastern leaders past and present: admired at street level and respected as a critical player by external powers, especially the United States. When Erdogan spoke with President Obama last week, the conversation centered on Turkey's anxieties concerning Iraq, Syria, and Iran – all countries with which it shares a border.

In the case of Syria, where the regime of Hafez al-Assad continues its bloody repression against opposition forces, rumors of outside military intervention are again circulating, centering on the idea of a no-fly zone over the country which Turkey, a NATO member, would play a critical role in maintaining. Turkey has also become a central consideration in terms of the West's response to Iran's nuclear program. With one eye on public opinion, Turkish leaders like Foreign Minister Ahmet Davutoglu have scorned the notion that Iran's nuclear ambitions represent a global threat, often adding that these concerns would be more appropriately directed at Israel's nuclear arsenal. At the same time, Turkey has offered to host talks with Iran's leaders over the nuclear stand-off – thereby insinuating that Turkey has the ability to succeed where almost a decade of previous such efforts have failed.

Publicly, Iran has reacted to the Turkish offer with enthusiasm. Its parliamentary speaker, Ali Larijani – a hardliner who once shocked an international security conference in Munich by making a speech in which he denied the Holocaust – breezily declared in Ankara, the Turkish capital, that "all issues can be easily solved through negotiations." The Obama Administration has shied away from criticizing Turkey, mainly because it sees Turkey as the primary counter to Iranian influence in the Middle East.

On one level, that assessment is correct; the conflicts in Iraq and Syria clearly demonstrate that Iran and Turkey are on opposite sides. And with Iran threatening to close the Straits of Hormuz, a transit route for one-fifth of the world's oil supply, no one would dispute the necessity of having friends in the region, even fair-weather ones. Yet none of that should lead us to conclude that Turkey is a solid, reliable ally, ready to assist with the overriding challenge in the Middle East today: neutralizing Iran's nuclear program. So why does the Obama Administration behave as though it is?

Much of the answer lies in the Administration's unwavering belief that there are "moderate" Islamists whom we must engage, indulge and respect. When Secretary of State Hillary Clinton rushes to deny American involvement in the assassination of an Iranian nuclear scientist, or when Defense Secretary Leon Panetta denounces U.S. Marines for urinating on the dead bodies of Taliban terrorists in Afghanistan, they do so in the hope of mollifying the anger of the so-called "moderates," who are exemplified best by Erdogan's government. If Turkey plays ball, the reasoning goes, similar political forces like the Muslim Brotherhood in Egypt and even the Hamas terrorists ruling Gaza are more likely to follow suit, and choose dialogue over conflict. The Administration also knows that Turkey, like the conservative Arab Gulf states, doesn't want Iran to weaponize its nuclear program, since such an outcome would cement Iran's position as the leading power in the region. Still, Turkey has cleverly ensured that this understanding works to its advantage. It can count on American sympathy for its aims in Iraq and Syria, and it can exert greater influence over Iran's leaders than might otherwise be possible. Of all the conceivable strategic pitfalls in the American-Turkish relationship, the most obvious one is the dilution of new sanctions on Iran. Turkey's stance that it will only respect sanctions agreed on by the UN has spurred other countries, including India, China and Japan, to make similar statements.

If the sanctions fail, will the Obama Administration be prepared to entertain military action? Indeed, will it stand in the way of those countries, like Israel, who may be willing to pursue the military option? Ultimately, if Turkey sabotages the sanctions strategy, will the Obama Administration continue smiling in Ankara's direction? The Administration's track record strongly suggests that it will. If so, the world will have been treated to another display of the strategy often derided as "leading from behind," which has dogged the U.S. in its dealings with other Middle Eastern flashpoints. Only this time, the consequent benefits to Iran could be fatal.

First They Came for the Bahai's...

"Contentions" @ Commentary Magazine, July 17, 2012

There is a common misconception that Iran's restrictions on the right to worship freely apply only to members of the Baha'i religion. But while the Islamic republic has reserved the most vicious forms of persecution for the adherents of this gentle faith – whose numbers, according to some estimates, have dwindled from around 500,000 at the time of the 1979 revolution to just 150,000 now – the situation of Iranian Christians is little better.

Through its treatment of its Christian and Jewish minorities, Iran's policies underscore that mythology behind the oft-heard claim that the followers of the "Abrahamic" faiths are accorded dignity and respect. Just last week, Iran's millenarian president, Mahmoud Ahmadinejad, told an Islamic conference in Tehran that Islam is the only true religion, denying at the same time the divine provenance of both Judaism and Christianity. "My dear ones!" Ahmadinejad declared munificently, "Islam is a world religion and God has only one religion, that of Islam, he did not send Judaism or Christianity; Abraham was a harbinger of Islam, as were Moses and Jesus!" The majority of Iran's 300,000 Christians belong to established churches like the Armenian and the Assyrian; for the time being, their fate is to walk on eggshells around the regime, which means they can't say or do anything that the mullahs might interpret as proselytizing. By contrast, it is open season on the followers of the smaller, evangelical denominations, all of whom risk being charged with the crime of *moharebeh*, or apostasy. Arguably the best known victim of this charge is the 35 year-old Pastor Youcef Nadarkhani, who marked his 1,000th day of incarceration In Iran's Lakan prison earlier this month. Nadarkhani, a leader of the evangelical Church of Iran who embraced Christianity as a child, has been given a choice: recant and return to Islam, or face the death sentence. So far, Nadarkhani has held firm. Nadarkhani's plight reflects a long-established pattern of harassment. In 1990, Pastor Hussein Soodman, like Nadarkhani a convert from Islam to Christianity, was executed after he repeatedly defied the regime's insistence that he recant. Soodman's execution set the tone for Iran's future dealings with converts to Christianity; in the last year, as well as Nadarkhani, several other pastors have been locked behind by bars, charged with offenses ranging from "crimes against national security" to the life-threatening accusation of *moharebeh*. What applies to these church leaders applies increasingly to their flocks. According to a report from ANS, a news service that highlights Christian persecution, Iranian Revolutionary Guards have closed down the

Central Assembly of God Church in Tehran, along with a campsite that holds Bible study schools and conferences. In tandem, the regime has imposed the sorts of restrictions that will be familiar to those who remember the persecution of Jews in the old Soviet Union: prohibiting the distribution of the Bible and associated Christian literature; allowing only small numbers of worshippers to attend services; checking IDs before worshippers enter services, which is a surefire way of depleting attendance through fear; and preventing the conduct of services in the Farsi language. A recent report on the treatment of Christian converts in Iran related the remark of an Iranian intelligence agent to the mother of two converts who were hauled away from their Tehran apartment for questioning: "Tell Jesus to come and rescue them." One will probably not find a better statement of the regime's true intent.

The reaction of western church leaders to the brazen demonization of Christianity in Iran has been typically nervous. Nadarkhani has been the subject of several press releases asking for clemency, but there is a clear reluctance to identify Iran's strategy for what it is: the first stage of a campaign to eradicate Christianity from the country. The "message of solidarity" issued by South African Archbishop Desmond Tutu last month illustrates this problem well enough. Tutu, who is best known in recent years for franchising the word "apartheid" to adversaries of the State of Israel, was at pains to point out that the torture and imprisonment which Iranian Christians face does "not reflect the Muslim faith." Given that the vast bulk of the many Christians around the world facing persecution reside in Muslim countries, it would seem that the archbishop is denying himself a much-needed reality check. Should the Iranian regime carry out its commitment to execute Pastor Nadarkhani, Iranian Christians will need much more than Tutuesque platitudes to soothe their wretched existence.

Mr. Rouhani, You're No Gorbachev

Moment Magazine, July 4, 2013

For several days after the election of Hassan Rouhani as Iran's new president, advocates of engagement with Tehran couldn't stop smiling. Jack Straw, the former British Foreign Secretary, praised Rouhani as "straightforward and pragmatic to deal with" and expressed hope that the tortuous saga of Iran's nuclear ambitions would "have a happy ending." A *New York Times* editorial solemnly concluded that a rare opportunity to reach a deal over Iran's nuclear program was now at hand, cautioning that

President Obama would have his work cut out dissuading potential spoilers – such as "congressional leaders and Prime Minister Netanyahu of Israel" – from raising objections. It's understandable, if not quite excusable, that the engagement camp is positively joyous at the thought of using the words "moderate," "pragmatic" and "Iran" in the same sentence. Rouhani's predecessor, Mahmoud Ahmadinejad, was always a thorn in the side of those who consider Iran what international relations scholars call a "rational actor." To cynics, he was a gift that kept on giving, someone who could be faithfully relied upon to say something outrageous – denying the Holocaust, threatening Israel with annihilation – just when everyone else was quietly waiting for a breakthrough. But does the engagement camp have a point, or is it, as a decidedly less sanguine Iranian friend of mine told me in an email, full of "half-wit mullah lovers"?

The expectation that Rouhani will become an Iranian version of Mikhail Gorbachev, the Soviet leader whose far-reaching reforms contributed to the eventual dissolution of the USSR, is certain to persist. After all, the hunger for political change inside Iran is as palpable as it was during the last days of the Soviet Empire, as is the worsening economic outlook. The strategic context, however, couldn't be more different. The bloodbath in Syria, in which Iran and its Lebanese Islamist ally Hezbollah have rushed to support the bestial dictatorship of Bashar al-Assad, offers inescapable proof that the conflict in the Middle East is less a confrontation with Israel and the U.S. than it is a civil war between the majority Sunni and minority Shi'a streams of Islam. To posit that Shi'a Iran would, with this epic struggle in the background, abandon its carefully calibrated nuclear ambiguity simply because Rouhani comports himself with more dignity than Ahmadinejad is the stuff of fairy tales.

Remember: Rouhani has not called on Assad to step down, in marked contrast to most Western and Arab states, nor has he expressed any reservations about Assad's crimes against humanity. Even if he does quietly harbor doubts, expressing them would risk the ire of Iran's top military brass and the country's Supreme Leader – and ultimate authority – Ayatollah Ali Khamenei, whose support for Assad is unflinching. That's one reason why, to my mind, there's a strong possibility that hailing Rouhani as a moderate will backfire spectacularly. Rouhani, after all, is a regime man through and through. Given Iran's stringent rules on qualifying for public office – out of more than 600 candidates for the presidency, only eight made it to the ballot – he couldn't be anything else. Consider, as well, Rouhani's career trajectory. Rouhani was an early confidant of Ayatollah Ruhollah Khomeini, the founder of the Islamic Republic. After the 1979 revolution, he served in a variety of prominent positions, many of them concerned with national security. Western diplomats know Rouhani because, from 2003 until Ahmadinejad's first term as president in 2005, he was Iran's chief nuclear negotiator. But the man dubbed by some obsequious admirers as the "diplomat sheikh" was tasked with sowing doubts about Iran's intentions on the nuclear front while the United States and its allies were tied up with the wars in Afghanistan and Iraq. His appointment as nuclear negotiator followed the revelation that Iran had been clandestinely developing a nuclear program whose ostensibly "peaceful purposes" were the subject of severe doubts on the part of the International Atomic Energy Agency (IAEA). In a 2006 speech to fellow clerics, Rouhani bragged about how the Iranians had continued work on the regime's uranium conversion facility in Isfahan – built with the assistance of the Chinese and the North Koreans – while negotiating with the Europeans. In the same address, he confessed that the Iranians were worried that providing a "complete picture" of their nuclear activities would lead to a fraught debate at the UN Security Council.

Since his election, Rouhani has repeated the mantra that Iran's nuclear program is entirely peaceful, declaring that "The nation will only be happy when we neutralize the plots of the U.S. We will protect the nuclear technology alongside any other technology." Essentially, Rouhani wants us to believe that Iran's nuclear program is benign simply because he says so. Yet he has given no indication that he will permit the IAEA to thoroughly inspect the nuclear facilities, nor has he even hinted whether Iran will reveal additional secret nuclear installations, such as the underground uranium enrichment plant at Fordow that was exposed by the American, British and French intelligence agencies in 2009. And, even if he did consider such a step, he would risk alienating both the military and Supreme Leader Khamenei, who recognizes the advantage of having a president perceived by the outside world as a reformist, but who will certainly not permit him to do anything that would irreparably compromise Iran's strategic position in the tempestuous Middle East. Put another way: Mr. Rouhani, you're no Gorbachev.

Putin, Russia and Iran's Nuclear Program

JNS/The Algemeiner, July 31, 2013

The victory of Hassan Rouhani in June's Iranian presidential election has once again thrust the word "moderate" into the center of the agonized debate over western policy towards Tehran's nuclear program – a debate whose latest iteration centers on the implications of Russian President Vladimir Putin's planned visit to Iran next month. But what "moderate" actually means in this context remains unclear. If the various western pundits and politicians who have embraced Rouhani are to be believed, this wise successor to the hyperbolic Mahmoud Ahmadinejad offers the best chance for a political deal over the nuclear program in years. Sure, Rouhani recently dismissed Israel as a "miserable regional country," but relative to Ahmadinejad's frequent expressions of Holocaust denial and threats to wipe the Jewish state off the map, that sounds rather, well, moderate. As Seyed Hossein Mousavian, a former Iranian official now engaged as a Princeton University research scholar, recently wrote, Iranian diplomacy under Rouhani can be expected to adopt a "professionalize[d] tone," which the U.S. should respond to with a "series of practical positive gestures." Rouhani is smart enough to realize that winning the confidence of the outside world simply by sounding like more of a statesman than Ahmadinejad is a darn good deal. And that is where the danger lies. For while Rouhani is certainly amenable to talking, he is far less reliable when it comes to the outcome – a final, transparent solution to Iran's nuclear ambitions – desired by the U.S. and its partners. As with the stalled Israeli-Palestinian negotiations, western policy towards Iran now places more emphasis on process – the simple act of sitting around a table – than it does upon the actual results of such parleys.

What that approach ignores, frankly, is the entrenched belief of Rouhani and his fellow mullahs that a negotiated solution to the nukes crisis is not in the interest of the regime. In strategic terms, Iran looks much stronger now than it did one year ago. Its policy of actively backing its monstrous regional ally, the regime of Bashar al-Assad in Syria, is now paying dividends, insofar as the brutal civil war there is turning in Assad's favor. Additionally, the crisis that has enveloped ruling Sunni Islamists in countries like Egypt and Turkey has not been replicated in Iran, where mass, sustained anti-regime protests have been largely absent since 2010. Most importantly, talks with the U.S. are not the only option available to Tehran. The last time Iran that took part in talks about its nuclear program, in Kazakhstan back in February, did not, unsurprisingly, yield any concrete results. During those negotiations, Iran received a proposal that would essentially involve a suspension of its uranium enrichment activities and greater openness towards inspection teams dispatched by the International Atomic Energy Agency (IAEA), a body that has consistently warned against the dangers of Iranian duplicity. In the interim, while western negotiators have anxiously awaited a response that, so far, has not been forthcoming, the Russians have gotten in on the act with a separate initiative.

The declared aim of Putin's Iran visit – the latest Russian media reports have it slated for Aug. 12 or Aug. 16 – is to try and get the negotiations back on track. Close behind is another aim; Putin wants Iran to purchase Russian-manufactured S-300VM Antey-2500 air defense systems. The price tag – $120 million – is a hefty one for a country whose economy has been badly damaged by international Iran sanctions, but then the Iranian regime has never placed the needs of its citizens above its military imperatives. Purchasing such a system would undoubtedly make the prospect of a preemptive strike on Iran's nuclear facilities far more risky.

At the same time that the Russians weighed in, the Iraqi Prime Minister Nouri al-Maliki, who is close to the Iranian regime, offered to play the role of broker between Washington and Tehran. The advantages for Maliki are obvious, in that taking on such a task would further endear him to the Americans without alienating the Iranians. And the initial State Department reaction – "We are open to direct talks with Iran in order to resolve the international community's concerns about Iran's nuclear program," said State Department spokesman Patrick Ventrell – was pretty positive. Again, this emphasis on process detracts from the far more important challenge of achieving results, thus enabling the Iranians to do what they have always done: buy time while continuing the nuclear program's development. The only foreign politician to openly express skepticism has been Israeli Prime Minister Benjamin Netanyahu. "On Iran, it is crucial that we see a change in Iran's policy, not a change in style, but a change in substance," Netanyahu recently said. Knowing that Netanyahu is far more isolated than, by rights, he should be in holding such a position, Iran has felt confident enough to lampoon him as a warmonger who is always crying wolf.

In fact, Netanyahu's anxieties are firmly based in reality. David Albright, the respected head of the Washington, DC-based Institute for Science and International Security, wrote in a July briefing paper that Iran "is expected to achieve a critical capability in mid-2014, which is defined as the technical capability to produce sufficient weapon-grade uranium from its safeguarded stocks of low enriched uranium for a nuclear explosive, *without being detected.*" (My emphasis.)

Once that capability is achieved, there is no going back. Moreover, for as long as western policy is bogged down in the bizarre game of talking about talks, the Iranians have no political incentive to scale the nuclear program back. The only measure that could conceivably slow the process involves tighter Iran sanctions and a stronger effort to close down smuggling routes, and even then, there is no guarantee that the west will gain the upper hand. As Rouhani himself said, back in 2005, "[I]f one day we are able to complete the fuel cycle and the world sees that it has no choice – that we do possess the technology – then the situation will be different." Yet here we are again, vainly hoping that this time, things will be different, that a regime that has consistently and successfully lied will somehow stop doing so.

Iran Nuclear Program: We Only Have Ourselves to Blame

JNS/The Algemeiner, November 5, 2013

One of the most irritating aspects of the international efforts to deal with the Iran nuclear program lies in the unrealistic expectations that negotiations create, even among those – like the American Jewish advocacy groups who met with the White House Oct. 29 to discuss the nuclear issue – who have every reason to be cynical. From Nov. 7–8, members of the so-called P5+1, which comprises the five members of the U.N. Security Council along with Germany, will meet with representatives of the Iranian regime in Geneva. These talks follow on from preliminary discussions whose content has not been revealed, yet we are assured that they were "very intensive and very important," (Catherine Ashton, EU Foreign Policy Chief) and that the Iranians brought with them a proposal "with a level of seriousness and substance that we had not seen before" (Jay Carney, White House spokesman). Hence, the sense we are getting is that one of the most intractable problems facing the Middle East is on the cusp of being resolved.

That's why I'm going to break ranks by issuing a spoiler alert. These talks aren't going to lead to a deal. Instead, they will function as they have always done, by allowing the Iranians to buy time, safe in the knowledge that the other options we are told are always on the table – from tighter sanctions to pre-emptive military action – are on the back-burner for now. There are three main reasons behind my assertion. Firstly, the P5+1 cannot for a moment pretend to represent an international consensus. On the inside, you have the Russians and the Chinese, who have consistently backed Iran during the nuclear dispute of the last decade. And on the outside, you have Israel and the conservative Arab states, whose trust in the Obama Administration when it comes to Iran is close to evaporating, and who thus may well reject any agreement framework. Secondly, all the attention paid to the apparently constructive atmosphere at the preliminary discussions, along with the public relations offensive unleashed by Iran's new president,

Hasan Rouhani, cannot camouflage some very basic facts. For example, if Rouhani really does want to reach a deal, how come he won't he explain why Iran's nuclear program was, from the beginning, a clandestine enterprise? The answer is simple: he is faithfully parroting the mullahs line that Iran's intentions were always peaceful, that the regime never intended to build nuclear weapons, and that anyone who thinks otherwise has fallen victim to an Israeli plot that seeks, in Rouhani's own words, "to divert international attention not only from its own clandestine and dangerous nuclear weapons program, but also from its destabilizing and inhuman policies and practices in Palestine and the Middle East."

Thirdly, we've already had the opportunity to test Iran's peaceful intentions outside the scope of the nuclear negotiations, and the result is an unmistakable F." A recent *BBC* report included footage of Iranian Revolutionary Guards fighting with the Assad regime in Syria, under the watchful eye of a commander named Ismail Heydari, who described Assad's bloody onslaught against his own people as a war "of Islam against the infidels." So rather than praising the Iranians over their willingness to talk about talking (about talking about talking...) about their nuclear program, we should be hauling them before the Security Council to demand answers over Tehran's decision to cross an international border in order to defend one of the world's most monstrous regimes. Yet it's unrealistic to expect the Americans or the Europeans to raise any of these objections. After all, they shamefully folded over the use of chemical weapons in Syria, so why should Iran be any different? Moreover, even if they agree a vague declaration of principles with the Iranians, these will collapse under the weight of details like the kind of monitoring regime to be put in place. For you can rest assured that whatever is acceptable to the Iranians will likely be unacceptable to the Israelis, the Saudis, and the Bahrainis, among others. And in any case, according to Olli Heinonen, a former International Atomic Energy Agency inspector, the Iranians have very little more to do on the uranium enrichment front before reaching weaponization capacity.

What's needed now is a bold domestic voice to challenge the Obama Administration's new-found confidence in Iran's rulers. But if you're looking to Jewish establishment organizations to play that role, forget it. Given that they've already been persuaded by Obama to drop support for further sanctions for now, it's unlikely that they will push for the stronger measures that will be necessary down the line. Remember that line about the all-powerful "Israel Lobby"? If only it were true. If only.

Defining "Mildly Islamist"

JointMedia News Service, February 27, 2012

I came across a vexing phrase while reading *The Economist* this week. In an article about political skullduggery in Turkey, the ruling Justice and Development Party (AK) of Prime Minister Reccep Tayyip Erdogan was described as "mildly Islamist." *Mildly Islamist.* Not as Islamist as some? Promoting Islamic rule by stealth rather than overnight decree? More open minded?

Over the last decade we have become accustomed to the rather crude division of the world's 1.6 billion Muslims into "moderate" and "extremist" camps. While this distinction is designed to look cognizant of internal differences, the questionable assumption behind it is that Muslims are, and will always be, uniformly distrustful of western liberal values. Therefore, those Muslims who are prepared to reach an accommodation are the "moderates," while those who advocate violent confrontation are the "extremists."

Being the louder camp, the extremists get all the attention. Several western commentators now assert that most extremists are moderate in their extremism, while some, like the AK Party in Turkey, can even be called mild. This seems to me less like logic, and more like prayer. If only we keep tightening the definition of who is an extremist, we'll get more moderates. And moderates are people we can talk to. The week before presenting Turkey's rulers as the acceptable face of Islamism, *The Economist* published an editorial headlined "Dialogue is the best defense." The editorial pointed out that the Islamist parties reaping the benefits of the last year's convulsions in the Arab world share a point of origin in the Ikhwan, or Muslim Brotherhood. However, the paper counseled, we need not fear that each country where Islamists come to power will end up like Gaza under the brutal rule of Hamas, which is the Palestinian branch of the Ikhwan. To avoid a Gaza outcome, *The Economist* recommends more dialogue and more cooperation with those Islamists who eschew violence, and who recognize immediate economic and social priorities. "...[T]he answer is to help ensure that reform-minded Islamists will not turn more radical themselves," the editorial stated. "Engagement makes that less likely, because it would reinforce the constitutional checks that cement a pluralist society."

On display here is the common western habit of playing down the ideological moorings of the Ikhwan, with the associated implication that its anti-western and antisemitic rhetoric is a cry of frustration that will become less anguished once power has been accessed.

Now, no-one would deny that Islamists are the flavor of the hour in Egypt, Tunisia, and Libya, and that they may well find themselves as the beneficiaries in Syria should the bloodstained menace that is Bashar al-Assad be overthrown. The challenge is how to approach them. Will western money, expertise and assistance combine to prevent the emergence of Sunni equivalents of Iran's regime? Will the Ikhwan approach its western interlocutors as equals, or will it attempt to trick them with the double-speak for which it is famous? One of the key flaws in the engagement strategy is that it accepts the self-image of the so-called moderate Islamists. A cleric like Yusuf al-Qaradawi, the main theological influence behind the Ikhwan, is thus able to pass himself as a "moderate" because he says he rejects violence – except when it is directed against Israelis.

A further key flaw was recognized recently by a most unlikely source, in the form of the pro-Arab British journalist Robert Fisk. On a visit to Tunisia, one of Fisk's friends, a prominent liberal, told him: "Do you know that of all the books now published in Tunisia, 92 per cent are Islamist? Don't you think we should be worried?" At the very moment of dialogue with the west, our interlocutors would be cracking down on women, minorities and freedom of expression at home. Even if we accept *The Economist*'s contention that full-blown Sharia law and confrontation with Israel are distant prospects for now, with each day of Islamist rule, we get one step closer. For what really counts in this situation is the street – and in large swathes of the Arab world, the Islamists are in firm control, pushing a message that is distinctly *un*moderate.

Jews know from their history that he who controls the street has the advantage. In the last months of 1932, right-wing politicians in Germany started reaching out to the Nazis, in the hope that Hitler would be moderated by the demands of high politics. But Hitler needed the street, where the only messages that counted were viscerally extreme ones, far more. Without this power behind him, he would never have been able to outwit Germany's elder statesmen. That's just one historical example to bear in mind – should our leaders decide to show the "moderate" Muslim Brotherhood some respect, let's not be surprised if we don't get the same favor in return.

Boko Haram's Spirit Comes to London

"Contentions" @ Commentary Magazine, May 24, 2013

Details are still emerging about the life and habits of Michael Adebolajo, the Islamist butcher who displayed the blood-drenched palms of his hands to a passing cameraman just moments after he and an accomplice murdered 25-year-old Lee Rigby, a soldier in the British Army's Royal Fusiliers regiment, on a south London street this week. As is common with any terrorism investigation, the focus is upon who Adebolajo was mixing with and which organizations he approached. A much-tweeted photo shows a stony-faced Adebolajo standing behind Anjem Choudary, a founder of the now banned Islamist organization al-Muhajiroun, at rally in London. It was Choudary who, in 2010, led a ceremony in which he and other supporters of al-Qaeda burned the poppies which many Britons pin to their lapels every November in commemoration of the British and Allied soldiers who fell in two world wars. And it was the same Choudary who justified Adebolajo's barbarous act by citing "the presence of British forces in Muslim countries and the atrocities they've committed."

When it comes to contacts with Islamist groups outside the United Kingdom, some press reports have mentioned that Adebolajo traveled to Somalia in the last year to join Al-Shabab, a particularly brutal al-Qaeda offshoot in east Africa, and may have even been arrested along the way. No solid evidence has, as yet, emerged to tie Adebolajo – a British citizen of Nigerian descent – with Boko Haram, the Nigerian Islamist terror organization that has instigated church bombings, pogroms and similar atrocities against the west African country's beleaguered Christian population. The prospect of a link with Boko Haram is of interest because Adebolajo was born into a Christian family who were regular attendees at a church in Romford, just outside London. Given the loathing with which Boko Haram regards Christians and Christianity, manifested in the more than 1,500 people killed during the group's attacks over the last three years, the very idea of a Nigerian Christian joining their ranks is as shocking as the hypothetical (so far, at least) example of a Jew who converts to Islam, joins Hamas and becomes a suicide bomber. But there is another, perhaps more important, observation to make here. The experience of Nigeria, which Christian rights activists say is now the most dangerous place on earth for Christians, illustrates the flaw of concentrating too narrowly on Islamist organizations, at the expense of the wider influence which Islamist ideas enjoy among the unaffiliated. As Ann Buwalda and Emmanuel Ogebe point out in a compelling study of Boko Haram and its anti-Christian fixations: While Boko Haram's bloody terrorist tactics certainly merit serious concern, the focus on this group has overshadowed a pattern of systemic religious violence in Nigeria. It obfuscates the pervasive history of the killing of Christians by Muslims in northern Nigeria going back over a quarter century.

Buwalda and Ogebe argue that Islamist activity in Nigeria has to be understood in the context of three concentric circles: sect (which incorporates Boko Haram), state, and street. Too much attention is paid to the sect circle, they say, and not enough to state policy or public sentiment. For example, the wave of anti-Christian violence that followed the 2011 elections in Nigeria was not orchestrated by Boko Haram, but "was an act of ordinary Muslims across most northern states." That particular carnage resulted in more than 200 Christians being killed, more than 700 churches destroyed, and more than 3,000 Christian families being driven from their homes. One can similarly make the case that it doesn't matter whether or not Michael Adebolajo engaged in direct contact with Boko Haram; like the young Muslims who rampaged against Christians in Nigeria two years ago, he is one of their number in spirit. And now that the killing methods of Boko Haram have come to the streets of London, perhaps Western leaders will pay serious attention to the fact that, alongside Zionism, Judaism and secularism, Christianity has been designated by the Islamists as a transcendental force of darkness – and that Christians across the Muslim world have to live with the consequences of that every day.

Turkey, Amid Islamization and Antisemitism, Fit for EU Membership?

JNS/The Algemeiner, June 25, 2013

The citizens of a Middle Eastern state explode with frustration against their corrupt, repressive government. They gather for noisy, impassioned demonstrations in their capital city. The authorities react violently. Images of middle-aged women and wheelchair-bound individuals being tear-gassed, clubbed, and sprayed with water cannon race across social media platforms like wildfire. The protests then spread to other cities. The authorities step up their repression.

And then, inevitably, the country's political leaders snarl that outside forces are stoking the discontent. Newspapers and websites are suddenly full of lists of American neoconservatives, illustrated with lurid graphics that superimpose the logos of organizations like the American Israel Public Affairs Committee (AIPAC) over pictures of demonstrations. No one needs to say the word "Jew" in order to know who's being referred to here. So where is this happening? In Bahrain? Egypt? Tunisia? Actually, no. What I'm describing is taking place in a non-Arab, inwardly Muslim but outwardly secular candidate nation for European Union (EU) membership. Turkey.

The protests there began on May 31, when an initially small group of activists gathered in Istanbul to voice opposition to the redevelopment of the city's Gezi Park. But the anger quickly escalated into an all-out confrontation with the Islamist government of Reccep Tayyip Erdogan. Many Turks are fed up with the slow yet inexorable Islamization of their country, which Erdogan has begun. Specifically, they are fed up with Erdogan's promotion of conservative Islamic dress codes; with his demand that married couples have at least three children; with his prohibitions on the sale of alcohol and his opposition to abortion; with his scolding of couples who dare to smooch in public; and with his clampdown on freedom of speech and of the media, which has resulted in Turkey having more journalists in prison than any other country in the world. As the German magazine *Der Spiegel* pointed out recently, Turkey's enthusiasm for incarcerating journalists – by some estimates, more than 60 are currently in jail – beats the records of even China and Iran.

It was always unrealistic to expect that an arrogant autocrat like Erdogan would actually listen to the demands of the protestors. His standard response has been to fulminate against shadowy plots hatched by Marxists, Kurdish separatists, and – most of all – Jews. As the Turkish demonstrations were reaching their height this month, the conservative newspaper *Yeni Safak* published an article which featured a "rogues gallery" of prominent American neoconservatives – Richard Perle, Paul Wolfowitz, Douglas Feith and so forth – as well as a photo of a masked protestor flanked by the logos of the American Enterprise Institute think tank and AIPAC. The thrust of the article was clear: the protests are being actively encouraged by a group of Jews hell-bent on war with the Islamic world. In tone and substance, it was thoroughly in line with other antisemitic screeds published by *Yeni Safak* – for example, a 2005 article that warned "Jewish paranoia" was at the root of the Middle Easts conflicts and predicted that this same paranoia would one day "destroy the Jews themselves." If you really want to see a plot, though, look no further than Erdogan himself. *Yeni Safak* is owned by Berat Albayrak, who is married to Erdogan's daughter (their wedding ceremony was broadcast live on Turkish television.) Berat's brother, Serhat Albayrak, is a press advisor to Erdogan, while their father, Mustafa, is the head of Albayrak

Holdings, a construction company that has prospered visibly under the present Islamist government. The company recently issued a nervous denial that it had been awarded the contract to build a shopping mall on the ground currently occupied by Gezi Park – the very same affront which sparked the protests in the first place. When this intimate network of famili-al and business ties is properly considered, it stretches credibility to think that Erdogan is somehow unaware of *Yeni Safak*'s vile Jew-baiting. Indeed, when you introduce Erdogan's consistent assaults on Israel into the equa-tion – like his recent, outrageous declaration that Zionism is a "crime against humanity" – you can see perfectly well how such attacks serve his broader political interests. After all, blaming the Jews is what Middle Eastern auto-crats do.

Which brings me to the issue of Turkey's bid for membership of the EU. There's a widespread impression that the bid, launched as far back as 1999, is unlikely to result in full membership. But that's not what Erdogan believes. He is adamant that Turkey is entitled to EU membership and his virulent reaction to the European Parliament's recent condemnation of his government's repressive acts – "I don't recognize you!" he roared in re-sponse – is a sign of his growing impatience. To their credit, EU leaders have, thus far, proven that they have something of the backbone that many ob-servers have doubted they possess. Stefan Fule, the EU's enlargement com-missioner, told an audience in Istanbul, which included Erdogan, of the need to "aspire to the highest possible democratic standards and practices... These include the freedom to express one's opinion, the freedom to assem-ble peacefully and freedom of media to report on what is happening as it is happening." Now Germany, led by Chancellor Angela Merkel, is stepping up the pressure on Erdogan. Following Merkel's description of the govern-ment's response to the protests as "appalling," the Germans are blocking forthcoming talks to move Turkey's accession bid further down the line.

But the fundamental question remains unresolved: Should Turkey be admitted to the EU? One can see how membership of the EU would boost the fortunes of those courageous Turks who have risked life and limb in their confrontation with Erdogan. Equally, the Europe that emerged after the Second World War cannot, by its very nature, tolerate the kind of govern-ment that has hospitalized more than 7,000 of its own citizens simply for exercising their right to peacefully protest. And it certainly cannot tolerate the kind of antisemitic agitation that brings to mind the worst excesses of the 1930s.

Is the Islamist Era Over?

JNS/The Algemeiner, July 18, 2013

With the overthrow of Mohamed Morsi's Muslim Brotherhood government in Egypt, one is almost forced to question whether the global Islamist movement has been dealt a mortal blow. The notion that the era of Islamism has come to an end is not as outlandish as it seems. While the faith of Islam crystallized in Arabia 15 centuries ago, the ideology of Islamism – which aims to place the imperatives of sharia law at the heart of a coercive and all-powerful state – is a product of the last century. Like its totalitarian cousins – fascism, communism and National Socialism – Islamism's point of departure is a visceral loathing of the political liberties that are integral to liberal democracies. All these monstrous political systems were convinced that, once empowered, they would stay empowered.

Hitler, for example, spoke of a "thousand-year Reich." At the height of the purges in the Soviet Union, Stalin told the writer H. G. Wells that, "socialist society alone can firmly safeguard the interests of the individual." But the Nazi Reich perished in the ashes of Berlin in 1945, while the communist paradise of the Soviet Union went out of business in 1991. Will 2013 go down as an equivalent year of defeat for Islamism? In answering that question, it's hard to overstate the importance of the current turmoil in Egypt. After all, Egypt was where the Muslim Brotherhood was formed in 1928. It is the cradle of Islamism, and it is the country that gave the Islamist movement a pronounced taste of bitter struggle as far back as the 1950s, when the Egyptian dictator Gamal Abdel Nasser crushed the Brotherhood. Yet Egypt is not the only Middle Eastern country where the Brotherhood's insistence that "Islam is the solution" is being sorely tested. In Gaza, where Hamas, the Palestinian branch of the Muslim Brotherhood, has been in power since 2006, the Egyptian crisis has exacerbated an already febrile situation. Infighting among its leadership, as well as worsening relations with its one-time allies, Syria, Hezbollah and Iran, is leading many ordinary Palestinians to question the competence of Hamas. In turn, Hamas is discovering that thundering slogans and terrorist assaults on Israel cannot feed, clothe, educate and employ a population in Gaza, or anywhere else for that matter.

In Turkey, a country that is light years away from Gaza in terms of its economic development, the Islamist government of Prime Minister Reccep Tayyip Erdogan has faced angry demonstrations at home and severe censure abroad. Here, too, the citizenry is beginning to realize that the Islamists cannot deliver when in government – corruption, nepotism and contempt for free speech are all hallmarks of Erdogan's regime, and its talk of Islamic values seems increasingly hollow against that context. It's a similar story for Islamist parties and governments elsewhere in the region. In Tunisia, the secular political parties in coalition with the Islamist Ennahda party have been alienated by Ennahda leader Rachid Ghannouchi's support for Morsi in Egypt. In Sudan, the Islamist government of Omar al-Bashir, an indicted war criminal, remains embroiled in conflict with South Sudan, a largely Christian and African state that declared independence exactly two years ago. Meanwhile, Qatar, the oil-drenched monarchy deemed by Forbes magazine to be the richest country in the world, is rethinking its disastrous policy of supporting and financing Muslim Brotherhood affiliates around the Middle East.

Ironically, among some western policy analysts, there's a widely held view that the current tribulations of the Muslim Brotherhood amount to bad news for democracy in the region. The military's removal of the Brotherhood in Egypt, they say, will turn Islamists against the democratic process, just as it did when a similar scenario arose in Algeria in 1991.

But the idea that the Muslim Brotherhood was committed to democracy in the first place is arrant nonsense. In certain countries, the Brotherhood has made a tactical compromise by participating in elections; in those cases, like Egypt, where the movement has won, autocratic and unconstitutional measures have quickly followed. Moreover, what this debate ignores is the critical point that democracy is about much more than voting. Elections in countries where the press is muzzled, where opposition parties are intimidated, and where the military plays an explicitly political role, are a farce. Platitudes about respecting the cultural differences of the Muslim world only cement the absence of those liberties that are integral to a healthy democracy.

A related argument asserts that election-friendly Islamists will, as a result of the Egyptian experience, now be pushed into the arms of violent jihadi groups. There's a certain degree of truth to that claim; western dithering in Syria has strengthened the al-Qaeda-linked al-Nusra Front, and boosted the likelihood of a new war between secular nationalists and Islamists in the event that Bashar al-Assad's bloody regime is removed. But that line gives the Muslim Brotherhood far more credit than it deserves. Under Morsi's rule, Egypt was as ugly and intolerant as it has ever been; any member of the Coptic Christian minority, which makes up 10 percent of the population, will confirm that. Having endured discrimination and pogrom-style violence during Morsi's tenure, the Copts know only too well that the Brotherhood's message to non-Muslims is simply this: convert or die.

Hence, there are many reasons to be both relieved and pleased that Islamism is now in marked retreat. Even so, we shouldn't conclude that the triumph of liberal democracy will inevitably follow. In my estimation, it's more probable that the Middle East will reflect the experience of Russia after 1991 – anti-western, anti-democratic, and dominated by the military and the intelligence services – than of Germany after 1945, where a constitutional, stable democracy took root as a direct result of the Allied occupation. That is why, while the Islamists may be down at the moment, they are certainly not out.

Rabbi Sacks on Multiculturalism's Dangers

Commentary, August 22, 2013

In the two decades that he served as the United Kingdom's Chief Rabbi, Sir Jonathan Sacks continued the tradition of his predecessor, the late Lord Immanuel Jakobovits, of positioning the office as a key voice in national debates. While Jakobovits was famously aligned with the views of Margaret Thatcher, in marked contrast to the established Church of England, Sacks adopted a more non-partisan approach, venturing insights into a range of issues – most importantly, on multiculturalism – that were not beholden to the orthodoxies of either the Conservative or Labor parties.

This week, Sacks again dived into the multiculturalism debate. In an interview with the *London Times* (subscription only) to mark his departure from office, Sacks reiterated his dismay at how the concept of multiculturalism has been interpreted and applied in Britain. "The real danger in a multicultural society," Sacks argued, "is that every ethnic group and religious group becomes a pressure group, putting our people's interest instead of the national interest." As Sacks explained in his 2007 book, *The Home We Build Together*, this societal Balkanization is inimical to a healthy democracy. "Liberalism is about the rights of individuals, multiculturalism is about the rights of groups, and they are incompatible," he stated baldly. In his conversation with the *Times*, Sacks honed in on Britain's unresolved anguish over the integration of its growing Muslim population. The radical contrast between the Jewish and Muslim experiences of living as minorities is, Sacks said, critical to understanding why uncomplicated integration has succeeded with the former, but not the latter: "The norm was for Muslims to live under a Muslim jurisdiction and the norm, since the destruction of the first Temple, was for Jews to live under a non-Jewish jurisdiction."

Ben Cohen

Interestingly, the firestorm of outrage that typically greets such remarks has centered not on Sacks, but on the unlikely figure of media mogul (and *Times* owner) Rupert Murdoch, whose appreciative tweet – "Good for UK Chief Rabbi Sacks! 'Let's put multiculturalism behind us'. Societies have to integrate. Muslims find it hardest." – angered Muslim activists in his native Australia. Mohammed Tabbaa of the Islamic Council of Victoria warned that Muslims "feel the full brunt" of such comments, while Nareen Young of Australia's Diversity Council bemoaned the fact that Murdoch's support for Sacks had left "a whole lot of Muslim Australians" nursing "hurt feelings."

One is tempted to say that these reactions deliberately miss the point. Sacks has contested neither the reality nor the desirability of a multi-ethnic society; instead, he has consistently argued that the communally-centered model of multiculturalism that prevails in Britain has frustrated attempts to forge an overarching British identity. No one is talking about how to persuade Muslims to *leave* the historically Christian nations in which they've settled, but rather how they might *remain* on peaceable terms. The example of Britain's Sharia courts, which provide an alternative venue for Muslims to settle their legal disputes, neatly illustrates the wider problem which Sacks has addressed. As the BBC, an estimated 85 Sharia councils are now operating in Britain, all of them dealing with a growing caseload. "On average, every month we can deal with anything from 200 to 300 cases," Sheikh Haitham al-Haddad of the Islamic Sharia Council told reporter Divya Talwar. "A few years ago it was just a small fraction of that."

What al-Haddad didn't say is that the judgments arrived at in Sharia courts routinely violate the sensibilities of a liberal democratic society. Indeed, al-Haddad himself is a notorious offender in that regard; as the blogger Ben Six has noted, here is an individual who "endorses genital mutilation, tells parents to marry their daughters off while they are young, orders women to obey their husbands, and tells people not to question men who beat their wives." (You can see a video of al-Haddad nonchalantly supporting the practice of female genital mutilation here.)

To paint objections to this Saudi-esque judicial philosophy as a hangover from the days when opposition to immigration was grounded upon race – as the British Muslim writer Sunny Hundal did in a recent piece for the *Guardian* – doesn't just willfully misrepresent what critics of multiculturalism, like Sacks, are saying. It also condemns the victims of Sharia courts, many of whom are women seeking a way out of abusive marriages, to an indefinite purgatory in the name of tolerance. While Hundal insists that multiculturalism's critics refuse "to get to grips with how Britain has changed," the truth is more nuanced: registering that these changes have occurred does not imply a duty to passively acquiesce to them.

In highlighting the historic unwillingness within Islam to accept that there are situations in which Muslims will be a minority, Sacks has captured one of the key reasons why British Muslim leaders are preventing their flocks from following the precedent set by other immigrant groups – like the French Huguenots, the Jews, and the Afro-Caribbeans–in maintaining their native identities while embracing the broader notion of Britishness. Perhaps the violent collapse of Islamist rule in Egypt, at the fulcrum of the Muslim world, will persuade nervous Britons that Sacks has a point after all.

Index

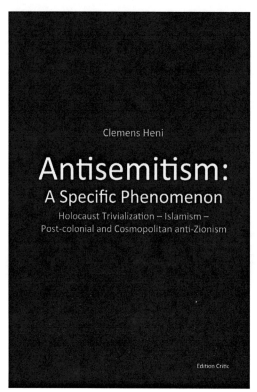

Clemens Heni

Antisemitism:
A Specific Phenomenon
Holocaust Trivialization – Islamism –
Post-colonial and Cosmopolitan anti-Zionism

Edition Critic

Clemens Heni holds a PhD in political science from the University of Innsbruck, Austria. In 2008/2009 he was a Post-Doctoral Associate at Yale University. He is the Director of the Berlin International Center for the Study of Antisemitism (BICSA), founded in 2011.

Clemens Heni: Antisemitism: A Specific Phenomenon. Holocaust Trivialization – Islamism – Post-colonial and Cosmopolitan anti-Zionism

Berlin: Edition Critic, 2013

This book analyzes the specifics of anti-semitism and Jew-hatred in the 21st century.

It includes a groundbreaking assessment of the political leanings of many prominent scholars in the field. Today's antisemitism extends far beyond right-wing circles and can be found among liberals, leftists, anti-racist communities, Islamists, and post-colonial scholars i the Western world.

Using English and German sources, the author demonstrates the need to oppose Holocaust trivializiation as well as other 'modern' forms of antisemitism like anti-Zionism and the defamation of the Jewish state of Israel.

xi + 648 pages 6" x 9" *Bibliography *Index
ISBN 978-3-9814548-5-7, 33€ | US $42 | £26
http://www.EditionCritic.de

A thorough, objective and intelligent analysis of the principal form taken by contemporary anti-Semitism.
Anthony Julius, London

Clemen's Heni's book is a very important document for anyone who wants to understand how Jews became the scapegoat of Europe in particular and the declining West in general.
Dr. Mordechai Kedar, Ramat Gan

Clemens Heni's "Antisemitism: A Specific Phenomenon" is a masterful and very sobering analysis of global anti-Semitism. It is an academically respectable "call to arms;" a passionate and yet dispassionate account of virulent Jew hatred in the Islamist world and its "politically correct" counterpart in the West. Read it and weep. Read it and join those among us who have not lost our moral sanity or historical post-Holocaust memory.
Prof. Dr. Phyllis Chesler, New York

CPSIA information can be obtained at www.ICGtesting.com
Printed in the USA
LVOW10s1657110914

403636LV00004B/378/P